Joomla! 1.5 Multimedia

Build media-rich Joomla! websites by learning to embed
and display multimedia content

Allan Walker

BIRMINGHAM - MUMBAI

Joomla! 1.5 Multimedia

First published: January 2010

Production Reference: 1250110

Published by Packt Publishing Ltd.
32 Lincoln Road
Olton
Birmingham, B27 6PA, UK.

ISBN 978-1-847197-70-2

www.packtpub.com

Cover Image by Filippo (filosarti@tiscali.it)

Credits

About the Author

Allan Walker grew up in New Zealand, and now lives in the United Kingdom, where he runs an online business consultancy and development company called "Amplify" (www.projectamplify.com). In recent years, Allan has been involved with a number of large-scale Joomla! projects, helping to establish Joomla! within the UK government and corporate sectors.

Allan has been a mentor for the 2009 Joomla! Google Summer of Code program, and is a member of the Joomla! Marketing Team.

When first starting to write this title, I assumed a couple of full-on weekends might break the back of the book. Nine months later, I have a better understanding of what efforts go into a project like this.

I would like to thank anyone who has contributed in some way to the development of Joomla!. The product provides a diverse solution for projects, and through the ever-growing extensions directory, most users can now configure a Joomla!-based project, rather than have to build it. It is the design and simplicity of Joomla! which leads to its success, thus allowing non-technical users to build complex projects easily.

For many of us who have based services around Joomla!, it has helped put food on the table. For this I am grateful. It is the generosity of people's time, skills, and the community support that keeps the project rolling, and Joomla!'s features improving with every release. If you are interested in helping the product and community, please see information about contributing at www.joomla.org.

For the lost evenings and weekends, my love and thanks go to my wife Georgina. Thank you for the continued support and patience.

About the Reviewers

Jose Argudo is a web developer from Valencia, Spain. After finishing his studies he started working for a web design company. Then, six years later, he decided to start working as a freelancer.

Now that some years have passed, he thinks it's the best decision he has ever taken, a decision that let him work with the tools he likes, such as Joomla!, CodeIgniter, CakePHP, jQuery, and other known open source technologies.

His desire to learn and share his knowledge has led him to be a regular reviewer of books from Packt, such as Joomla! With Flash (http://www.packtpub.com/joomla-with-flash/book), Joomla! 1.5 SEO (http://www.packtpub.com/joomla-1-5-search-engine-optimization-seo/book), Magento 1.3 Theme Design (http://www.packtpub.com/magento-1-3-theme-design/book), or Symfony 1.3 web application development (http://www.packtpub.com/symfony-1-3-web-application-development/book).

Recently he has even published his own book, CodeIgniter 1.7, which you can also find at Packt's site (http://www.packtpub.com/improve-coding-productivity-with-codeigniter-1-7/book). If you work with PHP... take a look at it!

If you want to know more about him, you can check his site www.joseargudo.com.

To my girlfriend and to my brother, I wish we will always be together.

Joseph L. LeBlanc is a freelance Joomla! developer specializing in Joomla!, PHP, and JavaScript. Joseph can be found teaching Joomla! classes and speaking at conferences. He has authored a book on Joomla! extension programming and a Lynda.com video series on using Joomla!.

Table of Contents

Preface

Joomla! is a Content Management System designed to organize and deliver content within a website environment.

Multimedia provides us with stunning interactive user experiences and wonderful design options, but it requires discipline and knowledge to utilize it effectively so that we do not alienate our audiences.

If you want to display more than just text on your Joomla! pages, this book has been designed for you and is a must-read. It takes you beyond the basics of Joomla! and helps to take full advantage of this powerful CMS structure to deliver media-rich web content to your site users. This book provides detailed information and all the required know-how for Joomla! administrators to create engaging, media-rich Joomla! websites. Utilizing core Joomla! features and the power of Joomla! Extensions, this step-by-step guide will show you how to include popular media elements into your website and collaborate with external web resources.

You will learn everything you need to know to present text, images, video, and audio in your content by manually embedding content, using more automated methods, and the power of specialized extensions. You will learn to create regular podcasts and utilize RSS to help publicize and deliver your site content.

Learn about the popular multimedia extensions for Joomla!; learn how they benefit your CMS with additional features, and how they are installed and configured. Utilize the abundance of external resources now available on the Web and learn how your Joomla! site can interact and present content from such sites as YouTube, Flickr, Twitter, and Google.

What this book covers

Chapter 1, *Getting Started With Joomla! Multimedia* introduces you to multimedia, breaks down the main elements, and is an overview of some of the things to come in following chapters. Your Joomla! Content Management System contains a number of built-in multimedia capabilities, these enriched with third-party extensions can turn your basic Joomla! CMS into a media-rich interactive user experience.

Chapter 2, *Managing Your Joomla! Media* tells us that one of the most important tasks when using multimedia in our Joomla! websites is the ability to upload and manage the files on your web server. In this chapter, we will look at using the built-in Joomla! Media Manager, as well as alternative methods for managing your website media and files.

Chapter 3, *Text, Characters, and Fonts in Your Joomla! Site* shows that text (and the styling of it) is one of the most prominent media types that has been, and still is used in website pages. Although it's such a major media element, web developers often pay little attention to this subject. In this chapter, we will highlight the use of fonts, characters, and text within your Joomla! site, and how we can not only change the site design by using another font typeface, but by doing so we can affect your site user's overall experience.

Chapter 4, *Adding and Managing Image Content* will provide the assistance to help utilize image content effectively within your Joomla! website, whether you need to create multimedia image galleries in your Joomla! website, or simply add images to your articles and modules.

Chapter 5, *Using Audio in Your Joomla! Website* highlights the use of audio in your Joomla! website. You will learn how to include powerful audio features such as audio players and podcasting capabilities into Joomla!.

Chapter 6, *Using Video in Your Joomla! Website* highlights the use of video media within your Joomla! website. We look at the process of embedding video content into articles, creating and maintaining video podcasts, and the powerful video solutions that third-party Joomla! Extensions provide.

Chapter 7, *Collaborating With External Sources* talks about how sharing of information between popular external resources, such as Twitter, Facebook, and Google, is an increasingly popular feature required by Joomla! users. Designed to extend the Joomla! Framework with new functionality, this chapter will look at the most popular collaboration extensions for Joomla! and the features they contain, as well as using good old fashioned HTML methods to embed external content into your site.

Chapter 8, *Joomla! Templates and Multimedia* describes how Joomla! Templates are the distinguishing factor between one Joomla! website looking just like the next. They contain the structural elements to display your Joomla! content, and deliver style and scripting information to the user's web browser. This chapter is an overview of Joomla! Templates, how they work, and how they can affect the display of multimedia content in your Joomla! site. Learn how templates can enhance multimedia capabilities, as well as how they affect the way in which your Joomla! site is displayed on mobile web devices.

Chapter 9, *Joomla! Multimedia Project* follows a cookbook style approach as we build a multimedia packed Joomla! website from start to finish, throwing in some of the previously mentioned techniques, as well as some new tips and tricks for good measure.

Appendix A, *Extension Types and How to Install Them* shows how installing extensions for Joomla! is an easy task, thanks to the design of extensions, and the Extension Manager tool that is included in Joomla!. It also shows us how to uninstall an extension.

What you need for this book

Most importantly, you'll need an installation of the latest, stable version of Joomla! 1.5, either locally or on a remote web hosting location.

To try out the techniques mentioned in this book (and follow some of the step-by-step tutorials), you will need a computer with Internet access, an HTML code editor (could even be Notepad or TextEdit), and an FTP client such as FileZilla.

Who this book is for

This book is aimed at Joomla! administrators and site developers who want to add media-rich content elements and interactive features to their site.

To get the most out of this book, you will need a basic understanding of what Joomla! 1.5 is, and how its main functions work. Regardless of your web development skill-set or level, you'll be walked through the clear, step-by-step instructions, but familiarity with a broad range of web development skills and Joomla! knowledge will allow you to gain maximum benefit from this book.

Conventions

In this book, you will find a number of styles of text that distinguish between different kinds of information. Here are some examples of these styles, and an explanation of their meaning.

Code words in text are shown as follows: "We can include other contexts through the use of the `include` directive."

A block of code is set as follows:

```
body {
    font-family: Arial,Courier,sans-serif;
    line-height: 1.3em;
    margin: 0px;
    font-size: 12px;
    color: #333;
}
```

When we wish to draw your attention to a particular part of a code block, the relevant lines or items are set in bold:

```
h1.logo a
{
    width: 208px;
    display: block;
    background: url(../images/logo.png) no-repeat;
    height: 80px;
    position: relative;
    z-index: 100;
}
```

New terms and **important words** are shown in bold. Words that you see on the screen, in menus or dialog boxes for example, appear in the text like this: "Your Joomla! site **Media Settings** can be found by going to the **Site | Global Configuration**."

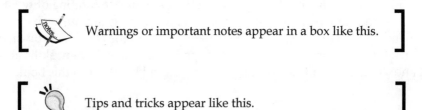

Warnings or important notes appear in a box like this.

Tips and tricks appear like this.

Reader feedback

Feedback from our readers is always welcome. Let us know what you think about this book—what you liked or may have disliked. Reader feedback is important for us to develop titles that you really get the most out of.

To send us general feedback, simply send an e-mail to feedback@packtpub.com, and mention the book title via the subject of your message. You can also share your feedback with the author at jmultimedia@projectamplify.com.

If there is a book that you need and would like to see us publish, please send us a note in the **SUGGEST A TITLE** form on www.packtpub.com or e-mail suggest@packtpub.com.

If there is a topic that you have expertise in and you are interested in either writing or contributing to a book on, see our author guide on www.packtpub.com/authors.

Customer support

Now that you are the proud owner of a Packt book, we have a number of things to help you to get the most from your purchase.

> **Downloading the example code for the book**
>
> Visit http://www.packtpub.com/files/code/7702_Code.zip to directly download the example code.
>
> The downloadable files contain instructions on how to use them.

Errata

Although we have taken every care to ensure the accuracy of our content, mistakes do happen. If you find a mistake in one of our books—maybe a mistake in the text or the code—we would be grateful if you would report this to us. By doing so, you can save other readers from frustration and help us improve subsequent versions of this book. If you find any errata, please report them by visiting http://www.packtpub.com/support, selecting your book, clicking on the **let us know** link, and entering the details of your errata. Once your errata are verified, your submission will be accepted and the errata will be uploaded on our website, or added to any list of existing errata, under the Errata section of that title. Any existing errata can be viewed by selecting your title from http://www.packtpub.com/support.

Piracy

Piracy of copyright material on the Internet is an ongoing problem across all media. At Packt, we take the protection of our copyright and licenses very seriously. If you come across any illegal copies of our works, in any form, on the Internet, please provide us with the location address or website name immediately so that we can pursue a remedy.

Please contact us at copyright@packtpub.com with a link to the suspected pirated material.

We appreciate your help in protecting our authors, and our ability to bring you valuable content.

Questions

You can contact us at questions@packtpub.com if you are having a problem with any aspect of the book, and we will do our best to address it.

1
Getting Started with Joomla! Multimedia

At present, the use of multiple media content in web pages is evolving at an astonishing rate. Each week there are new multimedia extensions launched in the http://extensions.joomla.org extensions directory. Launching almost as quickly are new social / media web portals, offering the ability to interact and stream media content into your site pages. Some of these popular portals are defining new multimedia features and setting new standards for website user interactions.

Your Joomla! Content Management System has lots of great built-in multimedia capabilities; these enriched with third-party extensions and streaming media sources can help evolve your default Joomla! website into a powerful media-rich interactive experience for your visitors.

This chapter is an introduction to multimedia, and how Joomla! interacts with these media elements.

What is multimedia?

The definition of **multimedia** is an ambiguous description, loosely used to define multiple types of media that are integrated and used with each other. Multimedia surrounds us in our daily lives and is utilized in many areas including marketing, advertising, art, medicine, engineering, and more!

Examples of multimedia can range from a simple mixture of two media types, such as a book containing text and images, through to an advanced interactive video game including images, video, text, and audio.

As the description suggests, "multimedia" contains different types of media content, and these different media elements can usually be defined into categories.

Categories of multimedia

From an academic approach, multimedia is often defined in two main categories: linear and non-linear. Hypermedia is the third definition, and although often viewed as its own classification, it falls under the non-linear multimedia category.

Linear

Linear multimedia content generally progresses as a presentation, without the requirement for the viewer to interact or navigate. Examples of linear multimedia would be a blockbuster movie at a cinema, or a television show.

Non-linear

Non-linear multimedia content is a media category which allows the user to control and progress through their own experience. Examples of non-linear multimedia could be an interactive video game or a computer based learning application.

Hypermedia

Hypermedia is a member of the non-linear category. It is an extension of the term "Hypertext", meaning linkable text that a user can click on and navigate to another area.

Hypermedia may contain text, images, video, and audio content that is linked. Hypermedia is the fundamental element for web pages due to its navigational properties. The best example of hypermedia is the World Wide Web (WWW) itself, which contains millions of web pages offering inter-linked media content.

Website multimedia

Website multimedia describes multiple forms of media and content that is delivered electronically to the end user via a web server, or website page. Website multimedia generally falls under the non-linear multimedia classification, as more often than not, it allows the end user navigational and control opportunities. The types of media used on websites can include text, images, audio, and video, but can also contain a number of other interactive features which fall under the "multimedia" description.

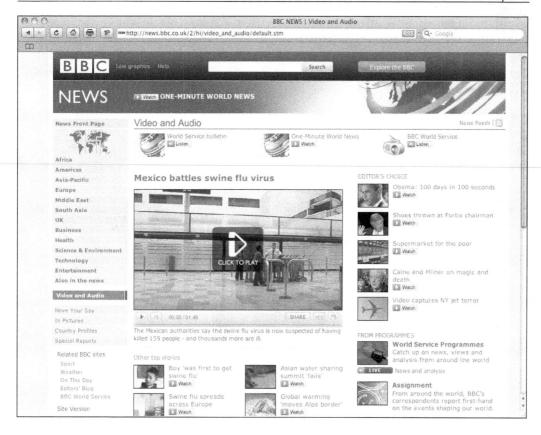

Throughout this book we will be looking at these multimedia elements, and how to display them effectively in our Joomla! website.

Various types of website multimedia

The Internet started with simple textual content. With the implementation of HTML and other coding languages, and the evolution of web browsers and connection speeds, media-rich applications and websites are now present everywhere on the World Wide Web.

Multimedia has directly influenced the growth of the Internet, just as the Internet has influenced multimedia. The expansion of information online is now becoming the most important multimedia vehicle. Web users now have the ability to control the delivery of data as they wish, and user interactivity is now a key process used in popular websites.

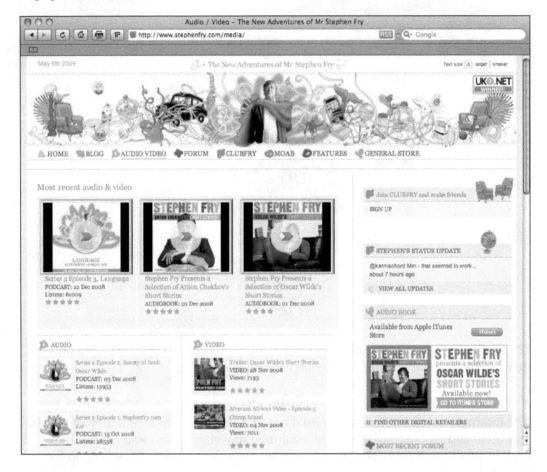

As mentioned earlier in this chapter, multimedia is the combination of multiple forms of content. These can include text, images, audio, video as well as scripting and numerous other site features, which help site users with navigation and interactivity.

What is Joomla!?

Joomla! is an award-winning open source **Content Management System (CMS)**, enabling you to build powerful database driven website applications.

Joomla! allows you to construct, organize, and manage your website content easily. Joomla! itself is a rapidly evolving product, as are the team and community supporting its growth:

Joomla! creates pages which are publically viewable and also contains a web driven administration area, accessible via a login screen:

Joomla! is utilized all over the world to power intranet and Internet websites of all shapes and sizes.

Examples of where Joomla! is used are:

- Online magazines, news portals, and publications
- Government applications
- School and church websites
- Corporate websites and intranets
- Personal web pages and blogs
- Audio and video portals

Joomla! has become a favored CMS to many people. Some of the reasons for its fast and continued growth include:

- Joomla! is an open source application that is freely available to everyone. For further information about this subject please visit `http://www.opensourcematters.org`.

- The product has a well structured roadmap for continued development and support.

- Joomla! has a vibrant growing community, creating an excellent help and support network.

- There are thousands of third-party extensions available which offer easily installable additional functionality. This allows powerful new features to be easily added to your Joomla! website, with just a few clicks of the mouse.

- A template structure allows you to completely customize the look and feel of your Joomla! website.

- Backend administration contains powerful features, is flexible and easy to use.

Including multimedia in your Joomla! site

Just like a hand-coded website, your Joomla! website can easily contain multimedia site content. In fact, the Joomla! CMS is constructed to easily create, manage, and present multiple content types, allowing you to publish these on your site pages.

The approach of including multimedia material into a software driven web framework (such as the Joomla! CMS) can be different than that of a hand-coded website. The media elements used will need to be included and deployed in a way conforming to the Joomla! CMS framework.

The Joomla! CMS web platform is designed for content management and to be as lightweight as possible in additional clutter. Out of the box it does a great job at managing content, but the application framework offers the ability for thousands of developers around the world to contribute additional features for the base CMS. These are called Joomla! Extensions.

Joomla! **Extensions** are third-party products which have been written to enhance the core Joomla! capabilities. They come in all shapes and sizes and can add powerful functionality to your default Joomla! There are thousands of Joomla! Extensions available in the **Joomla! Extension Directory (JED)** located at http://extensions.joomla.org as well as other Joomla! resources available on the Internet.

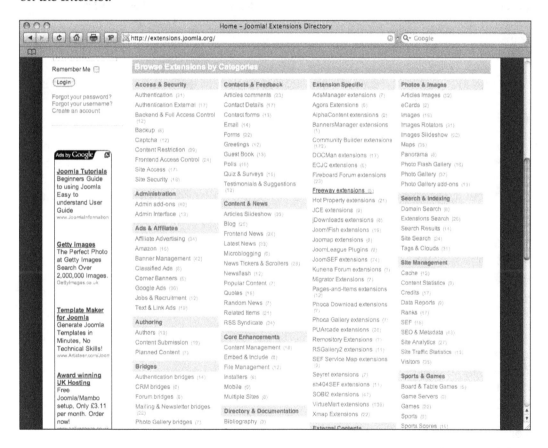

Multimedia extensions contribute to a large section of the JED, and we will be highlighting some of the most powerful and useful extensions in the following chapters.

Multimedia use in your Joomla! CMS

A powerful feature of the Joomla! CMS is its ability to organize and manage content. This content can be text, images, documents, audio, video, and anything else you can think up to deliver to your site users.

Joomla ships with its own "Media Manager" tool. This allows the ability to upload, organize, and delete different types of media to the images directory, or subdirectories if you wish. The media manager offers a thumbnail view as well as a detailed view of the file's properties, such as name, file size, and so on.

The purpose of the built-in media manager is to allow site administrators to manage media content from the website pages, without the requirement for File Transfer Protocol (FTP) access to the server. As a developer, using FTP is an essential transmission method, but when handing over a Joomla! based website over to the end clients, the need to restrict such access is commonplace.

Once files are in place on the web server, things start to get interesting. We have our media on the server, all ready to go, and now what? Before we get too much further, now is the time to highlight Joomla! Templates.

A Joomla! **Template** is a number of files within the Joomla! CMS which control the presentation of the content. Templates allow you to obtain a completely different "look and feeling" on your site pages. When combined with images, a Cascading Style Sheet (CSS) and the CMS database content templates contribute to the overall design and layout of your website.

When producing website pages, often the location of main elements will stay the same; these might be menus, banners, and so on. These pages will probably also require the same logo, colors, and styles, which is where our template and cascading style sheets come in handy. Templates also have the important role of allowing us to publish certain Joomla! content into specific areas of the template.

The CMS and template approach offers the ability to not only deliver our multiple media content in different positions around our website template, but we also have the flexibility of showing the content we want, when we want to. We will be devoting a whole chapter towards Joomla! Templates and how they can enhance our site multimedia features.

For now, it has been important to highlight the fact that "out of the box" Joomla! seems to offer basic web content management. With knowledge of the product as well as additional extensions and configurations, it can provide a stunning web solution that is brimming with multimedia features.

Text

Text is made up of letters, numbers, characters, words, and symbols. These put together form words, which convey an idea, belief, or fact. Text is the most widely used form of communication and is considered a fundamental element of visual multimedia.

Text is used everywhere on websites, it is even used in parts of the site that many users do not see. An example of this would be the HTML source code for the website pages:

```
 9  <?php if ($this->params->get('show_page_title', 1) &&
10     <div class="componentheading<?php echo $this->para
11         <?php echo $this->escape($this->params->get('p
12     </div>
13  <?php endif; ?>
14  <?php if ($canEdit || $this->params->get('show_title')
15  <table class="contentpaneopen<?php echo $this->params-
16  <tr>
17      <?php if ($this->params->get('show_title')) : ?>
18      <td class="contentheading<?php echo $this->params-
19          <?php if ($this->params->get('link_titles') &&
20          <a href="<?php echo $this->article->readmore_l
21              <?php echo $this->escape($this->article->t
22          <?php else : ?>
23              <?php echo $this->escape($this->article->t
24          <?php endif; ?>
```

Text can be used on page headings, main content, captions and help tips, documentation, error reporting, basically everywhere across your website.

A font is a particular style of text and plays a major role in the look and feel of modern websites. Fonts are used all over the Web now to style and define text. Without fonts, all of the text we see would have the same look to it, making things very uninteresting.

In modern websites, the text and the type of style you would like applied to it is usually defined using a stylesheet. Within a stylesheet document, it is possible to set font and text properties. These properties can apply to small or large areas of text used on your site pages:

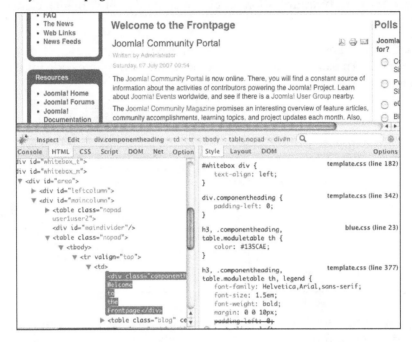

Images

Next to written text, images are probably one of the most utilized types of media in websites.

Images not only communicate information effectively (the old saying "a picture tells a thousand words"), but they are an important element of design, marketing, and branding which may distinguish your website from others.

The definition of an "Image" can often be used to describe the following elements:

- Photographs
- Graphics
- Diagrams
- Drawings

Images can be placed on web pages as a singular item to complement text, or they can be placed together to form galleries, which play a major multimedia role on some websites:

Indian Car Buyers Snap Up the Nano
By NANDINI LAKSHMAN / MUMBAI
Six weeks after launch, demand is far outstripping the supply of the world's cheapest car, giving automaker Tata Motors some financial breathing room

CDC: 20% of U.S. Homes Use Cell Phones Only
By AP / ALAN FRAM
For the first time, the number of U.S. households opting for only cell phones outnumber those that just have traditional landlines

Images can be created, edited, and saved into numerous formats. Some of these formats are more applicable for use on the Web than others.

For more detailed image information, please view Chapter 4, *Adding and Managing Image Content*.

Audio

Audio (or sound as we know it) can be used to inspire human emotion and deliver information. Audio is a major element of human entertainment, as well as a contributing element to videos, gaming, and other multimedia presentations.

The use of audio can add interest, be informative, and entertain. An often overlooked fact is that audio can also provide an interface for visually impaired users to attain the information they require:

Creative Photoshop With John Reuter Technology
Photoshop tutorials for fine art photographers. (Author: John Reuter)
Podcast Details

Typical Mac User Podcast Technology
Help for the Switcher and New Apple Macintosh User (Author: Victor Cajiao)
Podcast Details

Aots: Hardware Technology
Attack of the Show Host, Wil, brings you the hottest must have gadgets and gives you an insider's look at today's computers, games and tech. (Author: G4)
Podcast Details

Photoshop Killer Tips Technology
Get your daily video dose of the coolest Adobe® Photoshop tips, timesaving shortcuts, workarounds, and undocumented tricks with Matt Kloskowski, one of "The Photoshop Guys" from Photoshop TV. New shows are posted each weekday. (Author: Matt Kloskowski)
Podcast Details

Internet is now an audio-rich delivery mechanism, with audio being easily downloaded from websites and application portals. Most modern computer setups now include speakers, which depending on the way you look at it, has helped the evolution of audio usage within web pages. Possibly the equation goes the other way and greater audio usage on web pages has specified the requirements for computer users to need speakers.

All of that said, gone are the dancing Santas that used to load into web pages, and play a nasty Christmas MIDI file with no volume control! Now we are talking about websites containing "podcasts on demand", and "dial up your own personal radio station playlists", and impressive audio players including time counts and player controls.

Like images, sound files can be created and saved in many formats, including AAC, MP3, MIDI, WAV, as well as many others. Choosing the correct audio format to use on your website is imperative for the efficient delivery of the audio content to your site users.

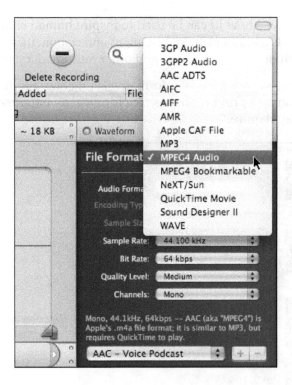

Video

Video can be defined as a sequence of still images put together and displayed on a screen to form the illusion of motion:

Video is one of the most powerful multimedia types, as it incorporates both images and audio. It can also contain text in the form of titles and descriptions.

Video has been known as one of the most demanding media types to work with due to the overheads of processing and working with large file sizes. Transmission and storage of video has often made it an unsuitable medium to use in certain conditions. However, things are changing rapidly, and video is now often linked to or "streamed" into an application, rather than the files hosted themselves.

Video can be saved in a variety of formats and compression types. Some of these will be very applicable, and others you should stay clear of for website use. More information about working with video can be found in Chapter 5, *Using Video within Your Joomla! Website*.

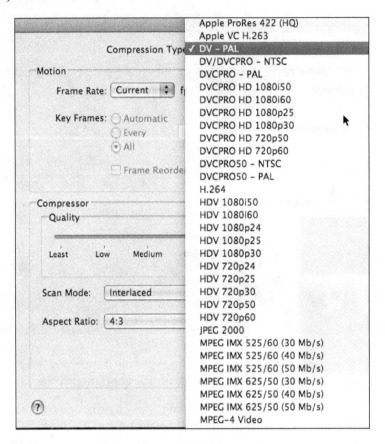

Multimedia and web accessibility

Website accessibility means that people who have disabilities can understand, interact, and navigate through web pages.

One of the main principles of web accessibility is to design websites and web software, which is flexible to meet different users' situations, preferences, and environments.

With the Web becoming an increasingly important resource for the sharing of information, many users are now going online for reference: health, commerce, government, recreation, media, and many other resources. It is essential that people wanting to utilize the Web have equal access and equal opportunities to these resources:

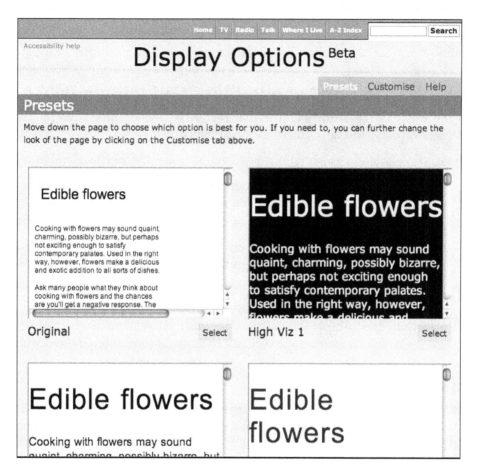

Another important consideration when building a website is that web accessibility has legal obligations in certain countries. Besides the important consideration to all of your site users, there could also be legal reasons why accessibility should be considered when building and maintaining your website.

Can a multimedia website be accessible?

It is possible for a multimedia rich website to also be an accessible website. However, the level of accessibility options you choose to implement into your website are decisions you need to make for your project. The decision basis will often include factors such as target audiences, country legalities, and project time and budgets.

There are a number of accessibility standards used around the Web, which provide accessibility guidelines and checklists to benchmark against. Examples of these are:

The Web Content Accessibility Guidelines (WCAG)

The **Web Content Accessibility Guidelines (WCAG)** have become a world standard for web accessibility, and falls into three 'compliance' categories:

1. **A** (also known as Level 1)

   A website must comply with all checkpoints in Level 1 otherwise one or more user groups will find it impossible to access information or functionality.

2. **AA** (also known as Level 2)

   A website should comply with all checkpoints in Level 2 otherwise one or more groups will experience significant barriers to access information or functionality.

3. **AAA** (also known as Level 3)

   A website may comply with all checkpoints in Level 3 otherwise one or more groups will find it somewhat difficult to access information in the document.

Section 508

Section 508 is a standard created by the US Federal Government. It contains 16 checkpoints for testing your website against. The first 11 checkpoints are exactly equivalent to the WCAG A (Level 1) guidelines. The last five checkpoints are partly based on the WCAG guidelines, but are more extensive. For further information about this standard, please search for Section 508 on the Net.

Site accessibility features are best considered at the start of a website project, and then having these addressed during development. It is much easier to take this approach rather than address this issue retrospectively. Fixing invalid site code and creating `title` or `alt` tags can consume hours of working time and often outweigh any budgets that have been put aside to make your content accessible.

There are a number of simple processes you can put in place to make your website more accessible. Trying to attain a higher level of accessibility will of course require a greater investment of time.

You may come across situations where the type of content you wish to offer on your site pages will never be accessible to certain audiences. This is where decisions must be made whether you make that content available in alternative formats. An example of this may be to include captions when playing a video, or to offer an audio version of text documents.

Throughout the development of your website, numerous software and online evaluation tools can be used to help determine the accessibility of your website pages.

An exhaustive list of these can be found on the Web, or at sites such as http://www.w3.org/WAI/ER/tools/complete.

More information on web accessibility

For further information and tools which can help you make your site accessible, please visit the following resources:

1. http://www.w3.org/WAI/: Guidelines and resources from the **World Wide Web Consortium (W3C)**.

2. http://www.bbc.co.uk/accessibility: Resources to help make the Web more accessible to you.

3. `http://en.wikipedia.org/wiki/Web_accessibility`: Wikipedia's page on accessibility guidelines.

4. `http://www.section508.gov/`: Section 508 requires that Federal agencies' electronic and information technology is accessible to people with disabilities.

Web browser support for multimedia

The Web was originally a text only medium, with browsers only being able to display text in a single font, size, and color.

With the explosion of the Internet, website browsers can now view images, play audio and video. A further development of the World Wide Web has been the evolution of "streaming media" which allows the media playback to begin without the files being fully downloaded first.

There are many web browsers available. Some of these are suitable for specific purposes and others pride themselves on being the most lightweight, or the fastest browser available.

Most browsers have built-in media capabilities, which is an acknowledgement of the growth of website multimedia. Other browsers require plugins to play multimedia content. **Plugins** are programs, which extend your browser capabilities by making making them compatible with additional media types. When your browser encounters a multimedia file, it hands over the data to the plugin in order to play or display that file.

You may have heard of the plugin "Adobe Flash Player", which enables you to play Adobe movies through your web browser, or the "Windows Media Player" browser plugin, which plays streaming audio, video, and presentations saved in Microsoft formats. Without these plugins installed into the web browser, this media content on website pages cannot be effectively viewed:

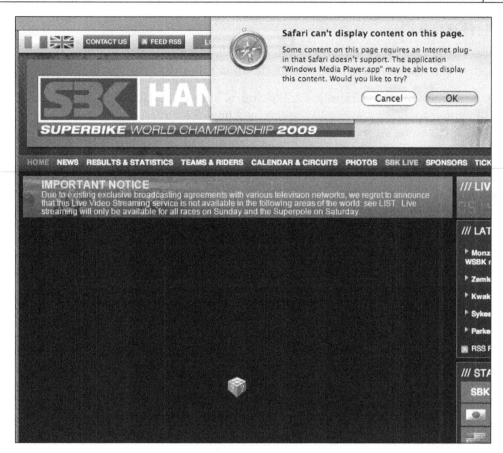

This highlights the importance of offering multimedia material in numerous formats, or if that is not an option, to provide the site users with clear instructions about the media trying to load, and when possible, where to go and find a plugin in order to play it.

Summary

In this chapter, we have looked at the terminology "multimedia" and how this description contains numerous types of media content.

We have highlighted the Joomla! CMS platform and recognized its built-in multimedia capabilities, as well as mentioned how these can be enhanced using Joomla! Extensions. As extensions enhance the default Joomla! installation, they will receive a healthy coverage throughout the chapters.

It is important to note website accessibility in this chapter, as it is much easier to consider and integrate web accessibility into the start of website development, rather than trying to address accessibility issues retrospectively. More information about accessibility and how it relates to specific media, is covered within each chapter.

2
Managing Your Joomla! Media

One of the most important tasks when using multimedia in our Joomla! websites is the ability to upload and manage the files on your web server. Once uploaded, this content may not require further attention, or you might need the ability for constant management and file revisions.

In this chapter, we will look at using the built-in Joomla! Media Manager, as well as alternative methods for managing our website media and files. This chapter includes:

- Overview of the Joomla! Media Manager
- Uploading media using the Media Manager
- The view
- Organizing your content
- Uploading your content
- Managing media using the Media Manager
- Alternative methods of managing files and media
- Third-party file management extensions

Overview of the Joomla! Media Manager

The Media Manager is a useful file management tool, which is included in the Joomla! CMS.

The Media Manager tool is located within your administration area and can be accessed by using the "Quick Link" icon on your **Control Panel**, or by going to the Menu: **Site** | **Media Manager**:

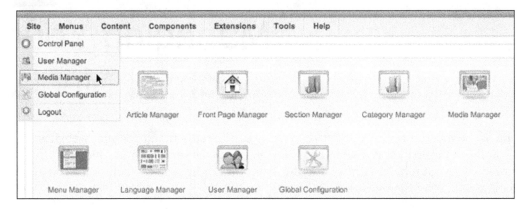

One of the main purposes of the Media Manager is to easily allow site administrators, and frontend users with permissions, the ability to upload and manage files for their Joomla! site. In circumstances where you do not have FTP (File Transfer Protocol) access to your web server, the media manager might be the only available tool with which you can add new images, videos, documents, and other files to your website.

Uploading media using the Media Manager

During initial site development, there are usually regular requirements to upload new files to your Joomla! site. Depending on the content for your website, this process can decrease as you move into the maintenance stages, or stay as a requirement for sites which are updated often.

Media Manager settings

As with all software applications, the Media Manager tool contains a set of predefined settings. Before using the Media Manager for the first time, it is recommended that you take a look at these as they offer the ability to customize media handling for your website. Depending on your file requirements, adjusting the media configuration settings now may save you time and effort down the line.

Your Joomla! site **Media Settings** can be found by going to **Site | Global Configuration**. Once the page has loaded, you will then need to click on the link named **System**.

The Media Settings area not only allows you to adjust settings related to the Media Manager, but also contains general settings for the media used throughout your Joomla! website. Information regarding each setting is as follows:

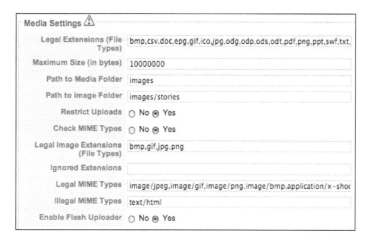

The fields are:

- **Legal Extensions (File Types)**

  This field is a comma-separated list of file types that you want to allow to be uploaded to your Joomla! website. This setting applies to the frontend of your site, as well as the backend which includes the Media Manager tool.

- **Maximum Size (in bytes)**

  This field holds the maximum size of the file (in bytes) to be uploaded. This can be set to "0" if you do not wish to restrict your file upload sizes. Most web servers will have their own file size limit that is usually configurable for the server by adjusting the server information file.

- **Path to Media Folder**

  By default, Joomla! has a media folder called `<joomlaroot>/images`. This is the area where all files will be uploaded to when using the Media Manager. You can change this value to a different directory if you wish, creating a default path for managing your media. The majority of Joomla! projects would probably leave this value as default.

If you do decide to use another folder name for your media directory, it is important to leave the current /images directory on the server as this can often be used by other components.

- **Path to Image Folder**

  This is generally a path where you put your images for your Joomla! Content Articles.

  By default, it is set to `<joomlaroot>/images/stories`. You can change this to be what you wish. If you want to access this folder from the Media Manager, then make this a subfolder of the "Media Folder" previously mentioned. For example, `<joomlaroot><mediafoldername>/<imagefoldername>`.

If you do decide to use another folder name for your image directory, it is important to leave the current /images/ stories directory on the server as this can often be used by other components.

- **Restrict Uploads**

  This feature restricts uploads by user type. The default is set to **Yes,** which means that users below the status of a "Manager" will only get one folder option to upload files into. That folder is your main "Media Folder". If you set this option to **No,** then users will also be allowed to upload to subdirectories within your main media folder.

- **Check MIME Types**

  This is a security feature, and uses MIME Magic or Fileinfo to verify your uploaded file types. By checking the MIME file information, you help ensure users don't upload malicious files to your site. Further information about **Fileinfo** can be found at `http://www.php.net/manual/en/book. fileinfo.php`.

- **Legal Image Extensions (File Types)**

  This is a list of legal image extensions that you and other users are allowed to upload to your Joomla! site. The default list includes **bmp, gif, jpg,** and **png** files. Adjust, if you require further image extension types.

- **Ignored Extensions**

  This setting checks the file types which should be ignored for MIME checking. By default, this is left blank so all files would be included if MIME checking is turned on.

- **Legal MIME Types**

  This sets the list of legal MIME types for uploading. By default, this setting includes some file types, and it is recommended that you do not adjust this setting unless you know what you are doing.

- **Illegal MIME Types**

  This sets the list of illegal MIME types for uploading. As with the legal MIME types, it is recommended that you do not adjust this setting unless you know what you are doing.

- **Enable Flash Uploader**

  The Media Manager contains an integrated Flash uploader tool. If enabled, this allows you to upload multiple files at once. The default setting is **No**.

 If you do decide to enable the Flash uploader and receive uploading issues, then disable this feature again. Issues can arise from incompatible Adobe Flash settings.

If you have made adjustments to the default Joomla! Media Settings, then you will need to save these by clicking on the **Save** button at the top right-hand side of the page in the **Global Configuration** section. A confirmation message to inform you that these settings have been saved should show on the following page.

Now that we have configured our site's Media Settings, let's head over to take a detailed look at the Media Manager upload feature.

The Media Manager tool is located within your administration area and can be accessed by using the "Quick Link" icon on your **Control Panel**, or by going to the Menu: **Site | Media Manager**.

The view

When you open the Media Manager, one of the initial options available to you is the choice of viewing your files and the associated information about them.

The two options are "Thumbnail View" and "Detailed View".

1. **Thumbnail View**: The first (and default setting) is called Thumbnail View. This offers a thumbnail preview of your files and a delete button below each file. Thumbnail View is great for a quick scan of your files (especially images), as you can actually see the list and a thumbnail icon in front of you. This view, however, can be cumbersome when dealing with larger quantities of files.

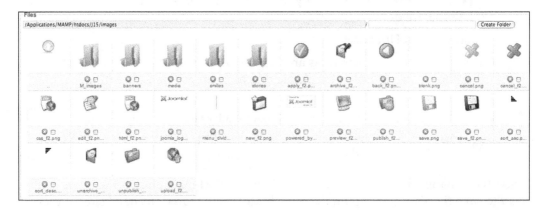

2. **Detailed View**: The Detailed View option shows a five column layout. This contains additional information about each file. The following information is offered in the Detailed View:
   - File Preview
   - File Name in alphabetical order
   - Image Dimensions
   - File Size
   - Delete option

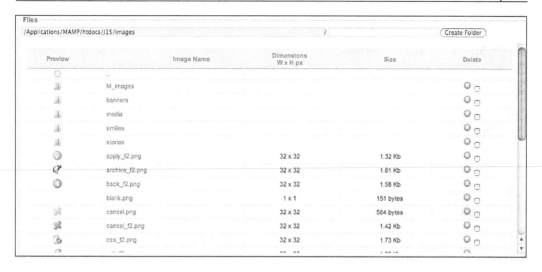

It is a simple click to switch between both of these view types. Depending on the directory you are in and how many files are contained within this, you may find that you often use both of these views.

Organizing your content

By default, the Joomla! Media Manager contains a number of subdirectories which will show up in a column to the left of the Media Manager. By clicking on the folders in this tree structure, you can show their content in the right-hand section of the Media Manager. Navigation through subdirectories in the Media Manager can be done using this method, or by clicking on the folders in the right-hand section which will also show the contents.

The organization of your website media content is of utmost importance. Just like with your Joomla! Articles, the correct structure of your files can save you time and frustration down the line when you want to easily find an image or media file.

One of the limitations in the current version of the Media Manager is that files cannot be moved into other directories. This means that it's important to get your file structure correct at the start of the project, and then files can easily be uploaded to their destination.

Creating a new directory

At the top of the Media Manager, you will see a horizontal bar showing the current directory location you are in. New directories can be easily created in the Media Manager by using the **Create Folder,** situated to the right of this bar.

To make a new directory, first make sure that you are in the directory where you wish to create a new folder. Populate the text field to the left of the **Create Folder** button and then click on this button to create your new directory with that name.

The page should reload, showing your new directory in place.

 A forward slash is already pre-populated, so you only need to enter the name of the directory and nothing else.

Just like with your Joomla! Articles, the better you organize your site files, the easier it is to manage these on an ongoing basis.

Deleting files

As with most things, a spring clean regularly can help in keeping things organized and efficient.

If you are not using your files any more or have created newer versions of them, then you can easily delete them by clicking on the red "X" icon next to the file type:

If you wish to delete multiple files at once, then you tick the checkbox next to each file, and click on the **Delete** button in the top-right of the Media Manager.

Uploading your content

Depending on your "Media Settings" in the Global Configuration, you have the option of using two types of upload features in the Media Manager.

Single file upload

The default uploader in the Media Manager is the single file upload tool, which is located at the bottom of the Media Manager. This tool will allow you to browse your local computer for a single file type, and upload this to your web server in the directory you have chosen.

To upload files using this method, first make sure that your destination for the file upload is correct. The easiest way to do this is by using the **Folder** Directory Menu on the left-hand side, and making sure the directory you want to upload your file to is highlighted.

To upload a file, click on the **Choose File** button. This will allow you to browse your local computer for the file to upload. Once selected, click on the **Start Upload** button to upload this file to your chosen directory on your web server. The Media Manager will refresh once the file is uploaded and you should see your new file inside your selected directory.

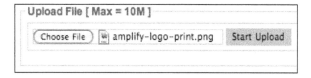

Multiple file uploads

If you have enabled the "Enable Flash Uploader" option in your Global Configuration Media Settings, then you should be able to benefit from the Flash based upload feature.

Like the single file feature, the multiple file Flash uploader is also located at the bottom of the Media Manager.

To upload multiple files, first make sure that the directory you wish to upload to is highlighted. Click on the **Browse Files** button and browse your local computer for a file. Repeat this process until you have a list of the files you wish to upload. Click on the **Start Upload** button to upload the files.

The process will show the status of each file upload.

At the time of writing this book, Flash 11s security settings have broken the built-in Joomla! Media Manager Flash Multi-file upload tool. This may be addressed in future releases of Joomla! However, the single file upload feature is the stable upload tool to use at present.

Managing media using the Media Manager

As mentioned earlier in this chapter, the necessity for good organization of your site content is very important.

Analyzing your project requirements at the start may save you hours of work in the future. A defined directory structure and clear descriptions of these folders can be very helpful for not only your own management, but for other administrators and users who may be uploading files to the site server. Even the default <joomlaroot>/images/stories structure can become challenging at times; now, did I put it in the /images folder or was it the /images/stories folder?

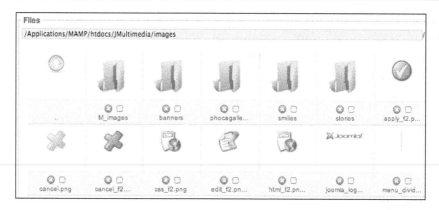

The built-in Media Manager is a wonderful tool for Joomla! administrators. In fact if you have a Joomla! website that has been built by someone else, then this may be your only tool for uploading new files to your web server.

So we agree that it's a cool tool; one, which can limit file types and allow you to create directories and upload files, but unfortunately one that is simplistic and has its limitations. One of these drawbacks is the lack of ability to move files about once they are uploaded.

Remember, we can create as many subdirectories as we wish (under our main media directory). So the trick is to analyze your site purpose at the start of the project, and set up these directories accordingly, which will save you time and frustration down the line. If your site is already established with files and links to these, then the job will certainly become more time consuming to do. A spring clean of the established site is possible though, and will require new directories to be created, files moved into these, and content and links checked to make sure they go to the correct destination.

Alternative method of managing files and media

Depending on your circumstances, you may or may not have login access to your web hosting server. If you do not, then one of your only options for uploading files will be to use the Joomla! Media Manager, or the option of third-party Joomla! Extensions.

If you do have web server access, then by using a method called FTP (File Transfer Protocol), you will be able to gain greater control over your file management.

FTP is a standard network protocol that is used to exchange and manipulate files over a computer network. A common use of FTP is to transfer files over the Internet between a local computer and a web server, which is exactly what we are after!

FTP clients

There are numerous FTP clients (programs) that can be used to transfer files. Some of these graphically show the file and transfer processes, making the management of your files from your computer to your web server very easy to do.

FTP programs

FTP programs range from no cost applications through to commercial software. Which one you choose to use will be down to personal preference. Most of these programs provide drag and drop features as well as easy directory navigation tools:

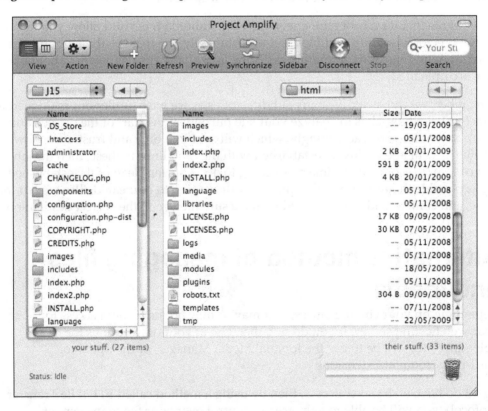

There are excellent FTP programs for all major operating systems. Some popular options for Windows and Mac are:

- Windows
  - ° FileZilla
  - ° CuteFTP
  - ° SmartFTP
  - ° WS_FTP
  - ° cURL
- Mac
  - ° FileZilla
  - ° Transmit
  - ° Cyberduck
  - ° CuteFTP
  - ° Fetch
  - ° FTP Command in Terminal

If you perform a search using a popular search engine, you will obtain a definitive list of FTP programs. A suggestion would be to download a trial version of these to see which one suits your operating system and requirements.

For the purpose of this topic, I have chosen to use and take screenshots from an FTP program called "Transmit". It is a commercial product, but personally one of my favorites. For those whose use MAC computers, Transmit is recognized as a wonderful FTP tool.

Connecting using an FTP program

Almost all FTP programs require similar information in order to connect to the web server. Depending on the program you are using, the naming of these fields may be slightly different.

In order to connect, we need the following information which is usually derived from setting up a user account (with FTP permissions) on your web hosting control panel:

1. **Server**

   This is the server address that you wish to connect to. Typically this can look like `ftp.yourserver.com`. Depending on the domain name settings, it can sometimes be your domain name, such as `www.yourserver.com`.

2. **User Name**

   This is your web server account username. Often this can be in the format of `yourusername@yourdomain.com`.

3. **Password**

   This is your web server account password.

4. **Initial Path**

   Some programs offer the ability to set an initial directory to navigate to upon login. If you do not have this option, then do not worry.

5. **Port**

   If the server requires connections on a port other than the default one, some programs offer you the ability to enter in a **port** number. It is best to leave this as the default setting unless you know what you are doing.

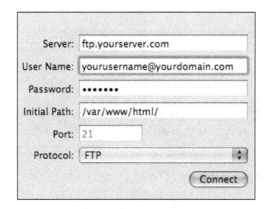

If you are having any issues connecting, then it's best to contact your web hosting administrator in order to check your login access details.

There are typically three types of FTP login methods available. These are:

1. **Anonymous FTP access**

   This is an easy connection method as you do not need to include any user information. Sometimes software companies offer updates or corporate and government websites offer forms and content to be downloaded via an anonymous connection method.

2. **Username**

   A simplified but restricted access level where you will be required to enter just a username. This type of FTP login is often used in school and intranet environments.

3. **Username and Password**

   This is a more restricted security access level where the user requires both a username and password in order to access the server. This method is often used by web hosting companies who offer people the ability to upload files to the web server.

If your FTP connection is set to username (or username and password), then you should see a dialog box on the screen. This will prompt you to enter your security access details:

Once connected, you will need to navigate to your webroot folder. Depending on your web server, this area may be named httpdocs, mainwebsite_html, public_html, or other naming conventions. It will be inside this directory where your Joomla! website files will reside.

When you have located your main `http` documents area and clicked to navigate inside this, you will see the default Joomla! media folder named **images**.

When you have successfully navigated to your remote main media folder (or any of the subfolders within this), you will need to make sure that you also navigate locally to the folders or files you wish to upload. Most FTP programs offer you the ability to create new directories, and drag and drop files from your local computer to the web server.

By using an FTP program, you can gain additional control over your website files and content.

FTP programs can allow you to:

- Create files and directories
- Rename files and directories
- Move files and directories
- Delete files and directories
- Set file and directory permissions

 FTP programs offer you the most flexibility in managing your website files, but it is important to take care when using FTP programs. By connecting to your directory structure on the web server, you are navigating amongst core Joomla! files.

FTP via a web browser

In addition to browsing the World Wide Web, modern web browsers are comprehensive internet tools containing additional features such as RSS readers, the ability to use e-mail, and work with FTP.

Although you can use dedicated FTP programs as we have covered, it's easy to connect to FTP servers using a typical web browser such as Firefox or Internet Explorer.

For the purpose of this example and screenshots, we will be using Mozilla Firefox.

Connecting to FTP via a web browser

There are some cases where web browser FTP access can be restricted by organizations, but in general, if you can use an FTP program to connect to your web hosting server, then you should be able to connect via FTP using your web browser.

The benefits of using a web browser are: Well... it's free and you probably already have it in front of you!

As when using an FTP program to connect, there are typically three types of FTP login methods available. These are:

1. **Anonymous FTP access**

    Authentication methods for FTP via a web browser are the same as when using a software-based FTP program.

2. **Username**

    A simplified but restricted access level where you will be required to enter just a username. This type of FTP login is often used in school and intranet environments.

3. **Username and Password**

    This is a more restricted security access level where the user requires both a username and password in order to access the server. This method is often used by web hosting companies, who offer people the ability to upload files to the web server.

There are usually two methods of connecting to FTP via a web browser. These are:

1. **Enter an FTP address into the address bar**

    For most web browsers that offer FTP support, it is possible to type in the syntax: `ftp.yourserver.com` or sometimes `ftp.yourdomainname.com`, and then press *Enter*.

If your FTP connection is set to **Username** (or **Username** and **Password**), then you should see a dialog box on the screen. This will prompt you to enter your security access details:

If you are having any issues connecting, then it's best to contact your web hosting administrator in order to check your login access details.

Once connected, you will need to navigate to your webroot folder. Depending on your web server, this area may be named httpdocs, mainwebsite_html, public_html, or other naming conventions. It will be inside this directory where your Joomla! website files will reside.

2. **Entering directly into the address bar**

The second method of connecting via FTP in a web browser is to enter the user information directly into the address bar. Although this can save you a step, I often find that users can make mistakes using this method, taking them longer than the previous connection method.

Different browsers may have slightly different syntax, but when using Mozilla Firefox you would enter something similar to the following directly into the address bar:

ftp://username: password@yourserver.com

For example, if my username was john and my password was 12345, then that would look like: ftp:john: 12345@yourserver.com.

Quite often the username can contain the domain name. If this is the case, the syntax would look like: ftp:john@yourserver.com: 12345@yourserver.com.

Uploading and downloading

Once you are connected to FTP by a web browser (by either of the previous methods), the uploading and downloading of files is usually quite intuitive.

```
Index of ftp://ftp.projectamplify.com
/mainwebsite_html/images/

    Up to higher level directory

  Name              Size      Last Modified
    AllanWalker.jpg  18 KB     19/3/09    16:21:00
    Box.jpg          15 KB     5/11/08    00:00:00
    M_images                   5/11/08    00:00:00
    apply_f2.png     2 KB      9/9/08     00:00:00
    archive_f2.png   2 KB      9/9/08     00:00:00
    articles                   18/5/09    11:44:00
    back_f2.png      2 KB      9/9/08     00:00:00
    banners                    5/11/08    00:00:00
    blank.png        1 KB      9/9/08     00:00:00
    cancel.png       1 KB      9/9/08     00:00:00
    cancel_f2.png    2 KB      9/9/08     00:00:00
    css_f2.png       2 KB      9/9/08     00:00:00
    edit_f2.png      2 KB      9/9/08     00:00:00
    favicon.ico      2 KB      21/11/08   00:00:00
```

To upload a new file, make sure you are residing in the correct remote directory for upload. Browse to a file on your computer and simply drag this file over into your web browser. Depending on the size of the file, this might take some time to upload and then the process should complete. You can download a file in a similar manner, or you might need to double-click on the file to start downloading it.

Web browser plugins

A number of popular web browsers offer you extension plugins, which can enhance the FTP capabilities when using the browser connection method.

The Firefox web browser has a useful extension called **FireFTP**. This plugin offers you a left and right view to easily manage and move files via FTP using your web browser. FireFTP is just like having a stand alone FTP program on your computer. It's free to use and works on Windows, Mac, and Linux. More information about FireFTP can be found by visiting http://fireftp.mozdev.org/.

The following screenshot shows the **FireFTP** plugin:

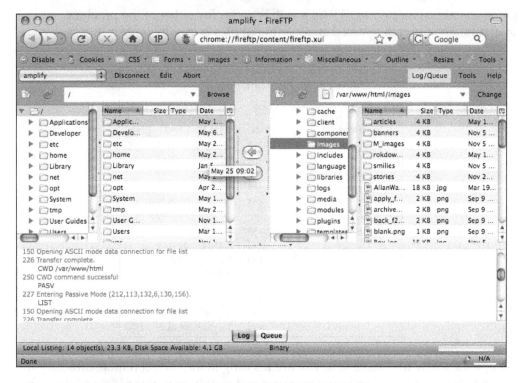

It is important to mention that, if you are performing regular file uploading, then using a specialist FTP browser plugin or FTP program will offer you additional features and make life easier for you. Usually you can save your favorite connections, so you can login to your web server with a few clicks.

With lots of free FTP programs available now that provide the options for file moving, renaming, and in some cases server-to-server file movement, there is no reason why you should not be using one of these if you have FTP server access and perform regular transfers.

SFTP

Secure FTP (SFTP) is a program that uses SSH to transfer files. SFTP encrypts both the commands and data being transferred, creating a secure connection between your computer and the remote server. You can use SFTP via an SFTP client, or the command line. Most FTP clients do offer SFTP support, but not all web hosts support SFTP, so it will pay to check with yours before trying to use this transfer method.

Third-party file management extensions

For the majority of users, the Joomla! Media Manager or using FTP will be more than enough to manage media between your computer and your Joomla! website. A number of file management extensions are also available in the `http://extensions.joomla.org` area. Some of these provide enhanced file uploading features, and others provide the abilities of an FTP program located within our Joomla! Administration.

Listed below are two popular extensions that provide an administrator with file management capabilities within the Joomla! Administration.

 There are also a number of excellent Document Management and Download Extensions to offer frontend document sharing and management. As mentioned earlier, for further file management extensions, visit `http://extensions.joomla.org` to see the available extensions.

eXtplorer

eXtplorer is a third-party file management application which runs natively under Joomla! 1.0 x and 1.5 versions. eXtplorer easily installs as a Joomla! component, but a requirement is to run in legacy mode for Joomla! 1.5.

You can use eXtplorer to access and modify files and directories on your server via FTP or direct file access. Rather than firing up an FTP client, using an extension like this can perform powerful file management actions from the backend of your Joomla! Administration:

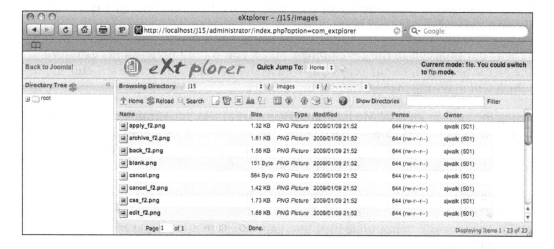

Joomla! Flash Uploader

Joomla! Flash Uploader is similar to the built-in Media Manager Flash uploader, but this extension contains extended features. It does not seem affected by the same issues that the Joomla! Media Manager Flash upload tool currently receives due to Flash security settings. This extension allows you to upload multiple files easily from your desktop to your Joomla! web directories. One nice feature of this extension is the ability to create "Upload Profiles" for your website users. This means you can give different website users different directories to upload to if you wish—a handy feature for larger sites requiring additional control over user uploading.

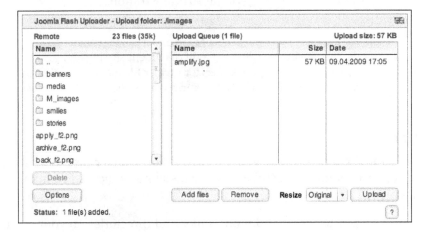

Summary

Good organization and structure of your website media is as important as it is to Joomla! Articles.

When your project is in the development stage, you should review and customize the Media Settings for your project, as well as define usable directory structures, which will make file management a simplified task.

Using the built-in Joomla! Media Manager is a great way for administrators (and frontend users with permission) to create directory structures and easily upload files from their local computer to the web server. Once uploaded, files can then be used in Joomla! Articles and in Components and Modules.

For developers (and site users with additional access to the server), the use of FTP is a powerful way to manage your files and site content, allowing you the ability to move and manipulate files, and gain access to other areas of your Joomla! file structure.

3
Text, Characters, and Fonts in Your Joomla! Site

Some may ask, why is a chapter about text and fonts being included in a book about multimedia?

The answer is quite straightforward: Text (and the styling of it) is one of the most prominent media types that has been, and is still, used in web pages. Although it's such a major media element, web developers often pay little attention to this subject.

In this chapter, we will highlight the use of fonts, characters, and text within your Joomla! site, and how we can not only change the site design by using another font typeface, but also affect your site user's overall experience by doing so.

Topics include:

- Overview of text, characters, and fonts
- Fonts and their effect on website users
- Which font is best to use?
- Joomla! Templates and Cascading Style Sheets (CSS)
- Alternative methods to use custom fonts in your web pages
- Joomla! text and typography extensions
- Browser support and accessibility around fonts

Overview of text, characters, and fonts

Text, and the use of it, is one of the largest contributions to most website pages. Text and characters are used to communicate and deliver information to the reader. When large blocks of text are displayed, it is important that it is styled to visually please the reader, as well as being easily readable.

Plain Text is a term, which is used to describe text that does not contain attributes such as fonts and styling. It is readable by almost all computer programs. In one respect, HTML code, CSS, and XML files are all plain text, but they also contain structural tags included with the characters.

A **Character** is a symbol. It can be a letter, a digit, or a punctuation mark, as well as a range of other informative symbols. Characters represent units of information.

A **Font** (also fount) is traditionally defined as "a complete character set of a single size and style of a particular typeface".

In the early days of the Web there was plain text on screens. This text could only have one style applied to it, making most web pages look very similar in text formatting, such as this screenshot of an early web page designed by Tim Berners-Lee in 1991:

Topology

Here are a few questions about the underlying connectivity of a hypertext web.

Are links two- or multi-ended?

The term "link" normally indeicates with two ends. Variations of this are liks with multiple sources and/or multiple destinations, and constructs which relate more than two anchors. The latter map onto logic description systems, predicate calculus, etc. See the "Aquanet" system from Xerox PARC - paper at HT91). This is a natural step from hypertext whose the links are typed with semantic content. For example, the relation "Document A is a basis for document B given argument C". From now on however, let us restrict ourselves to links in the conventional sense, that is, with two ends.

Should the links be monodirectional or bidirectional?

If they are bidirectional, a link always exists in the reverse direction. A disadvantage of this being enforced is that it might constrain the author of a hypertext - he might want to constrain the reader. However, an advantage is that often, when a link is made between two nodes, it is made in one direction in the mind of its author, but another reader may be more interested in the reverse link. Put another way, bidirectional linking allows the system to deduce the inverse relationship, that if A includes B, for example, that B is part of A. This effectively adds information for free. This is important when a critical parameter of the system is how long it takes someone to create a link.

KMS and hypercard have one-way links; Enquire has two-way links.

There is a question of how one can make a two-way link to a protected database. The automatic addition of the reverse link is very useful for enhancing the information content of the database. See also: Private overlaid web , Generic Links .

It may be useful to have bidirectional links from the point of view of managing data. For example: if a document is destroyed or moved, one is aware of what dangling links will be created, and can possibly fix them.

In general, the fonts that were used on computer devices (for screen viewing) were usually transpositions of popular offline printing styles, for example those for printed books. In early web pages, there were only a small number of typefaces available for use. The one main typographic constant that was used was a font called "Times New Roman" (for Windows), and "Times" (for MAC). These early computer typefaces were almost always members of the **serif** font family (or serified fonts).

Serif fonts are an imitation of hand written characters, and their style is usually enriched by (calli) graphic embellishments. A serif is a flick added to the tips of the lines that make up the character. An example of a serif font typeface (Times New Roman) is as follows; note the serifs (flicks) on each character:

The five main font families are:

1. Serif
2. Sans-serif
3. Cursive
4. Fantasy
5. Monospace

Next to "Serif" another popular font family is **sans-serif** or **sans serif**. A sans-serif typeface is one that does not contain the small character embellishments (serifs) at the end of the strokes. The term comes from the French word "sans", meaning "without".

Sans-serif fonts have now become the de-facto standard typeface for general body text that is viewed on screens. This is partly due to screen resolutions not being able to show the (serif) embellishments clearly, and a number of fonts residing in the "sans-serif family" have been created especially for screen view, such as the following example called "Helvetica". This having been said, do not write off fonts in the "serif" family, as these are also popular web font options.

Many tests have been performed regarding usability of typefaces residing within these font families, especially when they are delivered on computer screens. With the characters having to fit a relatively small pixel grid on screens, it is considered by designers that sans-serif fonts lend themselves more naturally to being digitized for screen view.

Fonts have been a popular method of stylizing plain text for centuries. You may be surprised to know that a number of the fonts installed on your computer will be older than you think. For example, Wikipedia quotes that the serif font "Times New Roman" was commissioned by the British newspaper "The Times" in 1931 and "Helvetica" first made its debut in 1957.

Fonts and their effect on website users

One of the most important (and often overlooked) area of web design is the use of text sizing and font choice. Many inexperienced designers fail to realize the effect these can have on the visitor's initial experience on their site pages. This in turn may cause a great effect on traffic conversions and the bounce rate of your site visitors.

Of course, the language you use throughout your website needs to be informative, make sense, and be of interest to your visitors. However, if this "wonderful content" is wrapped in a text size that is too large or small, and your users find it difficult to read, then those users are likely to leave your site and not return again. Equally, if you have given thought and consideration to your text sizing and font style, then this may help improve the duration your visitors stay on your site pages and possibly their return rate.

It's interesting reading about Joomla! text and fonts

It's interesting reading about Joomla! text and fonts

It's interesting reading about Joomla! text and fonts

It's interesting reading about Joomla! text and fonts

Preferences for visual appearance will always vary from person to person and the readability of a typeface may determine its appropriate use on a particular audience. Each typeface will produce some form of visual emotion to the user, and some fonts can portray a "take me seriously" emotion, while others a "relaxed" feeling while reading the text.

If you were going for a job interview, you might take time to dress up accordingly for the job-role. Presentation is everything; and the same goes for the typefaces used in your web pages. Typefaces attract attention; they set a tone and emotion to the text they embellish. Change your typeface and you can go from creating a casual feeling in your web pages to a formal one, unorganized to stylish, old fashioned to modern, and so on.

Typefaces are here to serve the text. They should be easy to read (especially when used in body text) and create a subtle style that does not overpower the reader. A number of font websites categorize their fonts into useful groups. If you would like assistance in choosing a font for your website, take a look at the font assistance tool at `http://www.esperfonto.com/`.

Which font is best to use?

When it comes to typefaces and fonts, there are plenty to choose from. A search for "fonts" in a popular search engine gave me 50,500,000 results and easily over 100,000 different typefaces were available.

Before you go out and buy a new hard drive to install all of these fonts, it is important to note that there are only a few fonts which are actually classed as easily readable fonts to use for the Web. These are fonts that are available on most computer operating systems and actually look good (as well as being easily readable) when viewed on screen.

If you are a designer, then you will probably have the web safe, major font groups installed on your computer. These typefaces would have been included in your computer when it was purchased. By visiting some of the popular font download sites, you could go ahead and install lots of additional typefaces. However, there is no point in specifying these interesting and custom typefaces on our websites, if the end user viewing the site doesn't have these fonts also installed on their computer. Without the same font available they won't see what we see. Hence, when choosing your font typeface we need to choose from a list of "Popular font families", in order to reach the majority of our site users.

The subject of "What font is best for the Web?" is an intriguing and long-winded one. Remember, it's best to play it safe for your body text and use one of the following popular choices:

Sans-serif fonts

The fonts in this family are as follows:

Verdana

Verdana was designed by Microsoft in 1996. Its purpose was specifically for screen use. The absence of serifs and the wide spacing make this font a popular choice for the Web.

Verdana

Arial and Helvetica

Helvetica (for MAC) and Arial (for MAC and Windows) is a common font style created over 50 years ago by Swiss designers. Although two different fonts, they are similar in properties with Arial being created by Microsoft as their version of the style. Arial and Helvetica are one of the most widely used sans-serif fonts.

Arial
Helvetica

Trebuchet MS

Trebuchet MS was developed for screen use and is common on Windows and MAC systems. It is popular for large headings and some consider it not quite as legible as Verdana for normal size print. It's best to try it out and see what you think!

Trebuchet MS

Lucinda Sans family

Lucinda Sans Unicode (Windows) and Lucinda Grande (MAC) were not created for the Web, but are remarkably legible when reading on screen. Lucinda Grande is the font choice used on MAC operating systems. They are considered the most calligraphic of typefaces within the sans-serif family.

Lucinda Sans
Lucinda Grande

Serif fonts

The fonts in this family are as follows:

Times New Roman / Times

Times New Roman (Windows and MAC) and Times (MAC) are primarily an offline print based font that is approximately 80 years old now. It is not the best font for screens but often a good second choice in your CSS file because it is such a prevalent computer font.

> Times New Roman
> Times

Georgia

Georgia is a font commissioned by Microsoft; again it was made especially for the screen. Although a serif font, Georgia tends to work well for screen viewing of small and larger text. Designers often substitute Times New Roman with this font due to its preferred web viewing properties.

> Georgia

Palatino Linotype / Palatino

Palatino Linotype (Windows) and Palatino (MAC) were developed over 60 years ago and are not screen fonts, but they render very well for web use. Microsoft distributed a clear imitation of this font; they called it "Book Antiqua".

> Palatino Linotype
> Palatino

The previous typefaces are recommended fonts to use for your main body text. However, there are methods for being able to show fancy custom fonts in your web pages, allowing all of your site users to view them without the need to install the fonts on their system.

If you are looking for examples of what various fonts look like on your screen, take a look at the **TYPETESTER** online tool at `http://www.typetester.org/`. This type tool allows you to include your custom text, and then format this with a variety of font and size options, viewing the output on your screen. There are many tools available that do this, but TYPETESTER is a great example of them:

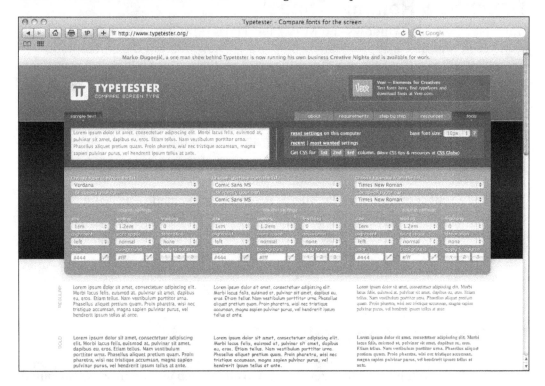

Joomla! Templates and Cascading Style Sheets

Before we launch into adjusting our Joomla! CSS font, it is important to include a brief introduction regarding Joomla! Templates.

What is a Joomla! Template?

A Joomla! Template is a set of files which control the presentation of your website content. Templates are packaged with a "formal file structure", meaning that they have certain requirements in order to work with Joomla! Each Template file plays a vital part in producing your final website design, its structure, and your site pages' interactive features.

Joomla! Templates are usually packaged up in a zipped format and installed using the built-in Joomla! upload / unzip feature. They come in all shapes and sizes and are designed in such a way that when they are installed and activated, they will display your Joomla! content with their designated structure and design:

Using templates has a number of benefits, including:

- A new template can be applied instantly to your website content. This flexibility means a completely different design may be given to your website with little effort.

- Multiple styles can be applied to your website by using a number of templates. If you are looking to provide different design layouts to different areas of your CMS, then this is an important feature.

- The template contains all CSS and website styling. This is all self-contained and can include overrides. By going into your "Templates area", you can easily make adjustments to your current template, and include custom changes into this folder, protecting the "Core Joomla! Framework".

An important styling element of a Joomla! Template is the CSS. These .css files contain important layout and style information, which contributes to your Joomla! website design.

Template CSS

Cascading Style Sheets are a web developer's best friend! They provide us with the opportunity to be completely consistent with our site styling, and provide additional layout and design options than plain HTML usage can offer.

Before CSS was used, nearly all of the styling in an HTML document was contained in the HTML code. Color, layout, styling, fonts, among others had to be specifically listed in the code, often repeatedly throughout the HTML document:

```
<html>
<body>
<p><font size="2" face="Verdana">
This is a paragraph of text.
</font></p>
<p><font size="5" face="Times" color="red">
This is another paragraph.
</font></p>
</body>
</html>
```

Here text is styled using an older HTML method, where the styling is within the HTML code.

By using a CSS method, it allows us to put most of this styling information into a separate document (.css file). This information can be referenced in the HTML easily, resulting in a more efficient process and considerably simpler HTML code.

The HTML code is as follows:

```
<html>
<body>
<p>This is a paragraph of text.<p>
</body>
</html>
```

The CSS code is as follows:

```
p {
    font-family:Helvetica ,Arial,sans-serif;
    font-size: 1em;
    color: #000000;
    text-align: left;
    width: 100%;
}
```

The previous HTML and CSS code shows the styling of a p tag.

CSS information can be embedded into the HTML document, but for a Joomla! Template it is usually included in a separate document. Quite often Joomla! Templates contain multiple CSS files to separate the design elements. When using CSS, a separate stylesheet for a handheld device may be used to accommodate the smaller screen resolution, a custom stylesheet could be used just for the Internet Explorer 6 browser, and so on. Your Joomla! Template can contain coding to tell the browser what stylesheet to load in, depending on what type of appliance the user is viewing your website with.

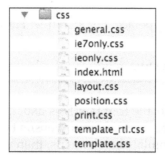

The Joomla! Template CSS file is usually located in the following directory `/templates/yourtemplate/css/template.css`. If you are using a pre-built Joomla! Template, you may see multiple CSS files inside the CSS directory. It is important to note that the names of these CSS files may differ between Joomla! Templates, but the `template.css` file is the standard naming convention for the main CSS file. Certain WYSIWYG editors rely on this naming convention to work correctly.

We could devote a whole book to the complexities of CSS. For this chapter, however, we are just going to highlight the font property, and its available values.

CSS font properties

Let's take a look at the numerous properties we can manipulate the text with when using CSS:

Font family

The font family property is a prioritized list of font names for an element. It is possible (and good practice) to specify more than one font typeface in case the user does not have the font you are specifying loaded on their computer system. In CSS, your browser will use the first font that it recognizes; hence we always list our font families in a priority order:

```
body {
    font-family: Arial,Courier,sans-serif;
    line-height: 1.3em;
    margin: 0px;
    font-size: 12px;
    color: #333;
}
```

In the previous example, the font `Arial` will be used ahead of the
font `Courier`.

There are two types of font-family values:

1. **Family Name**

   The name of the font typeface. For example: Helvetica, Courier, Arial.

2. **Generic Family**

   The name of one of the five generic font categories. For example, serif, sans-serif, and so on.

In a Joomla! Template CSS file, the font family is usually applied to the body tag. This specifies a main font to be used for your website body text. If you require additional styling to other Joomla! text elements, then we define those accordingly using further CSS.

```
body {
     font-family: Arial,Helvetica,sans-serif;
}
```

In the previous example, the browser will look for the font `Arial`, then `Helvetica`, and if for some unknown reason the user didn't have those fonts installed on their computer device, then the browser would substitute an available `sans-serif` font to use.

Where you use font families having more than one word in the name, it is important to surround these font names with double quote marks. While some browsers can read these fonts without the quote marks, problems can occur if the white space in between the words is considered or ignored.

```
body {
     font-family: Arial,"Times New Roman",sans-serif;
}
```

Note the `Times New Roman` in quotation marks.

Font size

The font size property in CSS sets the size of your text. Font sizing methods that you can utilize in CSS can either be of absolute (fixed), or relative size.

1. **Absolute:**

   ° Sets the text to a specific size

   ° Absolute sizing is useful if a fixed output or container is known. Using this method you can get the text to sit exactly as you wish into that defined area.

   ° Does not allow the user to adjust the text sizing in some browsers. For this reason it is considered poor for accessibility.

 2. **Relative**:

   ° Allows the user to change their text size in all browsers.

   ° The font size is based off the default font setting in the browser. The user can change this default value if they wish.

   ° Sets a size of the text that is relative to the surrounding elements.

The debate regarding which method to use is as on-going as which font typeface is best for the screen. Specifying in pt or px (absolute methods) has been classified as non-W3C accessible, but allows you to style text in a confined container with more design control. If the layout of your text is important, then you may require this styling method to align your text as you wish.

If text can just spill out on the page and be resized by the user if required, then relative is the preferred and accessible method of managing font size. Relative sizing can be done using em measurement or % (percent).

As a general rule:

```
1em = 16px = 12pt = 100%
```

Meet the units

In CSS there are four different units with which we can measure the size of the text as it is displayed in the web browser.

Setting the text size using em

To cater for all browsers and retain accessibility standards on your website, most designers are trying to adopt the em relative text sizing method. This is the preferred text resizing method by the W3C standards.

The way em sizing works is: 1em is equal to the current font size of the element in question. If you have not set a font size in other areas of your CSS, then it will take the user's default browser font size. The default text size in browsers is 16px, and usually a font such as Arial font or Times. This means the default size of 1em = 16px. If you were to set a font size for the body, say 18px, then 1em = 18px.

For general body text, you may see something similar to this Joomla! CSS file:

```css
body {
    font-family: Helvetica,Arial,sans-serif;
    line-height: 1.3em;
    margin: 0px 0px 0px 0px;
    font-size: 12px;
    color: #333;
}
```

Once the main body text font size has been specified, as in the previous example, other text elements in your CSS can then be set relative to this using em's:

```css
h2, .contentheading {
    padding: 0;
    font-family: Arial, Helvetica,sans-serif;
    font-size: 1.4em;
    font-weight: normal;
    vertical-align: bottom;
    color: #333;
    text-align: left;
    width: 100%;
}
```

Setting the text size using percent

Sizing using percentages works, as you would probably expect a percentage to work. Just like em's, using a percentage styling method is relative.

If the parent item has a font size of 24px, and the child has a percentage of 50%, then it will be displayed with font size of 12px.

Just like em's , one popular technique for sizing using percentages is to set a parent font size on the body of your CSS, and then use percentages for all other styling. Everything will be relative to that one parent size which is set:

```css
.tool-text {
    font-size: 95%;
    margin: 0;
}
```

Setting the text size using pixels

Pixels are fixed size units that are used in screen media. One pixel is equal to one dot on your screen and when using pixels to size your text you are telling the browsers to render the text exactly that number of pixels high. Using pixels to define our text size provides us with excellent control over the size and layout of the text. Using pixels, however, does not allow the ability to scale upwards for visually impaired users, nor scale downwards for mobile devices.

Sizing your text using pixels will allow browsers such as Firefox and Safari to still retain some text control, but when viewing with Internet Explorer 6 the user will not be able to resize this absolute styled text. All in all, setting font sizes with px is an accurate method, but do take into consideration the IE 6 lack of accessibility.

Setting the text size using points

The unit of points (pt) is usually associated with print media. Points are much like pixels in that they are of fixed size and cannot be scaled to size. Just like pixels are accurate for screen resolutions, points are accurate on paper.

```
72pts = one inch
```

It is not good practice to use pt styling for your Joomla! Template CSS, but it would be good to use points when creating a separate print.css stylesheet.

An example of print CSS may look like:

```
body {
  color : #000000;
  background : #ffffff;
  font-family : "Times New Roman", Times, serif;
  font-size : 12pt;
}
```

Font style

The "font style" property sets the style of your specified fonts.

The values are:

- **Normal**

  The browser will display a normal font style
- **Italic**

  The browser will display an italic font
- **Oblique**

  The browser will display an oblique font

When written down in the CSS, the font-style property may look like this:

```
body {
font-style: italic;
}
```

Font weight

The font weight property sets the width of the font. For example, how thick or thin the text should be displayed.

The values are:

- **Normal**

  Defines normal characters

- **Bold**

  Defines thick characters

- **Bolder**

  Defines thicker characters

- **Lighter**

  Defines lighter characters

You can also use the values: 100-900.

This method defines thick to thin characters and offers a further level of control. As an indication, the value 400 is the same as normal, and the value 700 is the same as bold.

```
p
{
font-weight: bold;
}
```

Using CSS, it is possible to define each of the font properties within your document, or you can define all of the values into one shorthand property. This is called simply font.

The "font" property in CSS can include the "line-height" value. This element allows you to set the space between the text lines:

```
p
{
font: italic bold 900 12px/14px arial;
}
```

Alternative methods to use custom fonts in your web pages

So, we really like a specific font and wish to use this for our menu or heading, but we know that the reader won't have this installed on their computer system. What can be done?

One of the most popular methods is to use images in place of the text. By using an image method, you can design your typeface in a graphics program (in the font of your choice) and then put that into your website page. This means that the user ends up viewing the words in your selected font. For Joomla! Templates, you will often see this method used for menu and module icons, among others.

Image replacement techniques can also be performed using a PHP / JavaScript Library called **FaceLift Image Replacement (FLIR)**, pronounced "fleer". This technique automatically replaces any text on the web page with an automatically generated picture if the font is not found on the user's machine. FLIR is open source and doesn't require other tools to be used on the server, nor any plugins to be loaded on the user's browser. FLIR requires PHP and the GD Image Library to be installed on the server.

The following is an example of FLIR in action on the home page at
`http://facelift.mawhorter.net`.

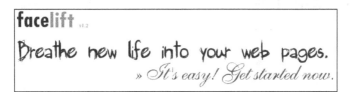

Scalable Inman Flash Replacement (sIFR) is another method of replacing short passages of plain text, with that rendered in the font of your choice. The sIFR method uses a combination of Flash, JavaScript, and CSS. sIFR is a new technology growing in popularity. sIFR is also open source, and requires the Flash player plugin to be installed in the reading browser.

Initiatives for real-time downloading of specific fonts to the user's browser are being developed and browser support being phased-in, and I'm sure in the near future will be available. There are even a number of sIFR extensions now available for Joomla! These will be mentioned in the following sections.

Joomla! text and typography extensions

The majority of professional Joomla! Templates now available have "Typography" and text / font features built directly into them. Pre-configured class styling have been included into the CSS sheets, allowing the end user a vast array of text styling at their fingertips.

From administration driven "What font do you want to use?" parameters, through to included `.class` styling, your template can take on a stunning new text look with small changes:

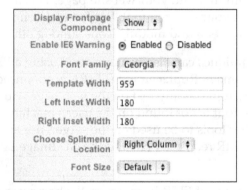

The majority of modern professional Joomla! Templates now contain pre-styled typography options which provide style and interest within your site pages:

In true open source fashion, there are a number of Joomla! Extensions available. These have been built to enhance the Joomla! Templates with all sorts of interesting text functionality.

Frontend font size adjuster (M)

This module allows visitors to increase or decrease the font size on the site pages. Visitors' font settings are remembered by use of JavaScript and a Cookie.

This module contains six different buttons and styles, and it is possible to assign a class to the module so you can customize these to suit your site:

To utilize this extension, visit `http://extensions.joomla.org` and search for "Font Size".

JsIFR3 (P)

Use any font in your Joomla! 1.5 website. This plugin incorporates Scalable Inman Flash Replacement (sIFR) into Joomla! 1.5.

There is a commercial version of this plugin, but this non-commercial version offers 14 plugin parameter settings to help refine the results for your project:

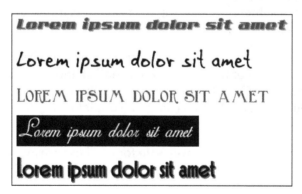

To utilize this extension, visit `http://extensions.joomla.org` and search for "jsIFR3".

capDropper (P)

capDropper is a simple plugin that makes the first letter of an article appear styled as a drop capital.

Styling can be adjusted to suit your template and the plugin activated or de-activated manually at an article level.

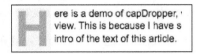

To utilize this extension, visit `http://extensions.joomla.org` and search for "capDropper".

There are numerous extensions which allow easy "text-resizing" and "drop capital" capabilities, alongside commercial versions of sIFR extensions. Visit `http://extensions.joomla.org/` in order to view the latest text and typography extensions that can spice up your Joomla! website.

Browser support and accessibility around fonts

As mentioned earlier in this chapter, there are a specific number of fonts which should be used for your main body text on website pages. The reason for these selected few is because they are easy to read and available on a diverse range of user computer systems, therefore offering the best opportunity to reach as large an audience as you can.

Fonts which usually fit into the previous categorization are called "web safe" fonts. Web safe fonts are a group of fonts which are installed and common among all versions of Windows, MAC, and Linux computers. By choosing a web safe font as a site designer, you increase the chance of your content being displayed in your chosen format.

The following is a list of recognized web safe fonts. These are available on Windows, MAC, and Linux operating systems:

Arial, Helvetica - sans-serif
Comic Sans MS - cursive
Courier New, Courier6 - monospace
Georgia - serif
Impact, Charcoal6 - sans-serif
Monaco5 - monospace
Lucida Sans Unicode, Lucida Grande - sans-serif
Palatino Linotype, Book Antiqua3, Palatino6 - serif
Tahoma, Geneva - sans-serif
Times New Roman, Times - serif
Trebuchet MS1, Helvetica - sans-serif
Verdana, Geneva - sans-serif
Symbol, Σψμβολ2
Webdings, ♦︎♏︎♌︎♎︎♅︎■︎♓︎♦︎▤
MS Sans Serif4, Geneva - sans-serif

Microsoft started a "Core Fonts for the Web" initiative back in 1996. This set contained existing fonts, fonts which were commissioned by Microsoft, and some licensed from Apple. The "Core Fonts for the Web" selections are classified as members of the "web safe" font category.

"Core Fonts for the Web" were designed to:

- Support an international market
- Be legible on screen
- Offer a range of typographic styles

The "Core Fonts for the Web" initiative included the following fonts. Note that these fonts are all the same font size.

Andale Mono
Arial
Comic Sans MS
Courier New
Georgia
Impact
Times New Roman
Trebuchet MS
Verdana
♦︎♏︎♌︎♎︎♅︎■︎♓︎♦︎
(Webdings)

As mentioned earlier in this chapter, using a generic font family which is defined in your CSS will be the safest option. Remember our generic font families?

- Serif
- Sans-serif
- Cursive
- Fantasy
- Monospace

One of these font families should always be specified at the end of your font family CSS definition, like this:

```
body {
    font-family: Arial,Helvetica,sans-serif;
}
```

The previous example shows the `sans-serif` font family that would be loaded in if neither the `Arial` or `Helvetica` fonts were available on the user's computer system.

As web browsers continue to evolve and adopt font typefaces, the real-time downloading and displaying of specific fonts will evolve our current "web safe" font limitations. For now, it's best to play safe (by choosing a web safe font) and make sure your site visitors (whatever their browser and operating system) can easily read and obtain your important textual information.

Summary

The use of text in our Joomla! web pages is usually the most prominent media element on the page. However, if a pre-built template has been used with an included font style, often little consideration has been given towards the font type and if it is suitable for the intended audience.

This chapter has highlighted the numerous fonts that are available to use and which ones are classified as "web safe", providing your users with the best opportunity to see the site text styling as you designed it to be seen.

Joomla! Template CSS files are an important and powerful styling mechanism that allows us to define and style our site text as well as other elements. In our CSS, we can use fixed text styling methods, or relative, allowing the user to resize their web page text as they require. Many Joomla! Templates contain enhanced "Typography" features including font-options and custom CSS styling. There are also some excellent third-party font extensions available at `http://extensions.joomla.org/`. Some of these include image replacement features which bring some exciting new font technologies to your Joomla! website.

Web Safe fonts are a safe choice to use for your main body-text. There is a great range of web safe fonts, which can provide different emotional responses from your site users. By choosing the correct font for your site, you can evoke numerous emotions such as a serious, humorous, or a classy feeling to your web text. You can also increase visitor "time on site", by providing correct font size and user-resizing controls for the text. Make sure you specify a font family in your CSS definitions, so if your specified fonts are not available, the browser will be able to choose a generic family-font to display your site text.

4
Adding and Managing Image Content

Next to text content, images are one of the most utilized multimedia resources in web pages. They can be used to inform and educate the reader, offer help with navigation, and to enhance the design and user's overall visual experience.

Whether you need to create multimedia image galleries in your Joomla! website or simply add images to your articles and modules, this chapter will provide the assistance to help utilize image content effectively within your Joomla! website. We look at:

- Why we use images in websites
- Image formats and which ones to use
- Including images in articles and modules
- Creating image galleries and slideshows
- Template images
- Joomla! Image Extensions
- Browser support and accessibility for images

Images and why we use them in websites

Research suggests that images enhance learning by illustrating the concepts visually and by providing visual memory cues to the viewer. We have been using images to describe, tell stories, and record history since our human evolution.

I have been in a few situations where, if a language barrier between me and the other party exists, we have resorted to a pencil and napkin in order to communicate effectively.

Pictures can convey a message, which might take many thousands of words to describe. This non-textual communication and the visual emotions that the use of images can generate mean they are the perfect medium to complement or replace the text in our web pages:

The previous image could easily take a thousand words to describe, which would look uninteresting to the reader and take up valuable space on our web pages. Instead the picture only utilizes a fraction of the space that our description would use and tells a story in itself.

Not only do images describe a story, a moment in time, or a fantasy situation; they can provide a visual stimulus, which portrays a style or theme and sets a mood for the viewer. Many Joomla! Templates now contain a high percentage of graphical images in order to produce interesting designs and effects, such as this commercial example from `http://www.yootheme.com`:

Many templates now utilize rounded edges for the graphics, or faded effects, and some create a 3D type effect on our two-dimensional computer screens. This is achieved by using shading and image layering effects. Others use images to create interesting navigation effects which could not be achieved without using these.

Besides the design, navigation, and branding effects that images help provide, inside our content and modules, we use images to advertise and communicate to our site visitors. One important trick as web developers is to make sure our images are as optimized as they can be before asking our viewers to load them into their web browsers. This ensures a pleasant user experience because if a site is slow to load, or images are missing, these can be a big turn-off to your site visitors.

Image formats and which ones to use

Images can often make up 50 percent of a Joomla! website; sometimes even more. These images that get loaded into the browser can be part of your template design, or site images we have loaded into our modules and articles. Choosing an appropriate format for this image content will help optimize the loading times of your web pages, which is one of the most important considerations when building a multimedia rich website:

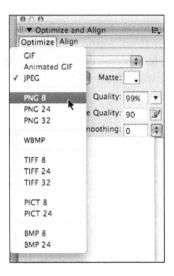

There are a few simple rules we can use in order to choose an appropriate image format. The most important criterion for the final file is the size. The previous image is exported using Adobe Fireworks on a Mac computer. External image editors such as the **GNU Image Manipulation Program (GIMP)** are good open source solutions for manipulating and optimizing images for the web. GIMP can be downloaded by visiting http://www.gimp.org.

With each image requiring loading by the user's browser, page-loading times can be easily affected with the quality and quantity of images you use in your web pages. This in turn results in end user frustration (especially on dial-up Internet connections) and loss of site traffic.

Digital images

Before we proceed further into file sizes and file types, it is important to mention a note about digital images. Because all of our web page images are stored or viewed on a computer device, they are in a digital format (an electronic file stored using zeros and ones). A digital image is built up of tiny elements called pixels. **Pixels** are the building blocks of all digital images and are small adjoining squares in a matrix across the length and width of your image.

Pixels are so small that you cannot easily see them when the image is viewed on your computer screen:

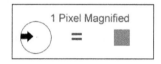

Each pixel is an element containing a single solid color, and when put together all of these tiny dots make up your final image. Usually, more pixels per area make up a higher quality image, but there is a point when viewed with the human eye on electronic devices that you cannot actually see the extra detail that the additional pixel's bring to the image:

The physical dimensions of a digital image are measured in pixels and all digital images have what is called an image resolution (the image height and width dimensions in pixels). It is possible to save your digital images in numerous formats and compressions in order to optimize the file quality and size. Image editing programs, such as Adobe Fireworks, are specifically designed with web optimization and export options:

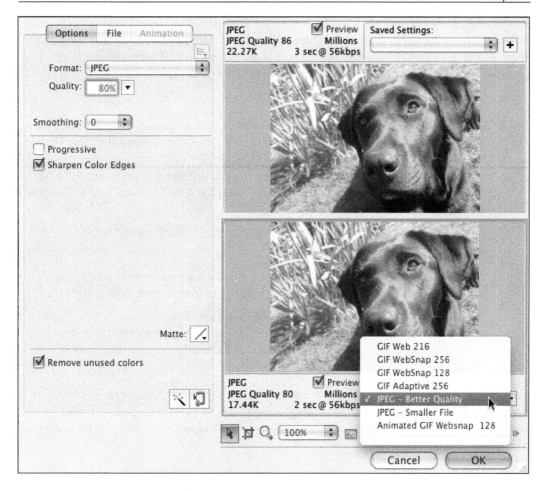

Lossy and lossless data compression

Data compression is an important part of our digital world. File compression is useful because it helps in reducing the consumption of expensive resources such as transmission bandwidth and computer hard disk space.

Almost all digital images that we use on the web have been resized or compressed to some degree. When editing or saving files in popular software editing programs, many options are provided to help optimize digital images.

Lossy and **lossless** compression are two terms that describe the compression type of a file, and whether or not the file retains all of the original data once compression and then decompression of that file has taken place. The preferred formats for digital web images (such as JPEG and GIF) all fall into one of the following compression types:

1. **Lossy**

    A lossy data compression is one where the compression attempts to eliminate redundant or unnecessary file information. Generally, once a file has been compressed, the information that was lost during compression cannot be recovered again. Hence, it is a degradable compression type, and as the file is compressed and decompressed each time, the quality of the file will suffer from generation loss.

    JPEG and MP3 files are good examples of formats that use lossy compression.

2. **Lossless**

    Lossless file compression makes use of data compression that retains every single bit of data that was in the original file before compression.

    Lossless compression is often used when an identical representation of the original data is required once a file has been compressed and then decompressed again. As an example, it is used for the popular ZIP file format. Image formats such as PNG and GIF fall into the lossless compression type.

For now, it is not so important to go into any more detail on these compression types, but the following image formats fall into both of these compression categories. It is possible to optimize your website images by choosing the correct format to save and present them to your site users.

Image formats

With hundreds of graphical image formats now available, it is understandable that there are some bizarre image formats being dished up on websites, mostly from inexperienced site designers who just happen to upload whatever they have been sent in an e-mail.

Having just mentioned the "hundreds" word, to help calm the nerves there are only four main formats that are commonly used and recognized as web suitable. These have been deemed suitable due to their format and compression properties (making the final file size and view quality suitable). Another important reason why these formats have become the standard is the accessibility of being able to open or view these file types on most computer systems. With the Internet bringing together millions of users across the globe, common formats that are easily viewed or saved had to evolve.

The following formats are members of both the lossy and lossless data compression formats:

- **Graphic Interchange Format (GIF)** pronounced "giff ".
- **Joint Photographic Experts Group (JPEG)** pronounced "jay-peg"
- **Portable Networks Graphic (PNG)** pronounced "ping"
- **Scalable Vector Graphics (SVG)**

Converting a digital image from one format to another is usually a "Save As" in a common graphical editor package. During this saving or exporting process, you will usually have options to choose the quality, file size, and pixel resolutions.

GIF

The GIF image format belongs to a family called "index-color" formats. This means they use a fixed number of colors to make up the image. The file size is usually related to the bit-depth or number of colors used. These are usually a small number such as 256 or "8 bit" color, and often contain as little as two colors. For optimum file size, you usually want to choose as lower bit-depth as possible while still retaining an acceptable image.

Due to its limited color properties, GIF images are usually perfect for a low number of solid flat colors and are often the format of choice for logos, buttons, and graphical text:

GIF images are an in-efficient format for images such as photographs, which contain lots of colors. Photographs that are converted to a GIF format will usually be of poor quality, look blotchy, or show jiggered edges due to the limited color range:

JPEG

The JPEG file format was designed to efficiently compress realistic true color or grayscale images such as photographs. This compression type was designed and is the perfect option to save and compress your photographic images.

The JPEG format works its magic by approximating blocks of pixels and during compression preserving the key details that are most apparent to the human eye. JPEG images can be highly compressed allowing you to save a good quality picture with a small file size. However, the JPEG format belongs to the lossy compression type which means every time you read, modify, and save your JPEG image, you lose some information. This derogation is very noticeable when you have text within an image, such as logos. This loss of data will still occur even if you set the quality slider to "100" when saving a JPEG image; hence it's an excellent example of lossy file compression.

JPEG is an excellent image format for multiple colors or toned images for your website, but it is not a good format to save your images in if you wish to edit or change them frequently:

PNG

PNG is a relatively newer file format that was created as the open source successor to the GIF format. Being a member of the lossless compression type, PNG images are best suited to images, which may require editing and saving again. Like the GIF format, the PNG file format excels when the image contains large uniformly colored areas. The PNG format also lends itself well to the use of transparency, which can be important for logos that may be laid on top of background colors, or graphics:

Mozilla Firefox, Internet Explorer 7, and most of the major browsers now offer PNG support. Many purchased Joomla! Templates will contain PNG images for logos, rounded module headings, and buttons / icons.

SVG

SVG is a new vector file format created by the **World Wide Web Consortium (W3C)**. It was developed to create a standard format for displaying vector graphics on the web.

SVG is a text based graphics format with the images and their behaviors defined in an XML file format, which means they can be easily searched, scripted, and compressed:

```
<?xml version="1.0" standalone="no"?>
<!DOCTYPE svg PUBLIC "-//W3C//DTD SVG 1.1//EN"
   "http://www.projectamplify.com/DTD/svg01.dtd">
<svg width="5cm" height="5cm" viewBox="0 0 700 600"
     xmlns="http://www.projectamplify.com/1000/svg" version="1.1">
  <desc>Example script01 - invoke an ECMAScript function from an onclick event
  </desc>
  <!-- ECMAScript to change the radius with each click -->
  <script type="text/ecmascript"> <![CDATA[
    function circle_click(evt) {
      var circle = evt.target;
      var currentRadius = circle.getAttribute("r");
      if (currentRadius == 100)
        circle.setAttribute("r", currentRadius*2);
      else
        circle.setAttribute("r", currentRadius*0.5);
    }
```

SVG images can interact with users in many ways due to their textural file format, and images can be used with scripting in order to trigger events in web pages and on mobile devices.

All major browsers except Internet Explorer offer SVG file support. However, a browser plugin for Internet Explorer is available. At this stage there are not many extensions around the subject of SVG, but there is a useful Joomla! Plugin called XHTML Headers. This plugin helps to see if the browser supports XHTML based technologies. For more information, visit http://extensions.joomla.org and search for XHTML Headers.

Including images in your content articles and modules

In the following section, we will cover inserting images into our Joomla! content articles and modules. This section assumes that you have a basic understanding of how Joomla! content articles function.

Adding an image using the Joomla! Article Image button

Images can be easily added to new and existing Joomla! Articles (and Modules) by using the **Image** button, which is an extended editor plugin that is configured to be turned on with new Joomla! installations. The Editor button loads in below the Content Editor window when you are in the **Edit Article** screen:

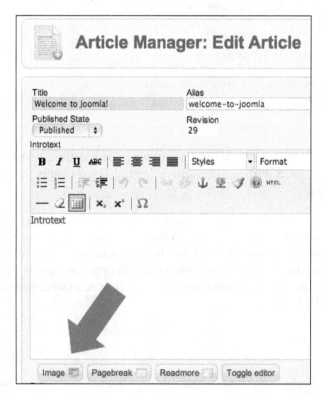

 It is important to note that this is a different method of inserting an image than that when using the Insert Image button on the WYSIWYG editor toolbar.

To insert an image into your Joomla! Articles, you will need to be in Article Edit Mode. Open your article for editing either by:

1. Clicking on the "Add New" Article icon when viewing the Control Panel.

2. Clicking on the Article option in the menu at the top, and then clicking on the "Article Manager" menu option. Select the article you wish to edit and click on the "Edit" icon in the top-right toolbar.

3. If logged into the frontend of your Joomla! website with the appropriate edit permissions, select the article you wish to edit and then click on the "Edit" toolbar icon.

Next, we need to choose where we would like our image to be placed. This is performed by inserting the image code in relation to the text that might be in your article. By clicking within the text content in the editor, you will be able to position your mouse cursor where you want your image to load:

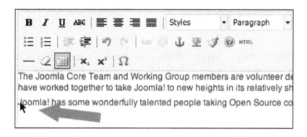

An Insert image screen will load on top of your Edit Article screen, which is the Joomla! Media Manager:

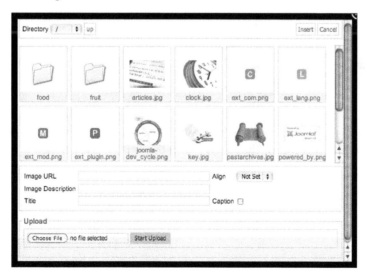

The Insert image screen will show all of the media in your Joomla! Media Manager. It contains the following features:

1. **Folder navigation**

    This is performed by using the **Directory** drop-down menu located at the top-left of the screen. You can drill down to subdirectories by using this or simply clicking on the folders that are available in the main Insert image window. The **up** button will quickly take you back up one directory:

    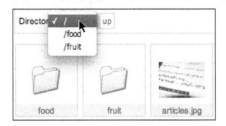

     You cannot move higher than your main "Media Directory" location, which is defined in the Global Configuration settings.

2. **Selecting an image**

    Simply click on the image you wish to use, and the **Image URL** location will be automatically populated with that image's location on your server:

    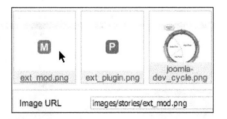

    If you wish to use an image from another web server or site, enter the full URL to the location of that image into the **Image URL** field:

    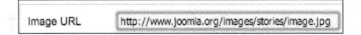

3. **Setting the image properties**

    We have three important fields (plus the **Align** and **Caption** boxes) to consider when inserting an image via the "Insert image" window:

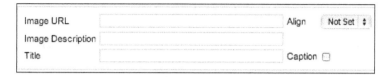

The "Insert image" window has the following fields:

*   The **Image URL** field holds the location to your image. This can be a relative URL to your website domain (for example, `/images/image.jpg`), or the absolute URL path to your image (for example, `http://www.mydomain.com/images/test.jpg`).

*   The image **Align** drop-down option allows you to align the image in relation to the text that the image surrounds. If the align is set to the left, the image will float to the left of the block of text, if aligned to the right, the image will float to the right of the text. If this option is left blank, there will be no image alignment set.

*   The image **Description** field is a Joomla! description which is the equivalent to an `alt` tag when using HTML. The Alt description is used to describe an "alternate-text" for an image. The `alt` attribute tells the viewer what they are missing on the page if the image is not loaded in. They are especially useful for people with screen readers, or those who choose to view the web with images turned off in their web browsers.

*   The image **Title** field specifies additional information about the image. This information is shown as a tooltip text to the user when their mouse is hovered over the image.

*   The image **Caption** checkbox will use the image title, and output this description as an image caption. This usually shows under your image, and CSS can be used to manipulate the look and positioning of this.

The Insert image screen also has a useful file upload tool built into it. Hence, if your images have not already been uploaded by FTP or the Joomla! Media Manager, then you have the option to upload when editing your content articles.

Before uploading, make sure you have selected the directory in which you wish to upload a new image to. To upload, click on the **Choose File** upload button located at the bottom of the Insert image screen:

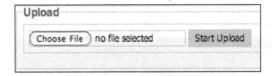

A screen will appear in which you should navigate to the file that requires uploading. Once you have selected your file, click on the **Start Upload** button to start the upload process.

A message at the top of the Insert image window will appear to tell you if your upload has been successful. If you have issues with uploading, check that your media directories and subdirectories have "read and write" permissions set on them to allow the upload.

Once your file has been uploaded, you can click on it to select that file, populate the image properties fields, and then click on the **Insert** button at the top-right of the Insert image window.

Adding an image using the Editor Image button

Your Joomla! install has one or two WYSIWYG (What You See Is What You Get) editors available. It is possible to change the editor type on a user basis within the User Manager. It is also possible to make a site-wide setting within the Global Administration:

A suggestion would be to download these and see which one (if any) makes your editing environment more suitable. Almost all of these editors offer the ability to insert images into your content articles, usually via an icon on the editor toolbar.

For this example, we will use the Joomla! default TinyMCE editor:

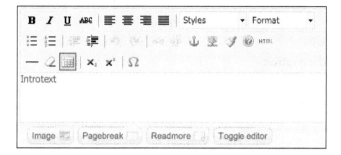

Firstly choose the article you wish to edit, or create a new article and go into the **Edit Article** screen.

As when using the Joomla! Image button technique, we need to position the cursor in an area of the article where we want the image to appear. In the editor toolbar, you will see numerous icons to perform editor functions. Look for one with a small photograph image on it:

When clicked on, this icon will open a pop-up window, which allows you to enter in the image location and properties. The main difference between this window and the earlier mentioned Joomla! Image button technique is that we manually need to enter in the image location in this area, and do not have the ability to upload images using this window:

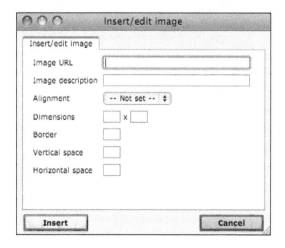

The fields available are:

Field	Description
Image URL	The Path to your image location.
Image description	The alt text for your image.
Alignment	Alignment of the image.
Dimensions	The height and width of the image.
Border	A border attribute for the image.
Vertical space	Vertical spacing around the image.
Horizontal space	Horizontal spacing around the image.

Using this method to input images into your content articles means that you have to manually enter the location to your site images (default is /images/stories/) and other properties into the fields provided, but it saves you having to enter the image code manually using HTML.

Image placement using custom HTML code

Depending whether you have chosen a WYSIWYG editor for your Joomla! account, you may choose to edit content articles and modules using an editor, or choose to format your site content using an HTML code view.

WYSIWYG editors can often add in additional characters to your site content, especially when content editors cut and paste the content directly from documents such as Microsoft Word, e-mail applications, and so on. They can allow users with no HTML experience to have wonderful functionalities for adding and updating website content, but can litter the code with unwanted or redundant code:

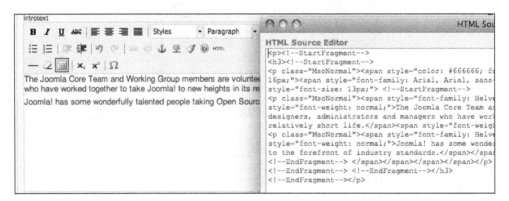

Image placement using HTML and CSS offers you options to align and style your website content as you desire. Let's look at how we can add an image into our content using pure HTML.

Just like using a WYSIWYG editor to insert an image, when using HTML we are performing a similar process, but this time entering in the image code by hand. In HTML, all images are defined using the <img> tag. Additional properties are given to this tag to make it perform functions. When using the WYSIWYG editor, we need to make sure that our image code is placed in the position where we want it to be displayed on the page:

In the editing window, position your mouse cursor where you want to enter your image. For our example, we will insert an image into the second (middle) paragraph of text (note each block of text has a <p> (paragraph) tag around it). The browser will show your image where the image tag occurs in the document. If we put an image in between two paragraphs, the browser will show the first paragraph, then the image, and then the second paragraph. In our example, we want the image to show at the start of our second paragraph, in line with our text content.

We will break this down as an example, so let's start off by inserting the basic <img> tag into our document:

```
<p>This is an interesting paragraph about inserting an image around
text</p>
<p><img>This is an interesting paragraph about inserting an image
around text </p>
<p>This is an interesting paragraph about inserting an image around
text </p>
```

Next we need to provide a location for the image. This is done by using the src attribute (src stands for source). The value of this attribute is the source location of the image you wish to display:

```
<p>This is an interesting paragraph about inserting an image around
text</p>
<p><img src="http://www.mydomain.com/image.jpg" />This is an
interesting paragraph about inserting an image around text </p>
<p>This is an interesting paragraph about inserting an image around
text </p>
```

Note how we have now added in a /> at the end of our image tag. This is required to end our <img> tag correctly and make our code XHTML compliant. Next we need to provide an alt (alternative text) description to our image. This is important to inform the viewer of what is loading into the page. Remember some web users have images turned off and use screen readers, so alt tags are very important for all images that you add into your site:

```
<p>This is an interesting paragraph about inserting an image around
text</p>
<p><img src="http://www.mydomain.com/image.jpg" alt="My Page" />This
is an interesting paragraph about inserting an image around text </p>
<p>This is an interesting paragraph about inserting an image around
text </p>
```

If we click on **Apply** on our content article now, this code will be saved and if the location to the image is correct, the image will show. The previous code will load the image in and then the text will load underneath:

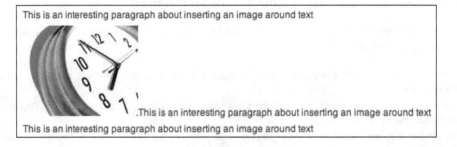

If you want the text to wrap around your image, we need to set an align attribute (alignment) for the image. Options for the align attribute are either left, right, middle, top, and bottom, which will result in the image aligning to each of these values in relation to any text block around the image:

```
<p>This is an interesting paragraph about inserting an image around
text</p>
<p><img src="http://www.mydomain.com/image.jpg" alt="My Page"
```

```
align="left" />This is an interesting paragraph about inserting an
image around text </p>
<p>This is an interesting paragraph about inserting an image around
text </p>
```

If you have set the image alignment to `left` and clicked on **Apply** to save your
Joomla! Article, you will see that your image is positioned to the left and at the same
height as the middle paragraph of text:

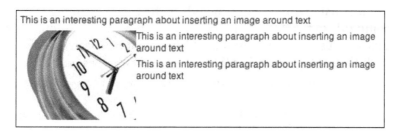

Next we need to specify a few more details about our image, mainly the height and
width of it. This is to ensure that when viewing across various devices, your images
will load in with the correct size. The `height` and `width` attributes are set as they are
spelt. These are in the value of pixels but there is no need to enter `px` to the attribute.
For example, if an image is `60 px` high and `100 px` wide, our code will look like:

```
<p>This is an interesting paragraph about inserting an image around
text</p>
<p><img src="http://www.mydomain.com/image.jpg" alt="My Page"
align="left" height="60" width="100" />This is an interesting
paragraph about inserting an image around text </p>
<p>This is an interesting paragraph about inserting an image around
text </p>
```

We can use HTML to perform additional functions such as image spacing. By using
the `hspace` (horizontal space) and `vspace` (vertical space) attributes, we can create
some padding around our image. This is especially useful when your text flows
around your images. In my example, I want to create some horizontal padding
between my image and the text flowing around it. The code now becomes:

```
<p>This is an interesting paragraph about inserting an image around
text</p>
<p><img src="http://www.mydomain.com/image.jpg" alt="My Page"
align="left" height="60" width="100" hspace="5" />is an interesting
paragraph about inserting an image around text </p>
<p>This is an interesting paragraph about inserting an image around
text </p>
```

The image will now look like:

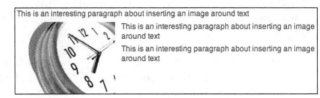

One final attribute that I would like to include is the `title` attribute (Title). This will provide a tooltip title to the image when the viewer hovers their mouse cursor over the image. Titles are useful for providing additional information and do have an affect on Search Engine Optimization (SEO). The code now becomes:

```
<p>This is an interesting paragraph about inserting an image around
text</p>
<p><img src="http://www.mydomain.com/image.jpg" alt="My Page"
align="left" height="60" width="100" hspace="5" title="A Nice Clock
Image" />is an interesting paragraph about inserting an image around
text </p>
<p>This is an interesting paragraph about inserting an image around
text </p>
```

The image will now look like:

If you want to insert numerous images into your articles and modules, it would be necessary to perform these steps for every image that you want to load in. It is possible to cut and paste the previous code and just change the values each time, but it can become time consuming.

Some image attributes such as the image padding (`vspace` and `hspace`) can be set in your CSS, creating a site wide stylesheet class for all of your content images. This CSS code may look like:

```
img { border: 0 none; margin: 3px }
```

The previous example will set a border of 0 and a margin of 3 on all of your site images, so you may need to specify the CSS attribute in more detail to suit your template.

Creating image galleries and slideshows

Joomla! is a Content Management System designed primarily for organizing and managing website content. It contains numerous multimedia features built into it, but its main focus is providing two roles: Powerful CMS features, and a well-designed framework which allows additional features to be added to the system, thus creating powerful functionality.

These additional features are called **Extensions** and are designed to plug in to the core Joomla! Framework and extend the functionality of it. With regards to the core Joomla! CMS, we have already looked at how images can be included into content items and modules. However, image galleries and slideshows are asking a bit more than just simple image management, and so require the power of extensions to provide these features:

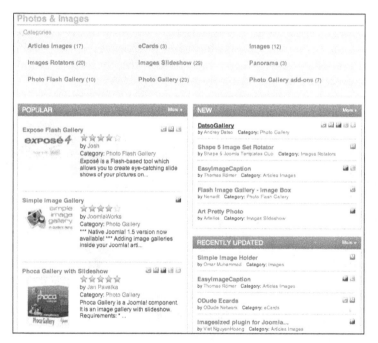

The number of multimedia extensions now available for Joomla! is staggering. We have extensions which can create complex galleries, stream in videos, and compile jukebox type audio features.

Having considered at great length the best approach for this section of the book, it has resulted in one option. That is to highlight some of the most popular and useful image gallery and slideshow extensions, and hope that these will provide understanding as to the complex image management capability that can be achieved by using Joomla! Extensions.

Image management extensions, and how to install them

Before proceeding with covering third-party extension functionality, let's quickly cover how image extensions are added to your Joomla! site.

As with most things in Joomla!, the process of installing extensions has had careful consideration from the development team, and is a very easy to perform. Most Joomla! Extensions come with their own installation instructions, and these general guidelines will help you get them installed on your site.

> Before installing anything, make sure you copy your file set and backup your site database.

For the purpose of this example, I am going to install one of my favorite Joomla! Multimedia Extensions—the RokBox extension by RocketTheme. RokBox is a MooTools powered slideshow plugin that enables you to display numerous media formats with a professional pop-up screen lightbox effect:

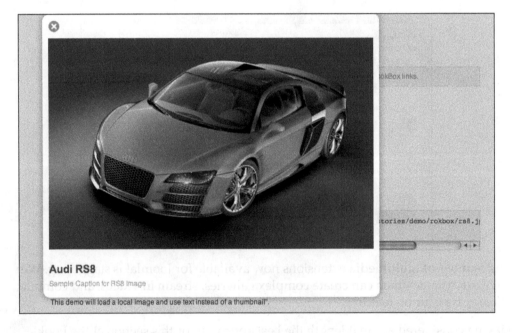

The installation steps are as follows:

1. Download the required extension and save this download on your computer. The file will be in a `.zip` format, or possibly a `.gzip` or `.tgz` format which may require unzipping before installation:

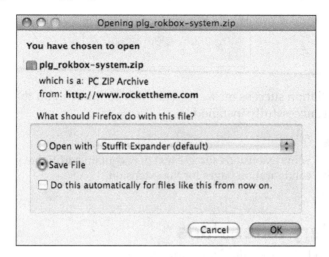

2. Log into your Joomla! Administrator's Control Panel, and navigate to the **Extensions** menu, then to **Extension Manger**. The page will default to the **Install** screen:

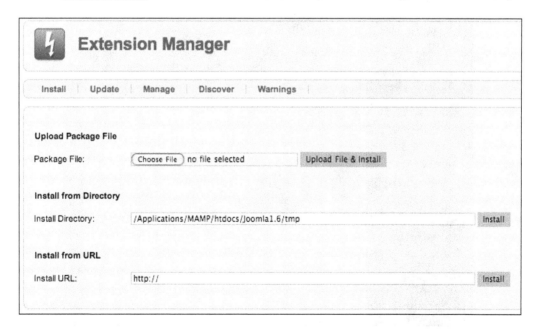

3. Browse your computer for the extension `.zip` file using the **Choose File** button on this page and once the file is located, use the **Upload File & Install** button. The Joomla! Installation Manger will perform all of the work and if your extension has been built correctly, the installer will place all files and documents into their correct directories:

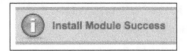

4. An installation success message will show to inform you that the extension has been successfully installed.

> Some extensions success text may contain additional links to configuration pages for the extension.

Image gallery extensions

The following is a list of Joomla! Extensions to create image galleries:

Simple Image Gallery

The Simple Image Gallery extension is a plugin:

The way the extension works is you add in a special tag — {gallery}myphotos{/gallery} — into your articles to display all of the photos correctly labeled in the myphotos folder:

The extension then goes to work. The gallery created contains features such as stylish shadows on each thumbnail, lightbox pop ups to display the original images, and automatically generated thumbnails for each image.

By utilizing the special tag method, you can display numerous galleries within your content articles and website. This offers great flexibility for a site-wide simple gallery feature.

Expose Flash Gallery

Expose is a component, module gallery extension that offers language support. It is a Flash-based tool for offering eye-catching slideshows of your images on the Web:

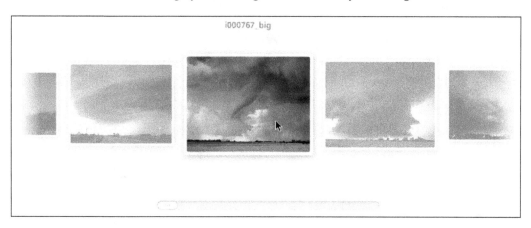

This extension is based on the stand-alone gallery software called "Expose" which has evolved to provide support for Joomla! websites. This extension offers numerous features, including nesting of albums, assigning thumbnails to albums, online picture upload, offline gallery management, watermark addition, and playing slideshows.

With Expose, you can link directly to images, categories of images, or full albums:

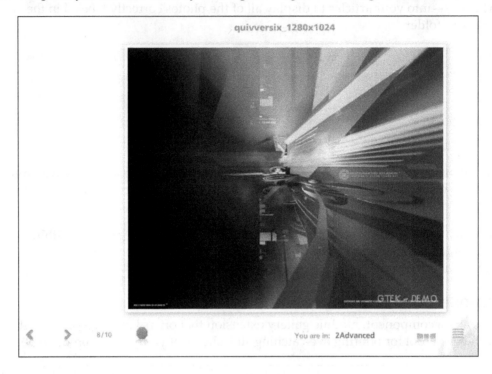

Phoca Gallery with Slideshow

Phoca Gallery is a fully-featured image gallery and slideshow extension for Joomla! It is a component with plugins and modules. It also caters for language support:

Phoca Gallery allows you to create image categories and subcategories, and place images into these. It is possible for images to belong to more than one category, which provides greater flexibility in displaying images.

Image thumbnails are automatically generated for the gallery, with added options such as watermarking, user access, YouTube support, and numerous gallery effects to display your image galleries in various ways:

Phoca Gallery comes with a range of available plugins and modules. It is possible to present image galleries and slideshows in both your articles and modules. There is even a search plugin to help Joomla! search through your image categories.

Ozio Gallery2

Ozio Gallery is a Joomla! Component, with available modules:

It can be used to develop complex image galleries with interesting effects thanks to the Flash features and gallery skins. These two features effectively turn this image gallery component into many different image gallery options:

Ozio Gallery offers you the flexibility of linking directly to the content, or by publishing your galleries into module positions using the Ozio Gallery module. Containing numerous parameters, this product should satisfy anyone requiring an interesting Flash-based image gallery feature with slideshow support:

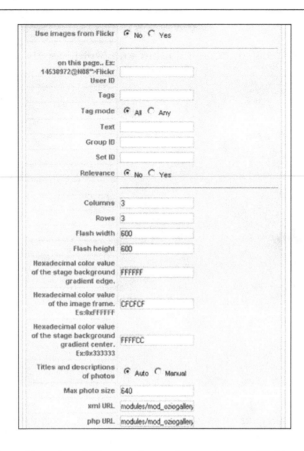

This extension also offers the ability to show photos from a **flickr** account, and to display your **flickr** images within your Joomla! site:

JoomGallery

JoomGallery is a Joomla! Component, Plugin, and Module with language support:

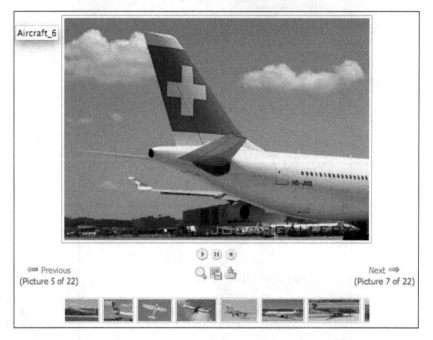

JoomGallery offers many features including defining subcategories of galleries, batch upload of images, user access rights to categories, configurable watermarks, slideshow support, and the list goes on:

Image slideshows

A list of Joomla! Image Extensions for creating slideshows is as follows:

RokSlideshow

RokSlideshow is a Joomla! Module that allows you to display a series of images and captions, and transition between them in a configurable manner.

The slideshow is driven by Mootools, providing fades, burns, wipes, and push effects between the images displayed. All in all, the module is capable of 30 different transition effects.

Image information can be displayed and images may contain hyperlinks, a title, and a description:

RokSlideshow is very flexible and easily customizable. It is a great way to display image slideshows in your Joomla! website and an excellent alternative to Flash image gallery players.

Simple Image Rotator

The Simple Image Rotator module offers a simple image rotating mechanism. It is a lightweight JavaScript alternative to Flash image rotation scripts, but offers a similar feel in terms of the fading transition. The previous image will fade within a few seconds to the next image, and so on. It does what it says on the tin!

Boncko Cooliris (PicLens) Gallery Plugin

If you happen to use Cooliris for your image galleries, then extensions such as the Boncko Cooliris Plugin will be right up your street:

You can easily add Cooliris image galleries inside your articles by using the special tag: {boncko}/img_dir/{/boncko}. This plugin will insert all images and Flash video files from the /img_dir/ directory into your Joomla! content, making your image gallery look good.

This process means you can store and organize your image galleries externally from your Joomla! site, and suck in the content that you wish. Boncko Cooliris Plugin can even play audio tracks while your image gallery is active.

Some of these have been highlighted because they are popular GPL extensions which offer great flexibility for creating image galleries and slideshow features.

There are many other image gallery extensions available at `http://extensions.joomla.org`:

Many new extensions are being made available each week. Some of these are free GPL, some commercial extensions, and others require club memberships to access. Whether they are free or commercial entities, I hope you find a solution for your image gallery and slideshow requirements.

Joomla! Extensions generally provide image solutions for creating galleries and slideshows within articles or modules. You may have a number of other images loading into your web pages, these are usually contained within your template.

Joomla! Template images

Joomla! Templates control the overall look and layout of your Joomla! website. They provide the framework that brings together common elements and they provide the glue for your layout to interact with modules and components.

Joomla! utilizes templates for both the frontend and backend (administration) of your site. When Joomla! is installed, it comes with a default set of templates included, and as you may be aware, you can find hundreds, if not thousands, of Joomla! Templates available on the Web. Some of these are feature packed and are commercial templates, some are ones without charge that fall under various licenses.

Templates utilize a defined structure, which allows all of the template elements to interact with each other correctly:

It is possible to make your own Joomla! Templates and now there are many tutorials available at http://www.joomla.org and a number of specialist Joomla! Template development books such as "*Joomla 1.5 Template Design, Tessa Blakeley Silver, Packt Publishing*". More information can be viewed at http://www.packtpub.com.

One important role of a Joomla! Template is to contain and load the site stylesheets. These help position the template elements in your site. An increasing number of these elements in modern Joomla! Templates are scripts, style information, and images.

Let's take a quick look at one of the popular included templates that are available for Joomla!:

It is easy to see a number of images that help make up this template. We have images for the logo and rounded images for the boxes. Here is the same template loaded in the browser with the images disabled:

The previous examples are of a relatively simplistic template, but you can see how the template images come together in greatly enhancing the site design. The advancement of Joomla! Templates are increasing every month, with many companies making extremely professional templates available for purchase each month.

These commercial templates often include preset color themes and styles, offering the ability to change the site color scheme, and layout in seconds. This flexibility offers the administrator powerful features to create a new look for their site, but also can mean that some templates contain an abundance of scripts and images that never get used once the administrator had made a decision on the color choice, among others. What used to be a simple path to your template image folder can now often be multiple directories in your template containing the image files:

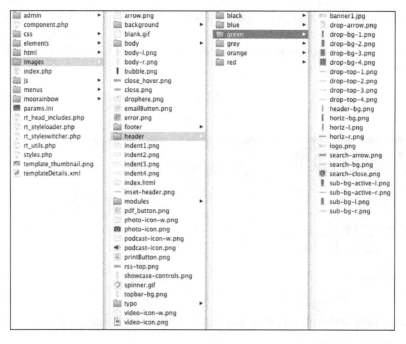

How to adjust your template images

The images for a Joomla! Template are generally located in the `<Your Joomla Home Folder>/templates/<yourtemplate>/images` directory. If you would like to adjust certain images in your template, the easiest way to do this is by viewing the template in your site browser and then making the necessary adjustments to the images.

It is worth mentioning that many web developers develop their sites locally. A local development process is easily created by setting up a localhost server environment on your computer. Utilities such as MAMP for MAC, and XAMPP for Windows provide easy software installs of all the necessary components for running a local server environment. If you don't already work locally, take two minutes out to look into these programs, as they not only save you time (as there are no connections to the live web servers), but also provide confidence when developing as you are never working on your live site:

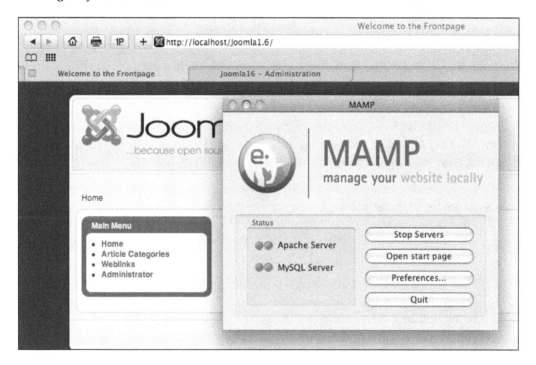

 There is more information about localhost development in Chapter 9, *Joomla! Multimedia Project.*

One of the easiest ways to find and manipulate your site images is to either use a browser element inspector tool (such as Firebug for Firefox or Web Inspector for Safari), or to simply right-click on the images in the web browser, and choose **View Image**. This option may differ depending on the browser you are using, but most browsers offer the ability to find the location (URL) of the image or to open it in a new browser tab:

Your image URL may look something like: `<Your Joomla Home Folder>/ templates/<yourtemplate>/images/logo.png`. This image URL method lets you know the path, so you can find the necessary image.

There are hundreds of available image manipulation programs, and we cannot go into the details of image manipulation in this book. However, if you stick to the following rules when adjusting your images, you will be on the right track:

- Copy the original file. For example, if your file is called `logo.png`, then name the original file as `logo.png.orig` (or something similar), so you always have a copy of that original file. Or if you will be editing your website regularly, consider a version control system such as SVN or Git.

- Make a note of the file name, size, and format before editing the file.

- Unless you are a pro, always keep the same image format as the original image. If this image is referenced in the CSS or original code, your new image name will be different and the image will no longer show.

- When saving an image, try to make sure the file size is as low as the original or as close to it as you can achieve through image optimization.

- If you do change the image dimensions, make sure you check if there are any CSS variables or other code that might specify the physical file dimensions.

With most templates, one of the first files you will adjust will be the Template Logo. The process for changing the logo is exactly the same as the previous steps.

I briefly mentioned the use of Web Inspector Tools. Probably one of the most common of these is a tool available for the Firefox web browser. This is called Firebug. Visit `http://getfirebug.com/` for more information. Firebug allows you to edit, debug, and inspect CSS, HTML, and JavaScript on any web page:

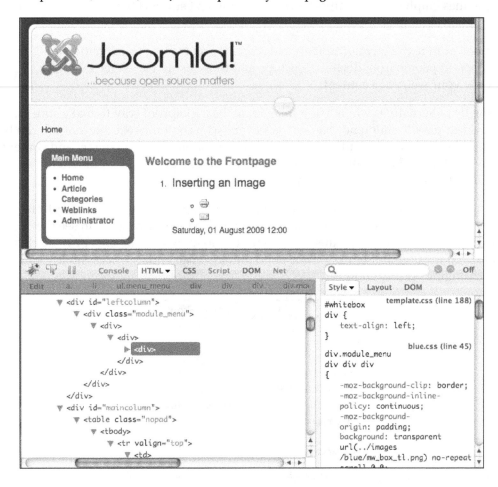

Firebug allows you to inspect web elements and edit these on the fly, in your browser. For example, if you wish to move your logo sideways or up and down a bit, simply inspect the image logo element, and then adjust the corresponding CSS which positions this element. This is just a brief example of what the Firebug tool can do, but its power comes in handy when you need to problem solve errors, and so on. If you are keen on enhancing and developing for your Joomla! Template, I suggest a tool like Firebug which will really help you out!

It is worth noting that Internet Explorer and Safari also have their own versions of an "Element Inspector".

Browser support and image accessibility

Almost all web browsers now offer image support. There are some considerations, however, when using images in your website content. The W3C Accessibility Guidelines emphasize the importance of offering text support (or text equivalents) to non-text content.

The power of text-equivalents lie in their capacity to provide "information and support" to people from disability groups and those using varied technologies to view your web page content.

Using text alternatives when using images can be a foolproof way to make sure that the widest possible audience has access to your web content. Text-alternatives can be visually read by screen readers, the size of the text adjusted for viewing, and content printed off to read in Braille, and so on, which makes a powerful argument for making alternative text content available.

Secondly when we do use images, it is important to specify the `alt` and `title` tag information, so users who have images turned off in their browsers can see the "alternative text" which explains what should be loading in. Title tags provide clear tooltips to the user and both of these tags combined can enhance accessibility and search engine optimization:

Up until recently, browsers such as Internet Explorer did not offer image transparency support, or PNG file extension support. Web developers had to use workarounds in order to show PNG files to users using these browsers to view their websites. Now Internet Explorer 7 and 8 both provide PNG support as a standard. SVG is a relatively new format, which required a browser plugin, for again the Internet Explorer browser. Web browsers, however, are improving every day, as is the support in them for various image formats.

Summary

Images are an important communication element. They are used to tell stories, show facts, advertise and sell, as well as visually entice the user with emotive feelings. Our Joomla! Templates usually contain many images, which create eye-pleasing and complex designs.

The use of images in websites has evolved quickly, from flat single color images to realistic high quality formats that cater to transparency and lossless compressions. The Web just wouldn't be the same without them! An increase in broadband and connection speeds has allowed the evolution of beautiful image-gallery scripts; a number of these being incorporated into powerful Joomla! Image Extensions. There has never been a better time to display images and galleries in your Joomla! site.

Take careful consideration when adjusting your existing template images, or when creating new ones for your site. Image file size and optimization is an important consideration to your site users. The use of good optimization tools and experience will help in providing quality images for your site while decreasing page loading time.

With a diverse range of user abilities and disabilities, varied connection speeds, and a vast range of hardware accessing the World Wide Web, it is very important to consider the correct use of images and make alternatives available for those who cannot or choose not to view them. The use of `alt` and `title` tags, as well as `height` and `width` properties are all best practice when loading images into your site pages.

5
Using Audio in Your Joomla! Website

Audio is a powerful and emotive media element. Most humans use audio as a primary form of communication and hearing. It is defined as one of our major senses. For those with good hearing, our daily lives are surrounded with thousands of sounds that influence us both consciously and unconsciously.

The Internet and audio have a very established relationship. The Internet has been a perfect delivery mechanism for audio and these elements have helped to re-define and rapidly evolve their respective technology and industries.

In this chapter, we will look at the use of audio in your Joomla! website. You will learn about:

- What audio is
- Audio and the Internet
- Audio formats
- Embedding and displaying audio in Joomla! Articles
- Creating an audio podcast for Joomla!
- Third-party audio extensions
- Browser support and audio accessibility

What is audio?

Audio is "sound" which is detectable to the human ear. Sounds are pressure waves of air that we hear because our ears are designed to be sensitive to these waves.

For humans, hearing is usually detected between the approximate range of 20 Hz and 20 kHz (20,000 Hz). 20 Hz is the lowest pitch (bassiest sound) we can interpret 20 kHz being the highest. It is recognized that as humans get older, the higher range of our hearing perception can often deteriorate.

In a computer environment, audio is often used to describe the sound system that is included with (or can be added to) a computer system, providing the processing and playback of audio files. Audio which is recorded or played back through a computer system is digital audio.

Audio and the Internet

Studies show how audio contributes to the human and computer interaction process, providing a more powerful experience than the delivery of text or graphical content.

However, in the early days of the Internet, it was inefficient to deliver a data-intensive format such as audio across our low bandwidth consumer connections. Audio was often placed on websites as digital files, which needed to be downloaded before a separate media player on the computer system performed playback. Finding audio players to play the format of the audio file was more difficult than it now is, and many amateur sites contained simplistic audio files which started playing when the web page loaded.

These were entertaining, but provided the user with no control over the audio, besides turning down their PC speakers! All that said, this was the evolution of audio on the Web, and it is now very different than how we once knew.

The delivery of audio and video have been two important contributing factors to the evolution of faster Internet connection speeds to the consumer, with these media elements now being commonplace when browsing web pages.

One of the most profound effects that the Internet, higher bandwidth speeds, and digital audio have had is on the music industry. With the nature of websites being the perfect "notice board" to communicate to users who you never could have before, artists and consumers have been by-passing the filter of record companies, who up until recently have been the only process for artists and music to pass through. Music is now one of the most popular search queries, and downloads of audio files and Internet radio have made it possible to reach mass audiences spanning across many continents.

An important element of the Internet is the tools we use to interact with it. The personal computer is now a multimedia suite, offering powerful audio recording and playback capabilities that only specialist studios used to have access to. With computer screens being a visual medium, the use of audio is a perfect delivery medium for those who are "sight impaired", and web audio has been a solution to the delivery of information for people with certain disabilities:

◀)) Listen to a message from the author.

```
<A HREF="work-e.wav">
<IMG SRC="audio.gif" ALT="Sound file: Let's work together for accessibility. ">
Listen to a message from the author. </A>
```

If the audio file contains lots of information, then you might want to link to a file that contains a complete transcript:

Let's listen to an excerpt from "The Walrus and the Carpenter," by Lewis Carroll.

Audio transcript: Excerpt from "The Walrus and the Carpenter," by Lewis Carroll.

Man:
"The time has come," the Walrus said,
"To talk of many things:
Of shoes-- and ships-- and sealing-wax--
Of cabbages-- and kings--
And why the sea is boiling hot--
And whether pigs have wings."

The previous image is taken from `http://www.w3.org`. It displays an accessible approach for an audio excerpt within a web page.

Audio formats

Just like video, hundreds of audio formats exist for recording and playing back digital sound and music files. Many of these are software dependant, requiring a specific program to play that particular file. These formats are not of much use when trying to provide audio to the widest possible audience, so we will be narrowing the choices down to a few well-known and well-supported formats that are suitable for web use.

Before we look at the choices of file types to use, it is important to mention that audio is data-intensive medium that has seen amazing developments in the way in which it is compressed and stored. This "data crunching" is performed using audio codecs. The word **Codec** stands for compression / decompression, which is the process that happens to the data.

Audio compression

Audio compression is very similar to video compression. Both use similar technologies to manipulate data and then offer it in a container suitable for playback to the user.

It is important to point out that an audio file format and audio codec (or compression) are two different things.

Audio codecs

The way that audio is compressed and stored is by using a codec, which has a major influence on the final file size. Specialist audio codecs have become available, which provide a balance of quality and file size options. As web hosting costs can become expensive to deliver data, codecs effectively reduce the storage space and bandwidth required for audio files on websites.

Codecs use algorithms to remove the data that is considered "not important" and hence our file sizes drop as this additional information no longer exists. A good example of audio compression is to remove the data that falls outside of our recognized hearing ability. Hence, if we have very high or low frequency data in there that falls above or below our hearing capabilities, it is of no use to us, so we get rid of it.

Most audio codecs are from the lossy compression family. This means the information that is removed during compression can no longer be recovered again. Lossy algorithms provide greater compression rates and are mostly used in consumer audio devices. They are also of interest to us because gauging the smallest file size (while retaining quality) is an important consideration when dealing with web audio.

An audio codec may not necessarily relate to its final file name or type. An audio file type such as .wav (commonly used on Windows computers) can be encoded using different codecs, for example, the GSM, MP3, or PCM codecs. Audio file types use different codecs for their compressions. This is generally due to licensing and ownership of the codec. Just to confuse the issue, some codecs are actually named the same as the file type, such as the .mp3 file format that always uses the "MPEG Layer-3" codec.

Audio file format

An audio file format plays a similar role to our video container file. The audio file contains the data file, but often also contains important header information, such as author, priority, notes, and other data.

Some of the most common audio file formats for use in a web environment are:

MIDI (`.midi`)	MIDI is short for **Musical Instrument Digital Interface**. MIDI files are very small and are well supported by computer software and browsers. MIDI files, however, are usually data-based audio rather than a recorded waveform, therefore making them small and easy to distribute, but unsuitable for music files.
AIFF (`.aif`/`.aiff`)	Developed by Apple, AIFF stands for **Audio Interchange File Format**. This file format is becoming increasingly popular for web audio. AIFF files are played using the QuickTime Player which is available on Mac and Windows. AIFF files can be compressed well, while retaining excellent quality.
MP3 (`.mp3`)	The **MPEG Layer-3** format is perhaps one of the most popular audio file formats in use on the Web. MP3 files are the audio part of a MPEG file and can compress audio to approximately one tenth of the original file size. This compression, while retaining good quality, has lead to their popular and widespread use. MP3 files can be played on many devices, making them an excellent choice for cross-platform capability.
AAC (`.aac`/`.mp4`/`.3gp`/`.m4a`)	Designed by Apple to be the successor of MP3, **AAC** generally achieves better audio quality at similar sizes. AAC's best known use is on the Apple iPod and it is the format used in the iTunes store and on Playstation 3.
WAV (`.wav`)	Developed by IBM and Microsoft, WAV stands for **Waveform** which is the standard audio format on Windows computers. WAV does not compress audio data, which makes it unsuitable for web use, but is commonly used for storing uncompressed audio. Although WAV does not compress the file, WAV files can be compressed using other codecs such as MP3.
WMA (`.wma`)	WMA stands for **Windows Media Audio** owned by Microsoft. It compares in quality and compression to an MP3 file, but has limitations on being accessible on all devices.
RealAudio (`.rm`/`.ram`)	**RealAudio** is a format owned by RealNetworks. It was in common use, and helped to shape the use of streaming audio on the Web. The RealPlayer is free, but this format seems to have taken a decline due to its proprietary format.

Bit rates

Bit rates refer to the speed at which a stream of data (compressed audio in this case) can travel. This is usually recorded in bits per second (kilobits per second, Kbps).

The more audio data that can travel during a period of time, the better the quality the audio will have. Logically, the higher the bit rate that is used when recording audio, the more audio data there is available, which results in larger file sizes.

We need to be aware of them because when exporting your audio, one of the options available is to choose the bit rate:

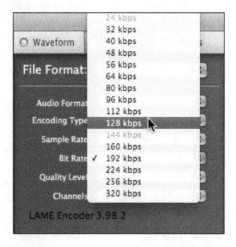

There is a benchmark currently being used for web audio which is 128 bits per second (**128 kbps**) for stereo audio. Depending on your audio data (it may be a voice podcast or music file), you can go higher or lower than this figure, and if your audio is in a mono format, bit rates can be reduced again. If your music file is very important and you feel that the majority of your audience has a good broadband connection, then going to 160 Kbps may be an option. Anything below 128 will affect your audio quality, but it is always worth experimenting to see how low your files sizes can be, while retaining the quality you require.

With an abundance of audio software being available, and modern home computers containing audio systems, you may already have the tools to convert and export audio for your website in hand. The trick is to export your files in different formats and compression rates, and then compare them with each other to hear the difference, and see the file size comparisons.

How to compress and encode audio

There is an abundance of audio editing and compression tools that are now available to help you manipulate audio files.

If you have specific requirements, then a quick search on the Internet will lead you to popular software. If you have an audio file and are looking to optimize this for the Web, or convert it into another audio format, then take a look at a Windows' open source solution, called LameXP, which can be downloaded at `http://www.snapfiles.com/get/lamexp.html`.

LameXP is a frontend graphical interface for the Lame MP3, Ogg Vorbis, and Nero ACC codecs. It allows you to convert your files into MP3, OGG, Wave, and ACC formats by providing an easy to use interface where you can drag and drop files:

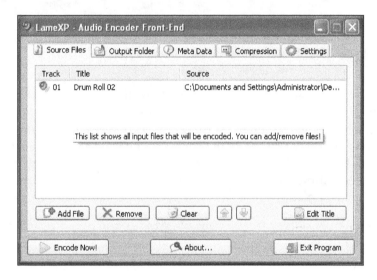

LameXP is powerful but easy to use. Once you have downloaded and installed the package, open it up and follow these easy steps to convert and optimize your audio:

1. Install any necessary codecs on your device. WAV files will require one, as will some others. Information boxes will talk you through these steps.

2. Drag your file into the LameXP window or click on the **Add File** button to add your audio files.

3. Use the tabs at the top to select your **Output Folder** and other file settings. The **Compression** tab is one to take note of. Within this tab, you can select the type of encoding you wish, as well as **Bitrate** for the encoded file. You can either use the **Quality** setting or pick a **Bitrate**, and the options will change depending on which radio button you select.

4. Use the **Encode Now!** button to start the encoding process:

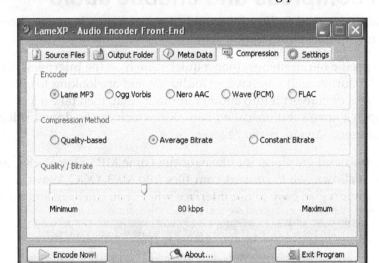

Hovering over the available options will provide further information to help you make choices. Due to the nature of audio, a suggestion is to encode your file using different settings, and then listen to these results and decide which bit rate / quality is most suitable for your piece of audio. Results will vary depending on the type of audio within your file. A piece of spoken audio such as an interview will react differently under compression than that containing a music track. With a few tests, you will find a happy compromise between the audio quality and the final file size.

At the end of the day, look to reduce your file sizes as much as possible, while retaining the quality you require.

Embedding and displaying audio in Joomla! Articles

One very powerful feature of Joomla! is the ability to include your own custom HTML into Joomla! Articles. This means we have the ability to completely customize the output of audio content in our articles and modules, which is what is required to insert audio manually into a Joomla! web page.

The source

Before throwing some audio content at our Joomla! site, we need to make decisions on the type of audio it is and the file format to choose.

As we have seen from the previous format listing, a good option is the .mp3 file format, due to its ability to be played via numerous audio players and devices.

The export functions in audio software applications allow various formatting and compression options. There is some trial and error when creating multimedia files, and I can only suggest trying numerous settings and then comparing the results to find the audio quality you desire while achieving a manageable file size.

The encoding

Your source material may be in a raw format or in a format different than the one you decide to use, so the conversion of this into a popular web format is an important step. Exporting audio for end use could be a book in its own right. If you are stuck, then you should use the standard for the Web, which is the MP3 format. The following offers you a guideline for MP3 export settings for web audio:

MP3 Voice Podcast	Mono, 64 Kbps, 44.100 kHz
MP3 Low Quality	Stereo, 96 Kpbs, 44.100 kHz
MP3 Medium Quality	Stereo, 128 Kbps, 44.100 kHz
MP3 High Quality	Stereo, 160 Kbps, 44.100 kHz
MP3 Higher Quality	Stereo, 192 Kbps, 44.100 kHz

You can see how the bit rate increases to provide more data per second, and a better quality sound. Unfortunately, this will be at the expense of a larger file size.

The upload

Audio can be uploaded to your web server either via FTP, or you can use the built-in Media Manager.

Via FTP

Open up your FTP program and log into your web server. In most graphical FTP programs, you will have two views; one for your local files and one for the remote files.

In your remote file set, navigate so you can see the Joomla! root directory structure. At this level create a new folder. In this example, I will call it audio. Browse your local computer for the audio file to upload and send it on up to the new **audio** directory:

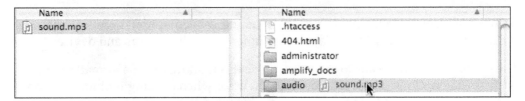

 It is good practice to make a blank .html file and upload it to your new audio directory. This will help stop anyone from being able to directly view all of the files inside your new audio directory. If you cannot create a new .html file, copy an existing Joomla! .html file that resides in the images directory.

Via the Media Manager

To upload via the Media Manager, log into administration and visit the **Content | Media Manager** link. Use the left-hand side directory structure to navigate to existing directories, or use the **Create Folder** feature to create a new **audio** directory:

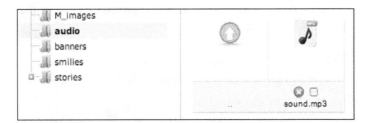

The previous image shows the Media Manager page with the folder structure on the left and files on the right.

The Media Manager location defaults to the setting in the Global Configuration settings. Usually this is within the /images/stories directory. If you wish to create a new root directory at the same level as the /images one (as we did using the FTP method), then you will need to change the default Media Manager path in Global Configuration and then come back to the Media Manager area to create your new directory. Your audio folder does not have to reside within the root of your Joomla! file system, but if you run a busy website, it helps for organizational purposes to contain your images, videos, and audio separately.

The Global Configuration also contains other media settings, such as maximum file upload size, which may need to be taken into consideration when uploading audio using the Media Manager. There may be "PHP max file upload" restrictions on your web hosting server, so FTP / SFTP will be a good option if you are struggling with the Media Manager.

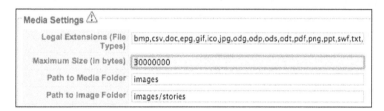

Once your audio directory has been created, simply use the file upload feature of the Media Manager to upload your file into the selected directory.

Editors

One of the most frustrating things that WYSIWYG editors do is to strip out or adjust your nicely entered code. Some are worse than others, but it will be in your interest to turn off your WYSIWYG editor when entering anything but simple HTML custom code into your Joomla! Articles. If you do not, then chances are your custom audio code will not work.

Although, I have just recommended to turn your editors off, I know they can be useful at times, and some users can't live without them. One simple trick is to create a new super administrator user and call it something like "noeditor". Then go and set the **Editor** choice for this user to be **Editor – No Editor**. Using this method you can login as the "noeditor" user whenever you wish. This saves having to switch the editor on and off regularly for a user.

User editor settings can be adjusted on a "User basis" by going to the **Site | User Manager page.** Click on the user you wish to edit and there will be a parameter setting labeled **Editor**:

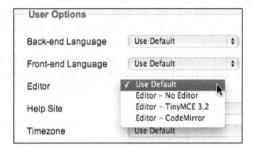

Select the option you require and click on **Save** on the User Edit page. Editors can also be set on a higher level in the Global Administration. Again visit **Site | Global Configuration** Menu to adjust this setting. Once in the Global Configuration page, you will see a setting labeled **Default Editor**. Select the option you require and click on **Save** on the Global Configuration page to save your changes:

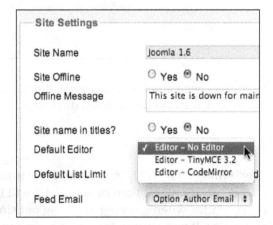

At Joomla.org, there are numerous editor extensions which can be easily installed and provide some fantastic functionality for editing your site content. These all treat the code differently, but as a blanket rule: When entering complex HTML code into your Joomla! Articles, it is best to have all editors turned off. Once your custom HTML code has been included into the article page and saved, be cautious about turning on your WYSIWYG editor and revisiting the article. When your WYSIWYG editor loads the source code, it may strip out all of your hard work, and leave you with an article, which will not display correctly.

Creating the article

New articles are created in the "Article Manager" view:

- Click on the **Article Manager** icon on the Control Panel, or under the **Components | Articles** menu link.

- Click on the icon labeled **New** at the top-right of that page. This will open up the **Add Article** page.

- One of few requirements your new article needs is a page **Title**, and some text within the article. Once these two things have been populated, you are able to click on the **Save** or **Apply** buttons located at the top-right of this page.

The audio HTML code

Audio can be presented in two ways within your Joomla! Articles and Modules:

Direct download

You can provide a hyperlink directly to the audio file, which will allow users to download the file, and when the download is complete, it can be played in the browser window via a plugin, or played on the users' machine via the help of an audio player application such as QuickTime or Windows Media Player.

The download method is the way that audio content used to be offered before web streaming and embedding content became commonplace. Direct downloads are useful if you want to allow your users to download and save the audio content as a file. The code to offer an audio download is a simple hyperlink to the file, and looks like this:

```
<a href="/audio/sound.mp3" title="Audio of Boats Download (1MB)" >
   Listen to my Audio File (1MB)</a>
```

The page looks like:

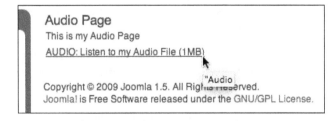

When creating a link to an audio file, it is good practice to always display the file size and additional information next to the link. This information can help the user to know what they are receiving, and the expected download times.

Streaming

Streaming is a process of delivering compressed multimedia content, and displaying this to the user in real time. Examples of web streaming include internet radio and television broadcasts.

In the case of streaming audio, once sufficient data has been downloaded, the user's player (QuickTime Player, Windows Media Player) can start to play the audio while the remaining portion of the audio stream continues to download. This process means users do not have to wait for the full file download to finish before viewing or listening to the content.

Streaming audio is often sent from prerecorded audio files located on a server, but the term "streaming" also relates to a "live audio broadcast (or feed)". Live audio feeds are converted into a compressed audio signal, which can then be delivered via a web streaming server which is able to multi-cast, or send multiple files to multiple users at the same time. This is the process that Internet radio stations use to deliver their media, and in a stricter sense it summarizes the true process of streaming.

Embedding code

As with most HTML code, different browsers interpret it in various ways. To ensure that your audio will play properly in all browsers, we need to use the W3C preferred method of using the `<object>` tag alongside the `<embed>` tag (which is recommended for Netscape and older browsers).

Using both of these tags allows our audio to be delivered correctly on all browsers, which provides us with the best possible chance of offering our audio to the widest audience.

The `<object>` tag is used to include multimedia objects such as audio, video and Flash into web pages. Within the object tags are parameters, and other tags which all have a function (some to different browsers) for displaying your content correctly.

The minimum valid code to embed audio in your Joomla! Article looks something like this:

```
<object width="350" height="50">
<param name="src" value="audio/sound.mp3">
<param name="autoplay" value="true">
<param name="controller" value="true">
<param name="bgcolor" value="#F4F4F4">
<embed src="audio/sound.mp3" autostart="true" loop="false" width="350"
       height="50" controller="true" bgcolor="#F4F4F4">
</embed>
</object>
```

Let's break down the elements of this code:

object	Used to include multimedia in a web page.
height and width	Used to define the height and width of the object.
param	Controls the parameters of the object.
src	The source of the file.
autostart	Set to true or false in order to start playing the audio automatically.
controller	Set to true or false in order to show or hide the controller.
bgcolor	Used to set the background color of the player.
embed	Use the embed tag to place the player on the page.
pluginspage	Takes the user to a plugins download page where they can download the specific player.

You will notice that the content within the <embed> tag is similar to some of that within the <object> tag. This is to cater for all browsers.

The previous code will embed the MP3 file into our Joomla! Article. This is assuming the audio track is called sound.mp3 and has been saved as an MP3 file in a directory named audio, which resides at the root level of our Joomla! file structure (at the same top level that the images directory does).

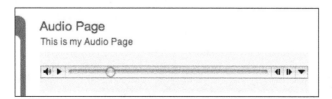

The previous code will use the user's default media player (that resides on their computers) to play the audio file. This is OK, but does not provide flexibility in player behaviors. Therefore, we can manipulate which player the audio file plays in by specifying a player in our code.

There are numerous Flash-based MP3 players now available; one I particularly like is from `http://www.flash-mp3-player.net` which is a powerful and free Flash MP3 Player containing some great features. There is even an easy code generator feature on the website which allows you to easily generate the correct code to embed the player into your web page. If you use the `flash-mp3-player` as an audio player, the HTML code looks similar to this:

```
<object type="application/x-shockwave-flash" data="http://flash-mp3-
  player.net/medias/player_mp3_maxi.swf" width="200" height="20">
<param name="movie" value="http://flash-mp3-
  player.net/medias/player_mp3_maxi.swf" />
<param name="bgcolor" value="#ffffff" />
<param name="FlashVars" value="mp3=audio/sound.mp3" />
</object>
```

 Audio players such as the Flash MP3 Player provide a tool for playing your external audio media. The path to your audio file, the filename, and its permissions will need to be set correctly for your audio files to play.

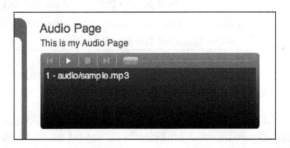

This code will produce a slick Flash-based audio player in your Joomla! Article, with minimal effort and code knowledge required. As mentioned, there are numerous players and online services around which contain their own features. The majority of these will be Flash-based players, because nearly 98 percent of web users' computers and browsers contain the Flash player.

If you are looking to manipulate your HTML audio code further, there are many parameters that can reside within the `<object>` tag. Unfortunately there are too many to cover in this book. For a list of more detailed parameters, visit the W3 Schools website at `http://www.w3schools.com/TAGS/tag_object.asp`.

Including audio using a Joomla! Plugin

Now that we have done the hard work of including an audio file into our Joomla!
Article using raw HTML code, let's look at the power of Joomla! Audio Extensions.

Joomla! Audio Extensions provide a diverse range of extended functionality to the
core CMS. Once a plugin is installed and configured, adding audio can be a simple
"few clicks" process. Specific Joomla! Audio Extensions will be highlighted later
in this chapter, but an example below will show you how powerful they can be
to administrators.

The extension chosen for this example is the **JosDewplayer**:

JosDewplayer is a GPL licensed MP3 audio player for Joomla!. The JosDewplayer
utilizes a Flash-based player interface, which takes MP3 files and streams them in
your HTML pages. The files can reside on your server, or remotely, and the latest
version offers support for multiple file playback.

To get the JosDewplayer for Joomla!, visit `http://extensions.joomla.org/` and
search for "JosDewplayer".

 Before installing any third-party code into your Joomla! website,
make sure you take a backup of your site database and file set
before installing extensions.

Log into your site Administration and click on **Extensions | Extension Manager** in the menu at the top:

Use the **Choose File** upload button to browse your local computer and find the `josdewplayer_plugin.zip` file. Once selected, use the **Upload File & Install** button to install this extension into your Joomla! website.

Once successfully installed, you should head over to **Extensions | Plugin Manager** to configure the new plugin. This particular plugin is classed as a **content** plugin, so you will be looking under that type for "JosDewplayer". Click on the text to load the Plugin Edit page:

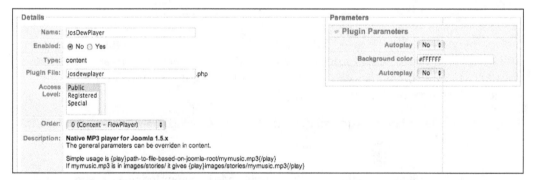

The set of fields on the left-hand side allow you to rename the plugin if you wish to do so, enable or disable the plugin, and set access levels for your site users. Underneath these is the **Description** field, which contains basic instructions to use this plugin. On the right-hand side, a set of parameters allow you to customize the **Autoplay**, **Background color**, and **Autoreplay** features. **Plugin Parameters** usually only need to be set once, and for our example we will be publishing the plugin and leaving the other parameter settings as they are.

 Make sure your plugin is enabled for it to work.

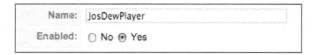

Let's head back to our Joomla! Article that we created earlier, the one with the raw HTML audio code and MP3 player code inside it. Now that we have our extension doing all of the work, all we need to enter into the article is a special tag which the plugin will recognize— {play} —, and then a URL link to our audio file, and then close the special tag again— {/play}. Enter the following code into your Joomla! Article:

```
{play}/audio/sound.mp3{/play}
```

In order to make an absolute link to the file, use the following code (replace the link with the full URL to your audio file):

```
{play}http://localhost/Joomla1.6/audio/sound.mp3{/play}
```

You can use either a relative link or an absolute link, depending where your audio file resides. The absolute link is useful if you are linking to external audio content, and this is one nice feature of the JosDewplayer.

The Autoplay, Background color, and Autoreplay features, set at a global level in the Plugin Parameters, can be overwritten with each instance of your tag usage. For example, to change the default color, we could use the following code:

```
{play}audio/sound.mp3|#000000[BGCOLOR]{/play}
```

The audio player will now look like:

A list of the available parameters is located in the **Description** field of the plugin's parameters. As long as your path to the audio file is correct, we can place an audio player into our Joomla! Article in seconds. Now view the frontend of your website in order to see your audio playing through the JosDewplayer plugin. You can use the player in your site as many times as you want just by inserting the simple tags specific to this plugin. Adding audio to your site pages is that simple when using an audio plugin for Joomla!.

There are numerous other audio extensions for Joomla! that contain their own features. Some play multiple audio file formats, some are JukeBox extensions, and others are players that support both audio and video files, making them a generic multimedia solution for your Joomla! site. More audio extensions will be covered later in this chapter.

Creating an audio podcast for Joomla!

Let's look at some powerful options for podcasting with Joomla!.

What is a podcast?

The word **podcast** is terminology used to describe the online delivery of an audio file wrapped in an RSS enclosure. The name is derived from the words "broadcasting" and "iPod" which usually take MP3 files and offer that content to other users. The name got associated with the iPod because it was one of the most popular devices that people were using to download the audio broadcasts, much like how the Sony Walkman is a brand name and "Walkman" became the default term for a portable music device.

What makes podcasting different to searching for an MP3 file and listening to it, is that files are delivered to you instead of you going to search for them. The podcast information is delivered via an RSS feed and can be subscribed to so that regular content is made instantly available to the subscriber of that feed. Podcasts reading (or listening) software can be configured to notify and automatically download the audio content if required:

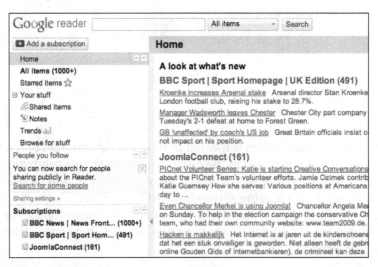

The previous image shows the Google RSS Reader

Before we proceed to build our podcast, let's take a quick look at the built-in RSS capabilities that Joomla! offers.

What is RSS?

The term RSS stands for **Real Simple Syndication**. It is, in its basic form, a simple method for people to stay updated with new content from your website.

RSS is very popular on the Web now with examples of its use being: the latest joke of the week, watching whether cheap airfares are released, and picking up the latest news releases from websites.

RSS feeds can be read by an RSS reader which can be desktop-based, web-based, or even run on a handheld device such as a mobile phone. A standard XML file format allows the information to be published and viewed by many programs.

Users subscribe to an available RSS feed by entering the **Uniform Resource Identifier (URI)** into their RSS reader, or by clicking on an RSS icon (if available) in a web browser, which then initiates the subscription process to that particular RSS feed. Once subscribed, the RSS reader checks the feeds regularly and downloads any updates it finds, therefore informing the user of news from that site without the user having to visit the website:

Joomla! and RSS

Joomla! 1.5 has some good functions to create RSS feeds, and even better ones to take RSS feeds and display the feed information within the Joomla! site. In Chapter 6, *Including Video In Your Joomla! Website*, we will look at how to manually create an RSS feed from a Joomla! Category containing articles with video content within it. It is possible to use a similar process to generate the audio podcast feed, but Joomla! does not create friendly podcasting RSS feeds, so we will utilize a third-party RSS service called FeedBurner to help us with this.

FeedBurner

FeedBurner is an RSS web feed management service introduced by Google in 2007. It is a free service providing bloggers, podcasters, and other web-based publishers with customer RSS management tools:

We will utilize the FeedBurner service to help provide podcast-friendly feeds that link back to our Joomla! content.

Creating a new podcast feed

Here is a step-by-step tutorial to creating a podcast using Joomla! and the FeedBurner RSS service.

Select and prepare your audio content

Using Joomla!, it is possible to deliver your own audio podcast files from your server. In this example, we will upload a self-contained audio file (called `audio` in `.mp3` format) to our web server.

If you are using FTP, simply move the MP3 file from your computer into the new directory. If you are using the Media Manager, then make sure you are residing in the directory you wish and use the file upload feature to load the audio into your desired directory on the web server.

Once your audio has been uploaded, we can proceed to include this in a Joomla! Article.

Disable the WYSIWYG editor

In order to place the correct HTML into our Joomla! Articles, it is best to make sure the built-in WYSIWYG Content Article Editors are disabled. You can easily do this by following these steps:

- Logging into your administration.
- Clicking on the menu item named **Site | User Manager**.
- Select the user to edit.
- Under the parameters for that user, select **Editor – No Editor** as the option for the **Editor** field.
- Clicking on **Apply** or **Save** to save your settings.

The editor can also be disabled on a global basis, by visiting your Global Configuration and changing the **Default Editor** field to **Editor – No Editor**.

Create the category

Follow these steps:

- Log into your Joomla! Administration and proceed to the Create Category area which is located under **Components | Articles | Categories**.
- In the top-right corner, click on the **New** icon, which loads the **Category Manager: Add Category** screen.
- Give your category a name. For our example, I am going to call it **Podcast**. The **Alias** can be left blank, but make sure the category is published. If you want, you can give this category a description.

That is all we need to do for now, so complete the process by clicking on the **Save** button at the top-right of the page.

You will see your new category created and shown in the **Category List**.

Create the article to display your audio

The next step is to create a new Joomla! Article, which will contain your audio content.

- If you are already in the Category screen, click on the link to the article view.
- If you are not, then click on the Article Manager icon on your Control Panel or go to the **Components | Articles** menu item.
- Click on the **Create New Article** button at the top-right of the page, give your article a **Title**, and select the **Podcast** category that was created earlier.
- We now need to include the HTML code into our article (refer to the *Embed and display audio in Joomla! Articles* section, mentioned earlier in this chapter).

 Make sure you don't have your WYSIWYG editor turned on in your Joomla! Articles when entering complex HTML code into your Joomla! Articles.

Once you have your audio code in place, click on the **Apply** button (top-right) to apply the changes and save the new article.

Create the menu link and RSS feed

Once you have created your audio article (or articles) and have it located in the applicable "Audio Podcast" category, it's time to utilize the Joomla! RSS feed menu feature.

Creating a menu link to the category is done by going to the menu you wish to place the new link on, for example, **Menus | MainMenu**, and clicking on the **New** icon at the top-right of the screen:

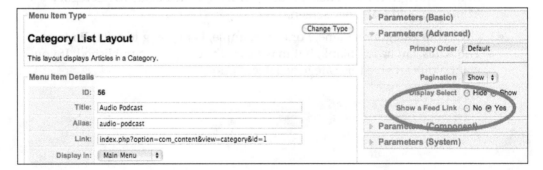

As this section is about creating a menu link for an RSS item, we will not take the time to go through all of the menu parameters, but for our RSS menu link the most important ones are:

- **Title**: Enter a title for your menu link. For our example, I am going to call the menu link **Audio Podcast**.

- **Type**: Click on the **Change Type** button to open up the menu **Type** options, which will open a lightbox with menu type options. Create a new menu type called **Link to Category** by clicking on the applicable link. The popup lightbox will disappear and the appropriate Menu fields will be populated.

- **Parameters (Basic) - Category**: You need to choose which category you wish the menu link to link to.

- **Parameters (Advanced)**: Make sure the **Show a Feed Link** radio button is set to **Yes**.

If you want to fill out any additional parameters or properties for the menu item, then please do, but the previous are the main requirements to create our new **Link to a Category** menu item.

Click on **Save** on that page to save the new menu item.

How it all works

If you look at the front page of your website, you should now see the new menu link you have created. If you cannot, then make sure your menu link is published, and your menu module is published to show the menu on your front page.

Click on this menu item, which will take you to the Category page, displaying the links to your podcast articles.

As most modern web browsers, such as Safari and Firefox, have built-in RSS readers, once you are on this Category page, you should see an RSS icon in your browser. In Mozilla Firefox and Safari, this will be an icon to the right of the URL field in your browser. Click on this to view the RSS feeds from this particular web page:

You may receive more than one option when you have clicked on the icon: **RSS 2.0** or **Atom 1.0**. These are syndication languages and will be covered in a chapter later in this book. For now, both will display your new RSS feed, and allow users to subscribe to and view them.

FeedBurner

Now the fun begins. We are going to create a podcast-friendly feed using the FeedBurner service by Google.

The FeedBurner service is located at `http://feedburner.google.com`. If you do not have one already, you will need to create a free account with Google in order to utilize this service.

When you are logged into your Google account, visit the previous URL, and you will be presented with a box to enter your RSS feed location into:

 Paste the URL to your podcasting category into this box, and not the actual RSS link itself. Then make sure you check the **I am a podcaster!** box to the right of this and click on the **Next** button.

If the link you entered is a valid URL link to your Joomla! Category, FeedBurner will accept it and take you to the next step. If you are having issues with your link, please create a new menu link in your Joomla! site that links directly to your "Podcast" category, click on that link, copy the URL, and then paste it in FeedBurner. This should be all that is required and FeedBurner will now report that it has found two valid RSS links from that URL—**RSS 2.0** and **Atom 1.0**. These are different syndication languages, and for this example, I will use the RSS 2.0 option:

Next we need to give our feed a descriptive **Title** that users will be able to view, and also provide the **Feed Address**, which will start with `http://feeds.feedburner.com/` and then have our suffix at the end. For this example, I will use the title, **Amplify Podcasts** and the Feed Address, **amp_podcast**. Once this information is populated, click on **Next**:

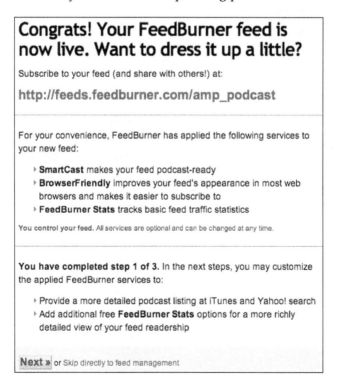

Unless the information you entered into your fields has already been allocated, you should be presented with your brand new sparkling podcast feed:

The FeedBurner service offers you additional features to customize your feed and even submit it automatically to iTunes. We need to utilize one of these, so click on **Next**.

At the top of this page, make sure the **Create podcast enclosures from links to: any rich media file** is selected. It should be the default setting:

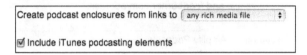

You can give your podcast a description, some keywords, and even add it to iTunes and the Yahoo! search engine. Then click on **Next**.

In this last page, FeedBurner offers you some powerful statistics, which lets you know who is subscribing to your podcasts and how often they have clicked on the content in your feed:

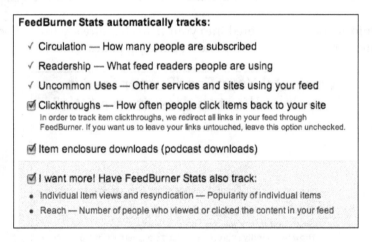

Click on **Next** and we are all done here!

Next, we need to let people know about your new podcast feed. In your FeedBurner page, you should see a tab labeled **Publicize**. Click on this and then on the left-hand side menu item labeled **Chicklet Chooser**:

Scroll to the bottom of the page where you can copy some HTML code:

Copy the code, go back to your Joomla! site, and create a new module, pasting in this HTML code linking to your new feed. Publish this on your podcast pages, and users will be able to subscribe directly to your feed:

To continue to produce podcasts from your website is now an easy process. When you want to create a new podcast, simply create a new Joomla! Article and either embed your audio player into it, or create a link to the podcast material and save this article into your "Podcast" category. Joomla! and FeedBurner will do the rest, automatically creating a new RSS feed entry for this new article.

Podcasting using extensions

There are other ways to podcast from our Joomla! site. These involve using the power of Joomla! third-party extensions, and one of the best tools for the job is the "Joomla! Podcast Suite" by Joseph LeBlanc:

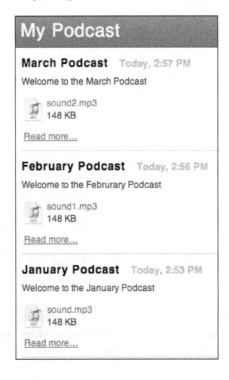

The Podcast Suite extension contains a Joomla! Component, Module, and Plugin which provides an extensive list of podcast tools at your fingertips. You can get your first podcast up and running quickly, and easily build and manage this ongoing.

We will highlight the Podcast Suite extension in the following section, which covers third-party audio extensions.

Third-party audio extensions

Joomla! Extensions provide us with a range of powerful audio solutions which can be installed and configured by administrators, with nearly no developer's knowledge required.

There is a huge number of extensions that are now available for Joomla!. The most difficult decision for a Joomla! site administrator is usually not finding an extension to do what you want it to, but finding the most suitable one out of the available options. The following section highlights some of the most popular, and non-commercial third-party audio extensions.

Podcast Suite

The Podcast Suite for Joomla! is in a world of its own. It does "what it says on the tin" and you can be presenting podcasts within Joomla! in as little as ten minutes:

The suite consists of a component, module, and plugin. These are installed via the Extensions Manager, and require minimal administration configurations.

The Podcast Suite works by creating an RSS feed for your podcasts, as well as a new article, which can contain a description and a special code enclosure for the podcast file. The plugin embeds a useful Flash-based MP3 player into the article, which means you can publicize an RSS link for your podcasts, as well as link directly to the article so your users can listen to them within your site. There is also a handy module to display the RSS feeds.

The Podcast Suite has some excellent author and metadata features, some of which are utilized by iTunes, helping to make your podcasts as iTunes-friendly as possible.

To download the Podcast Suite, visit `http://extensions.joomla.org` and search for "podcast".

MP3 Browser

The MP3 Browser plugin is a superb solution if you are looking to display and play multiple MP3 files in your articles. The plugin creates a table containing all of the MP3 files from a specific directory, for example, `/audio/training/`.

Download	Name	Play	Size	Length
	Tea For Two 30		0.5 MB	0:30 min
	Neptronic 30 (Freeplaymusic)		0.7 MB	0:33 min
	Maximus Hits 30 (Freeplaymusic)		0.8 MB	0:34 min
	Crunch mix 1990 - 1997 (Jon Hollis)		109.4 MB	79:41 min
	Breakbeat Classics 1999 - 2004 (Jon Hollis)		98.5 MB	71:44 min

The plugin displays the ID3 tag information for the title, album name, track length, and file size. It also produces a link so that users can download the MP3 files as well as play the files in your web pages using an embedded MP3 player.

The plugin is called by inserting the easy-to-use plugin tags within your Joomla! Article. The tag looks like this: {music}your/path/to/directory{/music} and will automatically scan the directory for files, and output them in a table listing.

The **Plugin Parameters** allow you to adjust the table's width and colors, replace the download image icon, and adjust column headings:

Plugin Parameters	
Max rows	20
Sort Filenames	⊙ Ascending ○ Descending
Table Width	
Header Height	
Row Height	
Table Header Color	#CCCCCC
Primary Row Color	#FFFFFF
Alt Row Color	#D6E3E8
Row Bottom Border	#C0C0C0
Show Download Column	⊙ On ○ Off
Download Header	Download
Download Colum Width	
Download Image	
Alternative Download Image	
Name Header	Name
Play Header	Play
Show Size Column	⊙ On ○ Off
Size Header	Size

To download the MP3 Browser, visit http://extensions.joomla.org and search for "MP3 Browser".

Simple MP3 Player

Simple MP3 Player is a simple Flash MP3 Player module. The module has various styling options and can be used as a single audio player, or works well with multiple files also, allowing you to create playlists:

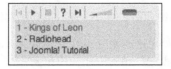

The Simple MP3 Player is based on the Flash MP3 Player mentioned earlier in this chapter and is located at `http://www.flash-mp3-player.net`. The developer of this module has used the power of Joomla! to allow administrators to easily adjust styling and configurations within the Module Manager.

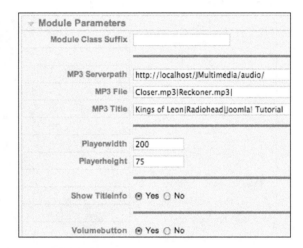

Containing a Flash-based audio player, the module should work for the majority of your audiences, and has been tested on IE 5-8, Firefox 2-3, Safari, and Opera.

To download the Simple MP3 Player, visit `http://extensions.joomla.org` and search for "Simple MP3 Player".

Jukebox

Jukebox is a component and module for Joomla! and is used for managing a music library and allowing your site visitors to listen to music displayed within categories. It has some great features for displaying a collection of music to your site visitors, and includes language support:

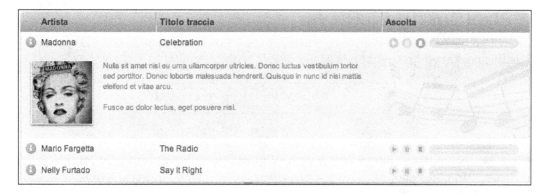

As you can see from the related image, the extension also has language support.

 If you download the com_jukebox.zip file from the developer's website, make sure you unzip this first before uploading it to the Extension Manager. The download file contains the component and a module, which both require installing.

The component allows you to create categories for your music files to reside within. You can add in descriptions, album art, and other music information, as well as use the easy upload feature for the audio file and album cover:

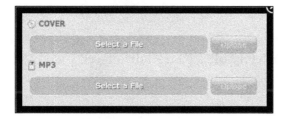

The included module will allow you to easily display a listing of the audio files:

To download the Jukebox, visit http://extensions.joomla.org and search for "Jukebox".

1 PixelOut Audio Player

The 1 PixelOut Audio Player plugin utilizes the 1 PixelOut Flash Audio Player, and has this packaged up so that it is easily usable within Joomla! as a plugin:

As with most Joomla! plugins, their beauty is in their simplicity of use. The 1 PixelOut Audio Player simply requires you to enter a code tag into your Joomla! Articles, and that's about it. This tag calls the player to load, and you will have a great looking audio player displayed within your Joomla! Articles.

The plugin contains a number of parameters that really help make this a player of choice. These parameters not only allow you to define a default path to your audio files, but you can completely customize the player's colors to suit your template:

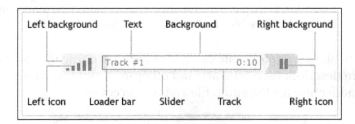

To download the 1 PixelOut Audio Player plugin, visit http://extensions. joomla.org and search for "1 PixelOut Audio Player".

Zina

Zina is a feature packed Joomla! Audio Component that provides a graphical interface for your music collection, a personal jukebox, a podcaster, and an MP3 player.

Zina has been built into a Joomla! Component, which can incorporate the search function, meaning your audio collection can be searchable via the Joomla! search box.

If you want to display music albums and offer sample songs from these, then Zina might be a good option:

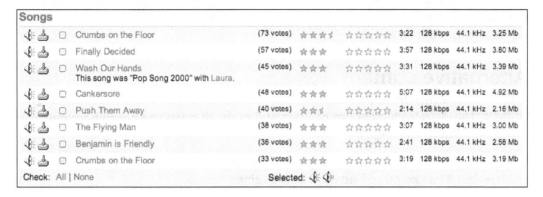

To download Zina, visit `http://extensions.joomla.org` and search for "Zina".

Browser support and audio accessibility

Audio is a great tool for entertaining and delivering information to your site visitors and is now very common to see on the Web. In fact, the sharing of audio files is now one of the most popular activities on the Web.

Audio is becoming a useful device for considerably enhancing the accessibility of your web pages. For people who are visually impaired, the ability to offer your visual content via an audio description is extremely valuable.

Problems arise when correct text alternatives are not made available, which then makes the audio content on the page inaccessible to certain audiences. Your audio will not be accessible to those whose hearing is impaired, so an accurate textual description could be made available to describe the contents of the audio file.

Good practice techniques

Here are some good practice techniques when using audio in your Joomla! pages:

Text transcripts

It is good practice to provide a text transcript to everything you do on your web page. For example, the `alt` tag of an image provides a text transcript of alternative text, allowing the user to know there is an image about that subject loading into that area of the page.

If your audio is about a meeting or product news, provide a text transcript of that content and make it available via a hyperlink to another area, or better yet, make it available on the same page somewhere. Text transcripts can be from a few words long to hundreds of them; your good judgment will be important to accurately describe your audio content.

Alternative content

Your HTML, which includes the audio in your web page, can also contain alternative content. The `object` element can be used to contain all types of information; much more than that of an image tag `<img />`.

Alternative content can not only help people with text-based browsers and screen readers, but it can be picked up by search engines.

Captioning

Captioning may not always be suitable. However, for audio content that is news or training-based, it might be suitable to add captions. Adding a caption to an audio file effectively turns it into a video file as it will contain audio and visuals. Many software applications offer a simple text captioning ability to complement the audio track.

Link to downloads

Providing a link on your web pages to the type of audio player that is required to play your content is very useful, and may just make a difference to your users listening to the audio content.

Audio controls

Offering controls to manipulate the playback of your audio is great practice and now almost an expectation. Audio controls let your visitors control the pace of the track, pause it, and adjust volume levels.

A simple feature such as playbar, pause and audio buttons on your audio player all help in making the player more accessible, than say a background audio track which loads without control features.

"Which audio format is best to use for the Web?" is a common question asked, and none of them are 100 percent compatible for everyone. The trick is to choose one, which will be suitable for a high percentage of your site visitors and then try to cater in other ways to other users.

According to numerous studies on the topic, Adobe Flash is now one of the most popular and widespread Multimedia Players on personal computing systems. Almost all modern web browsers now have Flash installed and statistics show over 98 percent of personal computers can play Flash files. This is why a large number of audio players in the Joomla! Extension directory are all Flash-based audio players.

If your audio content is important, take the time to export this and deliver it in a variety of formats. This provides your site users with choice, and for example, those who cannot run Flash will still be able to listen to it in another player.

Summary

Although Joomla! does not provide native audio features, the ability to enter custom HTML code into our site content provides us with great flexibility when we need to include audio.

Combining Joomla! and the FeedBurner RSS tool provides an automated and accessible way to deliver podcasts from your site, with the ability to easily generate new podcasts and monitor the statistics of the contents.

Joomla! Extensions add enhanced podcasting and audio players to your site, and the functionality of the extensions listed in this chapter will no doubt match and exceed other CMS audio features.

The options of audio formats and accessibilities of these can seem confusing at first, but there are a few standard formats (such as MP3) which are popular and safe to reach the widest audience. To adhere to the W3C accessibility guidelines, always try to offer alternatives for your audio, which could be a text description summarizing the audio contents.

6
Using Video in Your Joomla! Website

Video on the Internet is booming! Relatively recent improvements to factors such as superior video compression, increased connection speeds, and better hardware have all contributed to making the Internet a more reliable and accessible environment for the delivery of video content.

This chapter highlights the use of video media within your Joomla! website, and includes the following topics:

- Video on the Internet
- Video formats
- Embedding and displaying video in Joomla!
- Creating video podcasts for Joomla!
- Third-party video extensions
- Browser support and accessibility

Video on the Internet

The terminology, **video**, refers to the recording, manipulating, and display of a sequence of still images, representing scenes in motion.

Video is probably one of the most notable "media types" that springs to mind when the term multimedia is used. Video is a data intensive media format, requiring megabytes of data to display even short video clips. Limitations such as this have been a restricting factor for its widespread use on the Web, up until recently!

Over the past few years, the use of video on websites has rapidly increased and video has been used to sell, market, and for support and training purposes. New websites have evolved that focus entirely on hosting and presenting video clips to users, and this evolution of video potential has been because of the following contributing factors:

Bandwidth limitations

The growth of consumer broadband has greatly contributed to video evolution on websites. A large percentage of site visitors now have the bandwidth required in order to access quality video content via the Web. It is not as good as it will get, but this factor alone has been one of the biggest influences in "web functionality" growth. Bandwidths are becoming good enough in some areas, that Blockbuster Movie Streaming and Television are now targeting the Internet as a broadcast medium.

Integration of video with other web content

Until recently, most of the videos that were played on the Web offered no rich media capabilities, beyond that of playing back a simple video in a simple box player. Winding the clock back a few years, all video links on websites had to be downloaded to the user's computer, before playback could happen.

With the evolution of video formats, streaming video (content that can be played while it is still being downloaded), and the likes of the Adobe Flash Player, the delivery of video and its interaction with other web content has made for an enhanced user experience.

Authoring and playing video for the Web

With a diverse range of browsers and operating systems available, video on websites often required users to pause what they were doing and download a plugin so that they could access the video content. Modern browsers have become well equipped to play numerous formats of video content, often without the need for additional plugins.

Another contributing factor is the ease of creating content. In the past, you had to be an experienced video recorder / editor with specialist tools to create a video. More recently, new computer operating systems come pre-packed with a form of video editing software. The ease of creating videos and uploading them to websites has had a profound effect on its wide scale use as a popular media format.

With its evolution so far, video and the Internet are extremely well suited. We get to have as close to a real-life experience as possible, which is educational or entertaining, and we get to have this in one of the most interesting playgrounds available, the Web!

With the use of distribution channels, such as YouTube and Google Videos, there has been a dramatic evolution of video usage in websites. Rather than having to host your own video content (which usually causes increased web hosting costs), it is easy now to stream into your site's external video content from a distribution site. The ease of broadcasting and sharing this video content is another major contributing factor to the Web video boom.

Video formats

There are numerous video formats available. Each of these has an effect on the accessibility to different audiences, and some are licensed formats by corporate companies such as Microsoft and Apple. Video formats each contain their own algorithms, which process and handle the electronic video data in different ways:

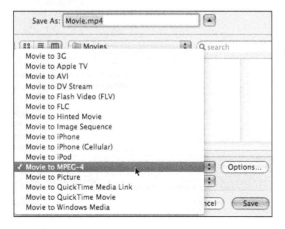

Some are more suitable for some purposes than others (such as storing videos on a DVD or playing videos on an iPod) and we will cover which video formats are suitable for a web-based environment.

Video compression

When using videos on electronic devices, an important concern is the file size. This has often been the restricting factor for using video on the Internet. However, video is becoming consumer friendly now, even mobile phones are able to record videos easily.

Video is a data intensive media format that uses a lot of space on a computer hard drive. Take this into a web scenario, and web-hosting server costs can become expensive due to the extended disk space required to host and play back video files.

The answer to this has been video compression. By compressing the video, it becomes easier to distribute and store it. Digital video compression can be achieved by compressing the data without impacting the perceived quality of the final product. Most of the video compression methods fall into the "Lossy" data compression format. This means that certain information gets deleted every time a video is compressed. Once exported, this information is lost and can no longer be reclaimed:

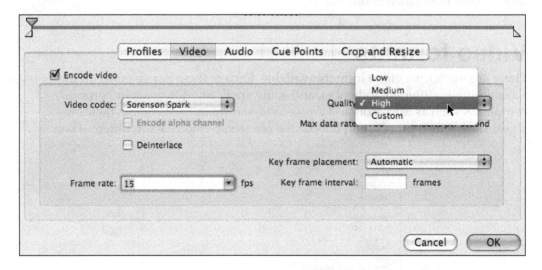

Compression works to remove the data that is considered "not important" and hence our file sizes drop due to this additional information that no longer exists. A good example of video compression is to remove the unrecognized colors from a video clip. There may be millions of colors in a movie (subtle shades of similar colors), but with humans only being able to perceive just over 1000 of them, it is in our interest to compress and remove this unwanted data.

Throw away too much data (over compression) and the changes become noticeable. When compressing video, the goal is to compress as much as possible to the point where you can notice a quality loss, and then nudge back a bit from this point, so you try to achieve optimum data compression and file size with minimal quality loss.

Video codec

Once upon a time, video codecs were a thing for "AV Nerds" and "Hardcore Illegal Video Downloaders", but believe it or not, you probably use them often if you use or watch movies either in a cinema, on a TV, or on your mobile phone.

A **video codec** is a device or software that enables video compression, and again the decompression of this data. The term **codec** stands for compression / decompression and various codecs are used in both the audio and video media formats.

Due to large media file sizes, mathematical codecs were built to encode a signal for transmission, and then decode it again for viewing. There are hundreds of codecs being used now and many of these come included with modern computer equipment. Some of the more common video codecs are VC-1, MPEG-4, and H.264.

It is important to note that a video codec is not a video container (or wrapper) file, by this I mean the final file format. You have probably noticed that none of your video files have an extension like `.vc-1`, or `.h.264`. This is because video files are packaged in containers or wrappers that hold all sorts of file information, such as additional audio and navigational information, as well as the video file itself. The codec does the compression and the container file holds the information for that file. Examples of video container files are FLV (Flash Video), MOV (Apple QuickTime), and so on. Each of these containers uses a certain type of video codec for their compression. Further information about video codecs and container files can be found at `http://en.wikipedia.org/wiki/Category:Video_codecs`.

We will be looking at these container files very soon because they are an important format for saving our web videos.

Bit rates

Bit rates describe how much information is processed per unit of time. Bit rates are an important part of video and audio compression, and all major video compression formats use various bit rates to crunch the data during compression.

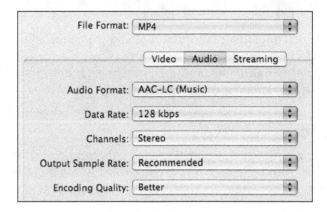

The unit of bit rate is bits per second (bps or bit / s) and can be used with prefixes such as (Kilo) Kbps, or (Mega) MBps, and so on. When exporting files from video editing applications, you may see the bit rate as an exporting option. What is important to remember is the higher the bit rate, the more information the file contains, resulting in a higher quality video file. A higher bit rate file will also result in more effort to encode / decode it, as well as a larger file size. Further information about video bit rates can be found at `http://en.wikipedia.org/wiki/Bit_rate`.

Video containers

There are many compression standards used to compress video file sizes into an efficient state. A compressed video file will be wrapped in a container file, which contains all of the relevant information to play back the video. In order to play this video, the viewing system needs to understand both the video codec the file has been compressed with, and the video container.

The following is a list of the most common video containers used for the Web:

- AVI
- FLV
- MOV
- MPEG

- WMV
- RM

Here is a brief introduction to each of these container formats:

AVI

AVI stands for **Audio Video Interleave** which is a well-known video container format developed by Microsoft in 1992. AVI files are of excellent quality, but this is usually at the expense of file size. It is a popular choice for video editors to save and view videos in, due to the quality.

There are many compression codecs for AVI files, so some of these cannot be played if the system does not contain the specific codec. This may mean a specific update may be needed in order to view some AVI movies. Most new computer systems, however, should be able to play a .avi movie file without the need for additional software.

FLV

FLV stands for **Flash Live Video**. It is a format owned by Adobe Systems and designed for web video playback. It offers high rates of compression and high quality video.

FLV is a popular format because it can be easily embedded into a web page for live streaming and is supported in most computer operating systems via the Adobe Flash Player and its web browser plugin.

At present, FLV is the chosen format for popular video broadcasting sites such as YouTube and MySpace and it is thought to be one of the most popular formats to deliver video on the Web.

Flash movies are an excellent format for web video, but they do have their limitations. Some companies will not allow the Flash player to be installed on their IT networks. There are also some search engine optimization limitations around full Flash authored websites.

MOV

QuickTime (the file extension is .mov) is the multimedia playback and storage technology developed by Apple. QuickTime files act as containers that combine file, text, audio, and video in a single file.

QuickTime movies are usually of great quality and the format offers good compression rates. The QuickTime player comes with Apple Macs, but Windows users may need to download the QuickTime player to view MOV files.

MPEG

MPEG stands for **Moving Pictures Experts Group**, which was established in 1988 as a working group to define a standard format for audio and video media types.

MPEG files are a common format for web use and offer good quality compression and file sizes. There have been numerous editions to the MPEG family since the 1980s with the latest and most popular format being MPEG-4 (`.mp4`).

MPEG files can be played with Windows Media Player or Apple QuickTime Player, which means they are probably one of the most cross-platform suitable file formats. This has led to their popular use all over the Web. The latest format, `.mp4`, offers superior compression, with great quality and small file sizes.

WMV

WMV stands for **Windows Media Video** and was created and licensed by Microsoft as a competitor to RealVideo. It is comparable in quality with other similar codecs and is supported by all Microsoft tools, which makes it the nature of choice for creating videos when using a Windows computer.

Anyone who isn't using a Windows computer will need to download the Windows Media Player, or an equivalent player, in order to play `.wmv` files. Therefore, in order to reach the largest audience, there are more suitable containers to use for your web-based videos.

RM

Real Audio/Video was one of the leading pioneers in streaming video. It is a propriety video format developed by RealNetworks and was first released in 1997. Its streaming format and good compression rates provided quality videos in relatively small file sizes.

RealVideo is usually packaged with audio and compiled in the container (`.rm`) file. The RealMedia format used to be very popular, but the propriety technology has led to the format's decline in favor of more easily available solutions.

There are many other video containers available for use in different environments. Further information on these can be found at `http://en.wikipedia.org/wiki/Video_container`.

Embedding and displaying video in your Joomla! web pages

Besides all of the wonderful features that Joomla! provides out-of-the-box, one very powerful feature is the ability to include your own custom HTML into Joomla! Articles. This means we have the ability to completely customize the output of content in our articles and modules, which is what is required to insert a video into a Joomla! web page, without the use of extensions.

The source

When preparing your video for the Web, one of the most significant choices is which video format to use.

Unfortunately, no single video format is 100 percent guaranteed to suit all of your site visitors. They will all be using different computer operating systems, screen resolutions, and web browsers, which means that consideration is required to allow your video to be seen by the majority of users, without the requirements for additional downloads or plugins.

We have already listed video formats earlier in this chapter. The three main players that make themselves noticed when providing support for these video formats are as follows:

Adobe Flash	SWF movies
Apple QuickTime	MOV, MPEG-1/2/4, AVI (depending on the codec used)
Windows Media	WMV, MPEG-1, AVI (depending on the codec used)

Adobe Flash claims they have a 98 percent presence in the market, and it is widely used as a format choice for video distribution sites such as Google, YouTube, and Yahoo!. If a high percentage of users can view Flash content, then this is one great reason to consider using Flash as a video format for your site.

There may be situations where installing Flash is restricted, such as on company computer networks. To cater for audiences such as this, making your content also available in an MPEG-4 video format may be a suitable option.

The encoding

An essential step for web video is preparing it for web delivery. Your source material may often be in a different format than the one you decide to use, and if it has been recorded by a mobile phone, a DVD camcorder, among others, it will probably be in a very unsuitable format for use on the Web.

There are a number of video exporting and conversion software applications available now, and although it would be great to go into detail, whole books have been written about editing and optimizing videos. The following is some basic information that can be taken as a guide when exporting your movie from video editing software. These are ideal for users viewing your sites with a broadband connection:

Adobe Flash format	Frame size and aspect ratio: (4:3) 384 x 480, (16:9) 270 x 480.
	Frame rate: 12-15 frames per second.
	De-interlace: Should be set to yes.
	Audio bit rate: 64 Kbps (speech) to 128 Kbps (music).
Apple QuickTime format	Frame size and aspect ratio: (4:3) 640 x 480 or 320 x 240, (16:9) 640 x 352.
	Frame rate: 15 frames per second.
	De-interlace: Should be set to yes.
	Audio bit depth: 16 bit.
Windows Media format	Frame size and aspect ratio: (4:3) 640 x 480 or 320 x 240, (16:9) 640 x 352.
	Frame rate: 15 frames per second.
	De-interlace: Should be set to yes.
	Audio bit depth: 16 bit.

Raw video will need to be encoded into a streaming format to produce an appropriate QuickTime, Windows Media, Flash, RealMedia, or MPEG-4 file. The length and time required to encode video is dependent on the export settings, software, and computer processing power. Many free and commercial software applications are now available to perform video editing, exporting, and file conversions.

An open source encoding tool worth mentioning is the MediaCoder from `http://www.mediacoderhq.com/download.htm`. MediaCoder is a free universal media transcoder that works with almost all popular codecs. MediaCoder can also transcode audio, providing you with a Swiss army knife for media encoding. A search on the Internet will provide you with editing tools to suit your computer platform, and there are lots available.

The upload

Whether you choose to use FTP or the built-in Media Manager, it is an easy process to upload video to your web server.

Via FTP

Open up your FTP program and log into your web server. In most graphical FTP programs, you will have two views, one for your local files and one for the remote files:

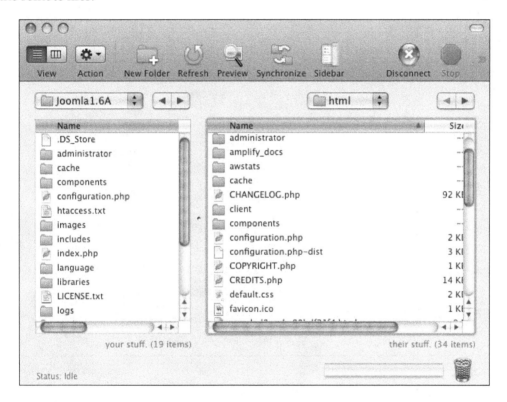

In your remote file set, navigate so you can see the Joomla! root directory structure. At this level, create a new folder named videos. Browse your local computer for the video file you want to upload and send it on up to the new video directory.

It is good practice to make a blank .html file and upload it to your new video directory. This will help stop anyone from being able to directly view all of the video files inside your new video directory. If you cannot create a new .html file, copy an existing Joomla! .html file that resides in the images directory.

Via the Media Manager

In order to upload a file via the Media Manager, log into the administration and visit the **Content | Media Manager** feature. Use the left-hand side directory structure to navigate to existing directories, or use the **Create Folder** feature to create a new `video` directory:

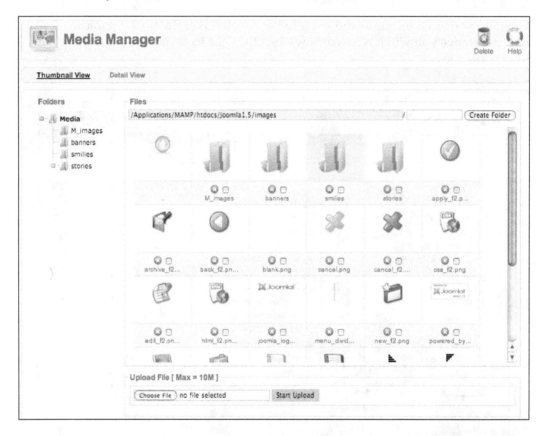

 The Media Manager location defaults to the setting in the Global Configuration settings. Usually this is within the `/images` directory. If you wish to create a new root directory at the same level as the `/images` one (as we did using the FTP method), then you will need to change the default Media Manager path in Global Configuration and then come back to the Media Manager area to create your new directory.

Media Settings ⚠

Legal Extensions (File Types)	bmp,csv,doc,epg,gif,ico,jpg,odg,odp,ods,odt,pdf,png,ppt,swf,txt,
Maximum Size (in bytes)	10000000
Path to Media Folder	images
Path to Image Folder	images/stories
Restrict Uploads	○ No ◉ Yes
Minimum User Level for Media Manager	Author ⬦
Check MIME Types	○ No ◉ Yes
Legal Image Extensions (File Types)	bmp,gif,jpg,png
Ignored Extensions	
Legal MIME Types	image/jpeg,image/gif,image/png,image/bmp,application/x-shoc
Illegal MIME Types	text/html
Enable Flash Uploader	◉ No ○ Yes

The Global Configuration also contains other media settings such as Max File upload size, which may need to be taken into consideration when uploading videos.

Once your `videos` directory has been created, simply use the file upload feature of the Media Manager to upload your file into the selected directory.

Editors

One of the most frustrating things with WYSIWYG editors is that they strip out or adjust your nicely formatted code. Some are worse than others at performing this role, but it will be in your interest to turn off your WYSIWYG editor when entering anything but simple HTML custom code into your Joomla! Articles.

Although, I have just recommended that you turn your editors off, I know they can be useful at times, and some users can't live without them. One simple trick is to create a new super administrator user and call it something like "noeditor". Then go and set the **Editor** choice for this user as **Editor – No Editor**. Using this method, you can log in as the "noeditor" user whenever you wish. This saves having to switch the editor on and off frequently.

User editor settings can be adjusted on a "User basis" by going to the **Site | User Manager** page. Click on the user you wish to edit and there will be a parameter setting labeled **Editor**:

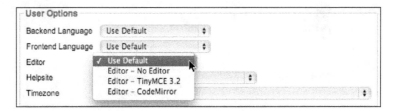

Select the option you require and click on **Save** on the User Edit page. Editors can also be set on a higher level in Global Administration. Again, visit the **Site | Global Configuration** menu to adjust this setting. Once on the Global Configuration page, you will see a setting labeled **Default Editor**. Select the option you require, and click on **Save** on the Global Configuration page to save your changes:

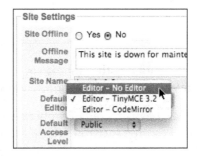

At Joomla.org, there are numerous editor extensions which can be easily installed and provide some fantastic functionality for editing your site content. All of these treat the code differently, but as a blanket rule: When entering complex HTML code into your Joomla! Articles, it is best to have all editors turned off. Once your custom HTML code has been included into the article page and saved, be cautious about turning on your WYSIWYG editor and revisiting the article. When your WYSIWYG editor loads the source code, it may strip out all of your hard work, and leave you with an article that will not display correctly.

To help make the Joomla! editor a bit more HTML friendly, you can adjust the security for your editor filtering. Here is how to do it:

- Within your Joomla! Administration, visit the **Article Manager** screen.
- At the top-right of the page, you will see an option to edit the Global Article "Parameters".

- Click on this and at the bottom of the screen, you will see the Editor Filtering List.
- Choose your Filter Group (for example, super administrator) and under the filter type, select "Whitelist".

You can also configure specific HTML to be ignored from the editor's filter list. Make sure you save these new configurations at the top of the page.

Creating the article

New articles are created in the "Article Manager" view:

- Click on the **Article Manager** icon on the control panel, or under the **Components | Articles** menu link.
- Once you are in the Article Manager, click on the icon labeled **New** at the top-right of that page. This will open up the **Add Article** page.
- One of the few requirements your new article needs is a page **Title**, and some text within the article. Once these two things have been populated, you will be able to click on the **Save** or **Apply** buttons located at the top-right of this page.

The video HTML code

Videos can be presented in two ways within your Joomla! Article:

Direct download

You can provide a hyperlink directly to the video file, which will allow users to download the video file, and when the download is complete, it can be viewed in the browser window with a plugin, or played on the user's machine via the help of a video player application such as QuickTime or Windows Media Player.

The download method is the way that video content used to be offered before web streaming and embedding content became commonplace. Direct downloads are useful if you want to allow your users to download and save the video content. The code to offer a video download is a simple hyperlink to the file, and looks like this:

```
<a href="/videos/boats.mov" title="Video of Boats Download 1.2MB" >
   My Movie about Boats (1.2MB)</a>
```

The page looks like:

> The Great Barrier Reef is the largest coral reef system composed of over 2,900 individu
> stretching for over 3,000 kilometres (1,600 mi) over an area of approximately 344,400 s
> mi).
>
> Download the Great Barrier Reef Movie (16MB)
>
> The reef is located in the Coral Sea, off the coast of Queensland in northeast Australia.
>
> http://en.wikipedia.org/wiki/Great_Barrier_Reef

When creating a link to a video file, it is good practice to always display the file size and additional information next to the link. This information can help the user to know what they are receiving, and the expected download times.

Streaming

Streaming is a process of delivering compressed multimedia content, and displaying this to the user in real time. Examples of web streaming include Internet radio and television broadcasts.

In the case of streaming video, once sufficient data has been downloaded, the user's player (QuickTime Player, Windows Media Player) can start playing the video while the remaining portion of the video stream continues to download. This process means users do not have to wait for the full file download to finish before viewing that particular content.

Streaming video is usually sent from prerecorded video files located on a server, but streaming can also relate to a "live video broadcast (or feed)". Live video feeds are converted into a compressed video signal, which can then be delivered via a web streaming server that is able to multi-cast, or send the files to multiple users at the same time.

Embedding code

As with most HTML code, different browsers interpret it in various ways. To ensure that our videos will play properly in all browsers, we need to use a W3C preferred method of using the `<object>` tag alongside the `<embed>` tag (which is recommended for Netscape and older browsers).

Using both of these tags lets our video play properly on all browsers, which provides us with the best possible chance of offering our video to the widest audience.

The <object> tag is used to include multimedia objects such as audio, video, and Flash into web pages. Within the object tags are parameters, and other tags which all have a function (some to different browsers) for displaying your content correctly.

The minimum valid code to embed a video in your Joomla! Article looks something like this:

```
<object width="320" height="240" classid="clsid:02BF25D5-8C17-4B23-
BC80-D3488ABDDC6B"
        codebase="http://www.apple.com/qtactivex/qtplugin.cab">
<param name="src" value="/videos/videofile.mov">
<param name="controller" value="true">
<param name="autoplay" value="false">
<embed src="/videos/videofile.mov" width="320" height="240"
    autoplay="false" controller="true"
    pluginspage="http://www.apple.com/quicktime/download/">
</embed>
</object>
```

Let's take a look at the elements of this code:

object	Used to include multimedia in a web page.
height and width	Used to define the height and width of the object. This is usually the same size or slightly larger than the video file size, as sometimes we need a bit of extra space to show the video controls around the actual video.
classid and codebase	Defines specific directions for automatically installing the ActiveX element.
param	Controls the parameters of the object.
src	The source of the file.
controller	Set to true or false in order to show or hide the controller.
autoplay	Set to true or false in order to start playing the video automatically.
embed	Use the embed tag to place the player on the page.
pluginspage	Takes the user to a plugins download page where they can download the specific player.

You will notice that the content within the <embed> tag is similar to some of that within the <object> tag. Using both of these tags will result in all major browsers being able to interoperate your content correctly.

Let's see our code in a working example. If we have a video called `boats.mov` that has been saved as a `.mov` file of 320 x 240 proportions, and this file is located in a directory named `videos` which resides at the root level of our Joomla! file structure (at the same top level that the `images` directory does). The code to embed that video will look like the following:

```
<object width="320" height="240"
        classid="clsid:02BF25D5-8C17-4B23-BC80-D3488ABDDC6B"
        codebase="http://www.apple.com/qtactivex/qtplugin.cab">
<param name="src" value="/videos/boats.mov">
<param name="controller" value="true">
<param name="autoplay" value="false">
<embed src="/videos/boats.mov" width="320" height="240"
        autoplay="false" controller="true"
        pluginspage="http://www.apple.com/quicktime/download/">
</embed>
</object>
```

There are many parameters that can reside within the `<object>` tag, too many to cover in this manual, but the ones listed previously are common parameters. For a list of more detailed parameters, visit the W3 Schools website at: `http://www.w3schools.com/TAGS/tag_object.asp`.

Including a video using an article plugin

Now that we have done the hard work of including a video into our Joomla! Article using raw HTML code, we will take a look at the power of a Joomla! Video Extension to include our video.

Joomla! Video Extensions provide a diverse range of extended functionality to the core CMS. Once a plugin is installed and configured, adding video can be a simple few clicks process. Joomla! Video Extensions will be highlighted later in this chapter, but for now we will look at how powerful they can be to administrators.

An example of an extension is the **Flow Player**:

Flow Player is a GPL licensed video player for web pages. The Flow Player utilizes a Flash-based player interface which takes numerous video formats and streams them in your HTML pages. It is a pretty advanced piece of kit, with advanced streaming technologies such as bandwidth, among others.

The Flow Player for Joomla! has been developed, which harnesses this wonderful player, and makes it work easily within your Joomla! website. There is a plugin version available that allows you to play media within your articles, and a module version which can be placed in any module position.

To get the Flow Player for Joomla!, visit `http://extensions.joomla.org/` and search for "Flow Player Plugin". Once you have downloaded this extension to your computer, we are ready to roll!

 Before installing any third-party code into your Joomla! website, make sure you take a backup of your site database and file set before the installation of extensions. There are some excellent backup extensions such as JoomlaPack and JoomlaCloner. Once configured, these help you to easily backup your Joomla! website with just a couple of clicks.

Log into your site administration and click on **Extensions | Extension Manager**.

Use the **Choose File** upload button to browse your local computer and find the `plg_flowplayer.zip` file. Once selected, use the **Upload File & Install** button to install this extension on your Joomla! website.

Once successfully installed, you should head over to **Extensions | Plugin Manager** in order to configure the new plugin. This particular plugin is classed as a content plugin, so you will be looking for something like **Content - FlowPlayer**. Click on the text to load the Plugin Edit page.

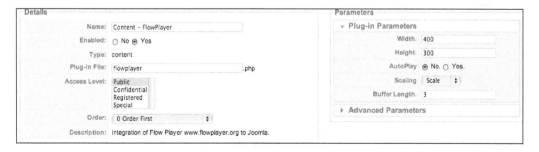

The set of fields on the left-hand side allow you to rename the plugin if you wish to do so, enable or disable the plugin, and set access levels for your site users. The set of parameters on the right-hand side allow you to customize the height and width of the player as well as showing movie controls and other player features. **Plug-in Parameters** usually only need to be set once, and for our example, we will be leaving the default settings as they are (except for making the plugin published).

Let's head back to our Joomla! Article that we created earlier; the one with the raw HTML video code in it. At the end of the `<object>` code, let's put in a few breaks `<br /><br />` to distinguish our new code from that already in place. Now that we have our extension doing all of the work, all we need to enter into the article is use a special tag which the plugin will recognize — `{flowplayer}` — and then a URL link to our video file, and then close the special tag again — `{/flowplayer}`.

```
{flowplayer}/videos/boats.mov{/flowplayer}
```

To make that an absolute link to a file, it will be:

```
{flowplayer}http://localhost/Joomla1.5/videos/boats.mov{/flowplayer}
```

 It is worth noting that Joomla! Plugin tags work with and without the WYSIWYG editor turned on.

You can use either a relative link or an absolute link depending on where your video file resides. The absolute link is useful if you are linking to external video content residing on another domain or server. They are not good practice when using internal site content. If one day you decide to change your domain name, you may have hundreds of broken links to revisit and change in order to reflect your new domain.

As long as your path to the video file is correct, we have now placed a video into our Joomla! Article in seconds. It's that simple! Now view the frontend of your website in order to see the your video playing through the Flow Player plugin. Adding a video to your site pages is that simple when using a video plugin for Joomla!.

There are numerous other video extensions for Joomla! that contain their own features. Some play certain video formats, some are gallery style components, and other players support both audio and video files, making them a generic multimedia solution for your Joomla! site. More video extensions will be covered in third-party video extensions.

Creating a video podcast

Creating a video podcast for Joomla! will allow you to display and promote your site or products to many users. Due to the nature of a podcast, they do not even have to be on your website to view the video podcasts, if produced correctly.

It would be easy for us to create a regular RSS feed to a category containing video articles. This would provide us with an RSS feed, informing subscribers that we have new content on our site. Unfortunately, the RSS feed capabilities of Joomla! are limited, and this method would not enclose the video content within the RSS feed. Hence, our users cannot download the video file for viewing without coming back to the website.

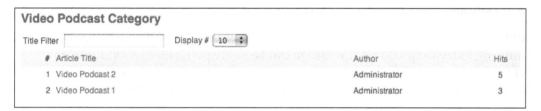

Creating a true video podcast requires the video content to be wrapped within RSS enclosures, which are a way of attaching multimedia content to RSS feeds. As Joomla! cannot provide this feature, we need to utilize a method mentioned in Chapter 5, *Using Audio in Your Joomla! Website*.

The external RSS feed creation service "FeedBurner" can generate RSS feeds that can contain our multimedia content. For further details about the process, please look at Chapter 5 for this topic. Following are the brief steps for creating a video podcast using the FeedBurner service:

1. Select and prepare your video content. A suggestion at first would be to insert your video code manually, as some video extension plugins may or may not work with this process.

2. Create a video article and place this within a designated "Video" category.

3. Create a "Link to Category" menu link so Joomla! can generate the RSS feed to that category.

4. View the menu link in the frontend of Joomla!, and copy the RSS feed URL.

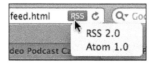

5. Visit `http://feedburner.google.com` and paste the URL into the feed creation box, making sure you click on the "I am a podcaster" checkbox.

6. Follow the rest of the FeedBurner process, giving your feed a title and address and making sure that you select "Create podcast enclosures from links to: Any rich media file".

7. Grab your new video podcast feed from FeedBurner and job done!

So what we have done here is that we used FeedBurner's powerful features to create a supercharged RSS feed, built off our Joomla! generated RSS feed.

Once your FeedBurner feed has been successfully created and tested, you should be able to add new video articles into the same Joomla! Category, with these automatically being added to the video podcast feed.

With the abundance of screen capture tools and video editing programs available, utilizing video to spread your message can be easily performed. As video is one of the most true-to-life media experiences, using it will inform and entertain your website visitors, and might just put you one step ahead of your competitors.

Third-party video extensions

It is the use of Joomla!'s video extensions that provide us with some really powerful video capabilities. So much so, that Joomla! has extensions ranging from placing a simple video into a content article, through to providing a mini YouTube style video distribution site.

Listed in this section are some of the most powerful, popular, non-commercial third-party video extensions for Joomla!. There are a number of commercial solutions also available; some of these are listed within the Joomla! Extensions directory.

AllVideos

AllVideos is an all-in-one media solution for Joomla!. AllVideos is a plugin which can easily embed video from distribution sites such as YouTube, Vimeo, and many more. As well as this, it can play back almost any video / audio file type directly from your server or a remote one.

AllVideos has the following features:

1. Dozens of video distribution sites are supported. For example, YouTube, Google Videos, Vimeo, Metacafe, Brightcove, Dailymotion, Revver, Spike, and more!

2. You can stream your own popular video formats, including `.fla`, `.swf`, `.mp4`, `.mov`, `.wmv`, `.wma`, `.mp3`, `.3gp`, `.divx`.

3. You can embed video content from your own server, or a remote one.

4. It is easy to use. Set the Plugin Parameters, make the plugin published, and you're ready to stream video content from your website.

5. You can customize your own display of the output from this plugin using a skinable template system.

It is worth mentioning that there has been a developed fork of this extension, called AllVideos Reloaded. Both extensions are popular, and have continued development and their own set of features. Please review both of them at `http://extensions.joomla.org` (listed under the Multimedia category, or search for "AllVideos") to view the comparisons.

hwdVideoShare

hwdVideoShare is a video sharing gallery extension consisting of a component and plugin. The purpose of this extension is to provide you with the features of a video gallery and distribution website, such as YouTube.

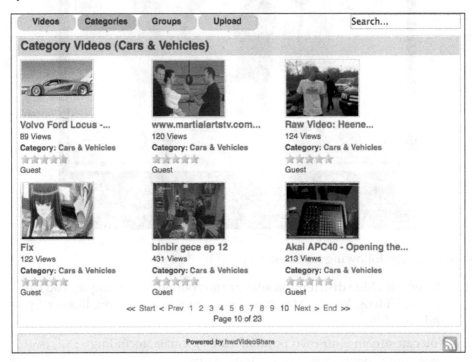

The component requires FFMPEG, MENCODER, and FLVTOOL2 to run, and can support the MPG, MPEG, AVI, DIVX, MP4, FLV, WMV, RM, MOV, MOOV, ASF, SWF, and VOB video formats.

Videos from third-party sources such as YouTube and Google Videos are also supported, and function seamlessly with uploaded media, while users can rate, comment, report, and add videos to their favorites.

The software uses the Joomla! Plugin Manager to support a variety of additional plugins:

- Template plugins can be used to style the gallery with a custom theme
- Language plugins can be used to translate the software
- Video player plugins can be used to change the video player
- Third party video plugins can be used to import videos from popular video sites
- System plugins can be used to trigger useful tasks on specific video events

This extension also integrates with the developers of additional products, providing further capabilities. To download this extension, visit `http://extensions.joomla.org` and search for "hwdVideoShare".

Simple Flash Video Player

The Simple Flash Video Player is a module for Joomla! 1.5, and is based on the JW player. It is easy to use and has the following features:

- Plays a single video file from a URL or unlimited video files from a playlist
- Plays YouTube videos
- Supports the playback of any format that the Adobe Flash Player can handle (FLV, MP4, MP3, AAC, JPG, PNG, and GIF)

The module contains the following parameters, which can be adjusted:

- Change player settings
- Video file properties
- Playlist settings
- Display a preview image
- Insert your own logo on movie load
- URL to an external page
- Autostart, repeat, and shuffle settings

To download the Simple Flash Video Player module, visit `http://extensions.joomla.org` and search for "Flash Video".

RokBox

RokBox is a MooTools powered JavaScript slideshow and multimedia plugin, displaying your content in an eye-catching lightbox type pop-up effect.

RokBox can display multiple media formats, including images, videos, videos from sharing sites, and audio. It is one of a new breed of plugins that can provide multiple media content capabilities right out-of-the-box.

RokBox comes with two default themes, but is designed so that you can tailor a theme for your site design, creating a tailored multimedia display for your site media.

Features include:

- MooTools v1.11 compatible
- Four customizable transition types: Fade, QuickSilver, Growl, Explode.
- Support for PDF, images, FLV, QuickTime (`.mov`, `.m4v`), Windows Media Video (`.wmv`), Flash (`.swf`), YouTube, DailyMotion, Metacafe, Google Videos, Vimeo, audio (`.mp3`, `.wav`, `.m4a`), local and remote sites
- Support for albums/categories

- Ability to pop up RokBox in pixels or percentages and in full screen, relative to the browser window
- Support for captions, including support for titles and descriptions
- Two predefined themes provided: light theme and dark theme
- Support for custom themes with the ability to customize styles and the RokBox configuration per theme
- Ability to auto-generate thumbnails when RokBox-ing local images
- Support for generating thumbnails or inline links from your Joomla! content

RokBox is a great plugin. Its simplicity, good looks, and versatility of media types, make it a very useful extension to your site.

To download RokBox, visit `http://extensions.joomla.org` and search for "RokBox".

Shadowbox

Like RokBox, Shadowbox is an online media viewer application that supports all of the Web's most popular media publishing formats.

Shadowbox is written entirely in JavaScript and CSS and is highly customizable. Using Shadowbox, website authors can showcase a wide assortment of media in all major browsers without navigating users away from the linking page.

Shadowbox can support images, audio, and video. The available video formats include:

- QuickTime
- Flash
- Windows Media

You can use Shadowbox to display media from links within your articles and modules, as it is the included `rel` in the hyperlink that activates the plugin. This means you can utilize the Shadowbox feature on any hyperlink you wish:

```
<a href="/myimage.jpg" rel="shadowbox">My Image</a>
```

As with RokBox, Shadowbox is a multi-use media plugin for your Joomla! website, so it may be all that you need for your multimedia requirements. The extension can be downloaded at `http://extensions.joomla.org` by searching for "Shadow".

There are numerous other video extensions and solutions for Joomla!. Many of these provide powerful features, but fall under commercial licenses and have not been covered in this section. If you require specific Joomla! video features, a search on `http://extensions.joomla.org` or via a popular search engine will provide you with additional solutions to those listed here.

Browser support and video accessibility

Video is a great tool for entertaining and delivering information to your site visitors and is now more common than it ever has been on the Web.

At first thought, it may seem that video is not the ideal media (in terms of accessibility) to have loading into a web page. If used correctly though, video can actually enhance the accessibility of a web page by becoming an additional means to deliver audio and visual content to site users. Due to these combined mediums, video is becoming a useful device for considerably enhancing the accessibility of web pages.

Problems arise, however, when correct text alternatives are not made available, which then makes the video content on the page inaccessible to certain audiences. For example, a video which has no audio content is inaccessible to those who are visually impaired, or to someone who is both visually and hearing impaired, it is of no use at all.

Text equivalents should always be made available wherever possible. For example, if your video is about "How to use our product", make sure that you offer a text description of the content available in the video, either on the same page or as a link to another area.

Good practice techniques

Here are some good practice techniques when using videos in your Joomla! pages.

Text transcripts

It is good practice to provide a text transcript to everything you do on your web page. For example, the `alt` tag of an image provides a text transcript of alternative text, allowing the user to know there is an image about that subject loading into that area of the page.

If your video is about a speech or news, provide a text transcript of that content and make it available via a hyperlink to another area, or better yet, make it available on the same page somewhere. Text transcripts can be from a few words long to hundreds of them; your good judgment will be important to accurately describe your video content.

Alternative content

Just like images, your HTML, which includes the video into your web page can also contain alternative content. The `object` element can be used to contain all types of information, much more than that of an image tag `<img />`.

An example would be, if you want to provide a Windows `.wmv` video on your webpage, then users who use Apple Macs wont be able to view this unless they have downloaded the Windows Media Player for MAC. Using the `object` element, you can specify that if the user can't play `.wmv`, then you should load a MPEG version (or alternative format) of that movie instead. If the MPEG movie isn't supported, you could specify that a text transcription be delivered instead.

Alternative content can not only help people with text-based browsers and screen readers, but it can be picked up by search engines.

Captioning

Captions on video content can be useful to the hearing impaired, or people with no speakers on their computers. Captioning may not always be suitable. However, for video content that is news or training-based, captions generally only enhance the video content.

Video controls

Offering controls to manipulate the playback of your video is great practice and now almost an expectation. Video controls let your visitors control the pace of the video, pause and re-view the video, as well as turn the audio on and off, and so on:

A simple feature such as playbar, pause and audio buttons on your video player all help in making that piece of video so much more accessible than one which just plays in a box without control features.

Web browsers are becoming more and more complex, containing powerful multimedia capabilities built into them. In days gone by, it was not uncommon to hit a web page and have to then go off and download a browser plugin in order to view the multimedia content displayed on that page.

These web browser plugins were optional software, which enhanced or added a particular function to the web browser. Users who do not have the capability to play your particular video format would need to download a plugin for their browsers in order to play that video format.

Some of the most popular video browser plugins are:

- Adobe Flash Player
- Apple QuickTime Player
- Real Media Player
- Windows Media Player

The problem with the question "Which video format is best to use for the Web?" is that none of them are 100 percent compatible for everyone. The trick is to choose the one, which will be suitable for a high percentage of your site visitors and then try to cater in other ways for other users.

According to numerous studies on the topic, Adobe Flash is now one of the most popular and widespread formats for displaying video on the Web. Almost all modern web browsers now have Flash installed, and statistics show over 98 percent of personal computers can play Flash files.

If you choose not to use Flash, then I suggest saving your movies to a MPEG-4 format (.mp4). These will also be playable by the majority of users across many devices.

Summary

Joomla! really is an excellent framework for displaying video content. Although, it does not have a built-in easy-click video function out-of-the-box, at its basic form the article pages display HTML code within your template structure. This means that we can upload, include, and embed all types of HTML for displaying video content within our Joomla! Articles, just as you would with hand-built HTML pages.

Taking this a step further, we have a wealth of video capabilities from Joomla! Extensions, which bring amazingly powerful video features into the CMS. From great looking players that can be played into module positions, to full blown "Host your own Joomla! YouTube" components, Joomla! Extensions are really where it is at for cutting edge web video solutions. If you use distribution services such as YouTube and Google Videos, then displaying this content within your Joomla! site can be a simple "few clicks process", and may save you money on web hosting bandwidth costs.

The choice of video formats and accessibility can seem confusing at first, but there are a few standard formats such as Flash and MPEG-4 which are good options to use, and will make sure that your content will be displayed to the majority of your site visitors. When including this video content, think about offering the video in multiple formats and make text-equivalent content available for accessibility reasons.

Video will bring a new dimension to your Joomla! sites. Use it with knowledge and consideration, and it will definitely enhance your site visitors' experiences.

7
Collaborating with External Sources

Sharing information between popular external resources such as Twitter, Facebook, and Google is an increasingly popular feature required by Joomla! users.

With new social networking sites and multimedia portals springing up every month, integrations between these and Joomla! continue to evolve through the use of powerful, third-party extensions.

Designed to extend the Joomla! Framework with new functionality, this chapter will look at the most popular collaboration extensions for Joomla! and the features they contain, as well as using good old fashioned HTML to embed content into your site. It includes:

- Social networking
- Using HTML code to include resources
- Using third-party extensions

Flickr, YouTube, MySpace, Twitter, Facebook, Google... the list goes on

Since its beginning, the Web has been used as a tool to meet people and share information. In recent years though, the interactions between web users have taken a rapid evolution.

Instead of using the Web as a tool to look up information, we are now inserting ourselves into it, and using it to connect ourselves to other people. The terminology "Web 2.0" was used to describe a more social, collaborative, and responsive web, and we see that these features are now well engrained into the modern "Web".

The phrase "What came first, the chicken or the egg?" springs to mind when trying to summarize recent evolutions of the Web and popular networking sites that are on it, for example, Facebook and Twitter. These two "social tools" required the Web to be where it was for their evolution, but yet they have dramatically helped to shape the way the "Web" now is, creating new paths into website development, third-party collaboration and interactions.

"Where is it going?" and "Where will it go to?" are questions often asked. When I was five years old, I watched a Star Trek episode with the actors using handheld flip-type devices, and using the term "Beam me up Scotty", communicating with their Starship. Now every day I carry a handheld computer / phone that is trackable by satellites, and with a few clicks I can post and receive information to a global notice board, the World Wide Web. It scares me in one respect how quickly we are socially evolving around this increasingly corporate driven entity named the Web, but I get excited with the technology and opportunities it brings:

So, it may be Google, Facebook, Twitter, MySpace, YouTube, and so on; Joomla! can collaborate with them all. At the end of the day, it is electronic information that is contained in one location, and then presented on another. Certain Joomla! Extensions have developed because there was a requirement to show this information and display it on the users' Joomla! based website. This chapter will highlight some of the most popular extensions and tools currently providing these solutions.

Using HTML code to include resources

When using Joomla! as a framework for your website, not only do you get a database driven Content Management System with bells and whistles, you get the ability to use custom HTML within your site by including it into articles and modules.

There are even specialized Joomla! Extensions that allow you to take this one step further and insert custom PHP, JavaScript, and HTML. For popular external resources, the code to share content usually comes in an accessible HTML format, which Joomla! can manage without the requirement of custom code plugins.

This key feature means that we can customize the content of our Joomla! pages and embed and share content from popular external resources with just a few clicks. Many popular multimedia web resources such as YouTube, Google Video, MySpace, and Flickr offer the ability to share content; in fact this feature is one of the main purposes behind each of these distribution services.

Using the content from these distribution services means that we can share it more easily with the world, but also save money on bandwidth costs. With data-intensive multimedia files having to be stored and then delivered to your site visitors, hosting your own multimedia content can quickly end up costing you a considerable sum in web hosting fees.

Inserting custom embedded code from an external resource such as MySpace, YouTube, Google Video, and Flickr is actually an easy process thanks to the distribution site packaging and delivering the content ready for us to use. The important point is that the code generated by your external resource needs to be valid and designed to work in an HTML environment. If this is the case, then the process to embed it into your Joomla! Article or Module should be very similar for most of them.

For this example, we will insert a *video clip sourced from Google Video*, and enter this into a Joomla! Module. As Google Video is delivering the content and is designed to offer us easy code to share this content, adding it into our Joomla! website is no more than a simple copy and paste exercise.

Here are the steps required:

 When starting to insert custom code into your Joomla! Articles, it is important to turn off WYSIWYG editors for your user account. This is because these editors cannot always process the custom HTML code. If the code is not recognized by the editor when loading in the content, it will remove the code altogether. The editor settings can be adjusted in the Global Configuration, or on a user basis via the User Manager.

- Select your resource, in this case we will use a windsurfing video sourced from Google Video. On the Video page, we see numerous options for sharing the content. We want the option to **Embed Video**:

- Copy the code to your clipboard:

- Log into your Joomla! Administration and navigate to the **Module Manager** area. Select the **New** button from the top-right menu icons to create a new module.

- On the **Add New Module** page, select the **Custom HTML** option, which allows you to create a new module with your own content in it:

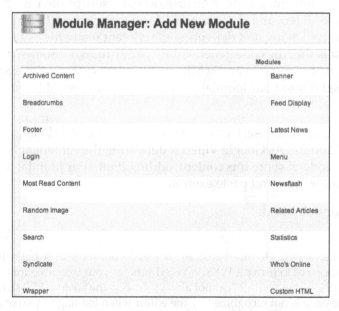

The Custom HTML option allows you to enter in custom text or code within a module position.

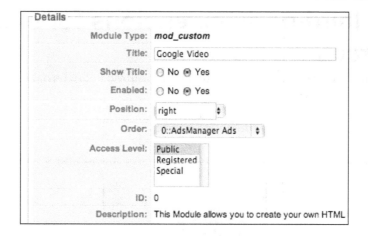

- You will need to give your new module a **Title**. Select its **Position** on your template and select the other options available for module publishing.

- In the **Custom Output** box, paste your "Google Video embed code":

Custom Output

```
<embed id=VideoPlayback src=http://video.google.co.uk/googleplayer.swf?docid=-16969836779916 78306&hl=en&fs=true
style=width:400px;height:326px allowFullScreen=true allowScriptAccess=always type=application/x-shockwave-flash> </embed>
```

- Navigate to the frontend of your Joomla! site to see the **Google Video** content now showing in your Joomla! website.

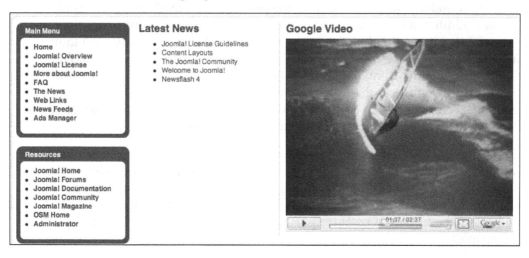

This method of embedding external content can be applied to Joomla! Articles also, and content can be utilized from almost all distribution sites, as long as their supplied HTML code is accepted by Joomla!.

Using third-party extensions for external resources

First of all, the opportunity for the inclusion of hundreds of external resources would be a possibility for this chapter.

Instead of this approach, listed are some of the more popular GPL-based extensions residing at Joomla.org, and those that are feature packed and have stood the test of time. Further information about GPL can be found at http://en.wikipedia.org/wiki/GNU_General_Public_License.

We have also taken the opportunity of trying to list only non-commercial extensions in this chapter. Professional commercial extensions may also be available for collaborating with external resources.

Without sounding like a stuck record, the purpose of Joomla! Extensions is to provide additional functionality to your Joomla! Framework. Some extensions are so useful that if you build more multiple Joomla! websites, you may even think of installing a particular extension always as a default. An example of this might be Community Builder from http://www.joomlapolis.com which, besides many other features, enhances the user registration and profile options. Different Joomla! users will collect or design their own tools which they are happy to utilize, and this is one of the reasons that Joomla! has such a thriving community.

Out-of-the-box Joomla! is a slick CMS that is lightweight, and the true power of Joomla! is in the application framework which has been developed to allow the extension of its core features. The majority of the multimedia features are added to our Joomla! sites via extensions, and with the popularity of social networking and external multimedia resource portals, the extensions around these sites have rapidly grown.

The extensions have been organized under popular titles such as Social Networking, Video, Audio, Weather, among others. There may be some extensions that fall under more than one of these categories, so they have been organized within the most applicable area. Each extension listing will contain a summary of its purpose and a feature list. The letters to the right of the following extension titles denote whether the extension is a component, module, plugin, language, or template.

> Due to lengthy URLs and the possibility that Joomla! Extension Directory (JED) listings could change at any time, search terms for the following extensions have been included, rather than direct links to the extensions. Performing a search on the JED for the related terms will help you find these extensions easily.
>
> The letters after the extension titles denote the following:
>
> M = Module
>
> C = Component
>
> P = Plugin
>
> L = Language
>
> T = Template

Joomla! and social networking integration

Social networking is the ability to define communities or groups of people that share interests and can interact. Traditionally, these would be small groups of people who were often located within a similar regional area, but with the growth of the Internet and social networking websites, these communities are now available to a global audience.

Twitter Follow Me (M)

The "Twitter Follow Me" module places a Twitter link image icon on your website pages, so visitors can click on this to go to your Twitter page. The Module positioning may be situated outside of your Joomla! Template so that the icon sits in relation to the users' browser window, rather than being contained within your site template.

It is a simple approach, but effective eye-catching icons, and this module's easy installation and configuration, make this a perfect professional-looking solution to add to your Joomla! site.

Configuration settings are all self contained within the module, so once installed visit the Module Manager area in order to configure.

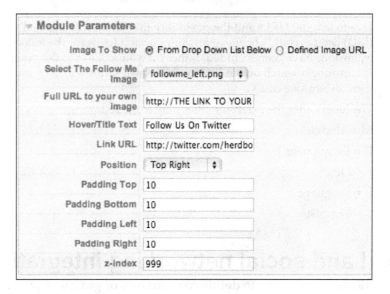

Module Parameters include:

- Select from one of the included PNG images or use your own custom image hosted on a web server
- Include custom text when the image is hovered over
- Adjust what position in the users' browser window you wish for the icon to be published

To download this extension, visit http://extensions.joomla.org/ and search for "Twitter Follow Me".

AutoTweet NG (C, P)

This plugin posts the title and URL for new Joomla! Articles automatically as Twitter messages (tweets) to a Twitter account. You can even limit the content posted to particular Joomla! Categories:

A nice feature of the AutoTweet extension is the additional plugins that are available, which post tweets from Joomla! related software and extensions. Examples of these are Kunena forum posts, K2 Article Manager, Phoca Download, EventList Event Management, and more.

Once installed, configurations are performed within the **Plugin Parameters**:

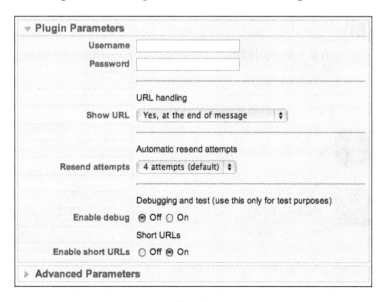

Some of the features in the new version include:

- Uses the Twitter REST API to post messages.

- All plugins are customizable: Account, category/section to post to, link position, show section/category, post private articles, post modified articles, exclude sections/categories, use a title or text for messages, additional static text (for example, for hashtags), short URL service provider (now bit.ly is also possible).

- Also works with sh404sef and JoomSEF and Joomla! native SEF support.

- Automatic support for short URLs.

- Automatic message resending: Sometimes you will get an error message when posting. This can happen from time to time when Twitter or Facebook is overloaded or the API is down. AutoTweet resends the status message automatically if there is an error on the API site.

- AutoTweet also posts later published or republished articles.

- AutoTweet NG comes with a backend component. The component logs all posted messages (including error and pending messages) and you can manage and resend these messages in the component's backend.

- AutoTweet NG supports articles with the current publish date. (These articles are posted automatically to Twitter when published by Joomla! or you can post them manually from the AutoTweet NG backend component.)

To download this extension, visit `http://extensions.joomla.org/` and search for "AutoTweet".

JTweet (M)

The JTweet extension is a module that publishes your Twitter tweets in your Joomla! site:

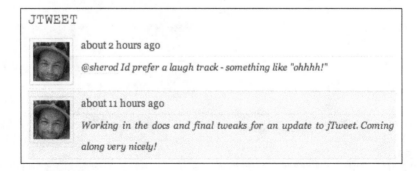

The module's features include:

- Set the number of tweets to display.
- Choose whether to display your avatar or not.
- Select whether to display just your tweets or all tweets related to a particular topic.
- Select auto join phrases according to the nature of your tweet. For example, specific intro text for replies, verbs, replying to tweets, and more.
- Set the text to appear while the tweets load.
- Filter your own tweets via keywords. For example, only display tweets that contain the word "Joomla!".

Once installed, all configurations are performed within the **Module Parameters**:

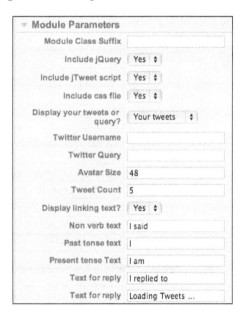

The latest version now loads the scripts on the fly, making the module XHTML compliant.

Please note that the module now requires the JB Library plugin in order to work. The JB Library plugin loads the jQuery library automatically into the head of your template. The jQuery library is required for the jTweet module.

To download this extension, visit http://extensions.joomla.org/ and search for "JTweet".

Tweetboard (P)

From the makers of the "Twitter Follow Me" module comes "Tweetboard". Utilizing the Tweetboard API plugin will allow you to display a Twitter Tweetboard on your Joomla! website:

Tweetboard is a fun and engaging micro-forum type application that pulls your Twitter feeds in and reformats them into threaded conversations. This is a great marketing technique in order to improve traffic flow to your website. Conversations that have spun off from the original are also captured, effectively providing a discussion layout to your site visitors.

The Tweetboard extension is a Joomla! Plugin. Once installed, the configuration settings are located in the plugin, under the Plugin Manager area:

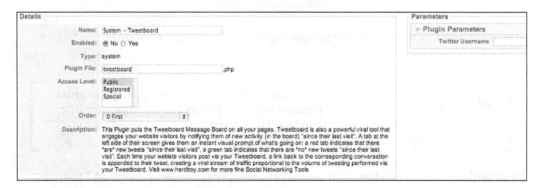

Before enabling the plugin, please visit the Joomla Exclusive Invite Portal (a link on the author's downloads page) and use the specially generated code: `joomlainvites01`. This will allow you to quickly use Tweetboard with your Twitter account.

To download this extension, visit `http://extensions.joomla.org/` and search for "Tweetboard".

WebScribble jConnector (C,M,P)

jConnector allows your Joomla! members to sign in using Facebook Connect, which is a powerful set of APIs that lets developers bring identities and connections into other applications:

If users are registered with Facebook, they can simply click on the **Facebook Connect** icon next time they visit your site, and they will be logged in automatically. This integration will add these users to your Joomla! database, so you can administer their accounts through Joomla!.

Installation is easy with one `jConnector.zip` package file to be uploaded via the Extension Manager. Following a successful installation, you will need to go to the Module Manager in order to configure the **Module Parameters**:

To begin using Facebook Connect, you must obtain **API key** and **Application Secret** from Facebook. To do so, you should first sign into Facebook at `http://facebook.com`.

After signing in, you need to go to `http://facebook.com/developers/` and follow the process for creating a new application. Once you have the Facebook API key, you will need to populate this parameter within the plugin management screen.

To download this extension, visit `http://extensions.joomla.org/` and search for "jConnector".

Facebook Fanbox Free (M)

Facebook Fanbox is a Joomla! Module that displays Facebook FanBox in your Joomla! website:

The Fanbox lets users:

- See how many users are already fans, and see some of their friends
- Read recent posts from the page
- Become a fan with one click, without needing to visit the page

Before you add a Fanbox to your website, you need the following:

- A Joomla! 1.5 website, and the ability to install modules
- A Facebook page that promotes your website (you must be the administrator of the page)
- Your Facebook page ID and profile ID to enter into the **Module Parameters**

There are a number of parameter options for control over this extension, and it has received good feedback from users requiring this type of feature in their Joomla! site:

To download this extension, visit http://extensions.joomla.org/ and search for "Facebook Fanbox".

jwFacebook Comments (P)

The jwFacebook Comments plugin utilizes Facebook's comments feature and allows you to place these at the end of your Joomla! Articles:

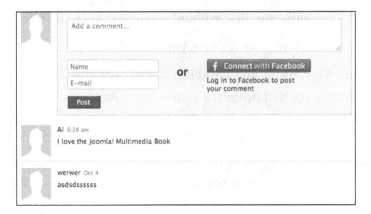

If your site visitors have a Facebook account, they can easily place comments on your Joomla! Articles, but one nice feature of this system is that anyone can place comments (you don't need a Facebook account). It utilizes Facebook's comments feature instead of using your own, possibly saving you hosting bandwidth costs.

Installation is easy, but there are few additional steps to perform in order to get this feature working. These are clearly listed on the developer's website, but in short are:

- Install the plugin using the Joomla! Extension Manager
- Upload an included .htm file to your web server and then navigate to the Plugin Manager to configure the **Plugin Parameters**
- Configure your Facebook API, the path to the uploaded .htm file
- You will then need to log into Facebook to enter the domain of the site you are installing the comments on

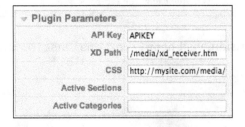

To download this extension, visit http://extensions.joomla.org/ and search for "jwFacebook Comments".

Joomla! and video channel integration

Video is the coolest thing on the Web at the moment, and there are some great Joomla! Video Extensions available to display content from external video distribution sites.

 It is important to mention that there are a number of specific video solutions for Joomla! that also provide support for streaming external video content. Please see the extensions listed in Chapter 6, *Using Video in Your Joomla! Website* for further video solutions.

easiertube (P)

easiertube is a Joomla! Plugin that couldn't get any easier to manage and use. It is designed to display videos in your articles from the following sources: YouTube, Google, UStream, Revver, and MySpace.

To use it, simply install this plugin and configure its settings in the Plugin Parameters area. Enter the remote video link within your content articles and the plugin will automatically convert the URL and embed the player in your page.

Parameters can be set for:

- Front page display width and height
- Main content display width and height
- Fullscreen
- Autoplay

The latest version (5.5) now includes:

- YouTube support
- Related videos (YouTube), also can disable search
- Disable show info
- Disable annotations
- Show border (with color option)
- Metacafe videos
- Show statistics
- Show video title

Install the plugin using the Extension Manager and configure its parameters in the Plugins Manager area:

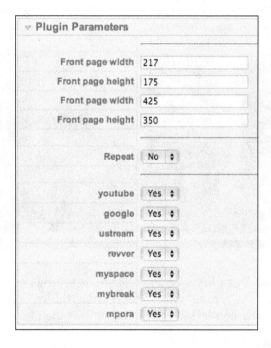

To download this extension, visit `http://extensions.joomla.org/` and search for "easiertube".

QTube (M, P)

QTube is a module and plugin designed to embed YouTube videos into a Joomla!
Content Article:

The plugin allows you to play videos within your Joomla! Articles and contains
parameters which allow you to adjust the look and feel of the video container object.

The developer of QTube has also developed a QTube module, allowing the ability to
include videos into modules.

The module and plugin are installed via the Extension Manager and its default
parameters can be set in the Plugin and Module Manager areas:

To download this extension, visit http://extensions.joomla.org/ and search
for "QTube".

JMultimedia Suite (C, M, P)

The JMultimedia Suite is a kit of multimedia extensions. It can automatically detect and display videos from many streaming sites and in many media formats. It offers the administrator numerous video options:

	#Title	Added	From	Views
	test tet	Qua, 22 de Abril de 2009 12:21	Gavin King	12110
	U - Judain	Qui, 04 de Junho de 2009 16:00	kimbrasil	4445
	U - Judain	Qui, 04 de Junho de 2009 15:55	kimbrasil	2536

Key features are:

- Create/edit video categories
- Create/edit media items
- Customizable CSS
- Multi-media formats are supported
- Integration with commenter comments system

A requirement of the JMultimedia Suite is for the extension "denVideo" to be installed. It will then automatically recognize video links within your articles, and support all video formats that denVideo does, including:

- SWF (Flash applications)
- FLV and H264 (Flash videos)
- CLASS (Java applet)
- MOV and MP4 (QuickTime)
- RM and RAM (RealMedia)
- MP3 (audio)

- DIVX and AVI (HD videos)
- WMV and WMA (Windows Media)
- PNG, JPG, GIF (images)
- Metacafe.com
- Brightcove.com
- YouTube.com
- video.Google.com
- video.Yahoo

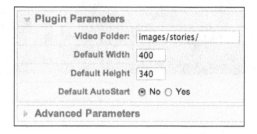

To download this extension, visit http://extensions.joomla.org/ and search for "JMultimedia Suite".

Joomla! and audio and radio channel integration

Presenting audio and radio from external sites is an ever increasing request, and extensions have been springing up regularly that provide solutions.

As with video, a number of audio solutions are available for Joomla! that also collaborate with external resources. See the extension listings in Chapter 5 for some Joomla! audio solutions.

LCPlayer - Radio / TV (M)

The LCPlayer allows you to enter in any URL of a radio feed, or television feed, and have this played in your Joomla! site via the LCPlayer module:

The module works by an administrator adding in the URL of a radio or TV feed. These stations will be available to the user from a drop-down menu. The administrator can set permission for this user menu as well as adjust the player width and logo image.

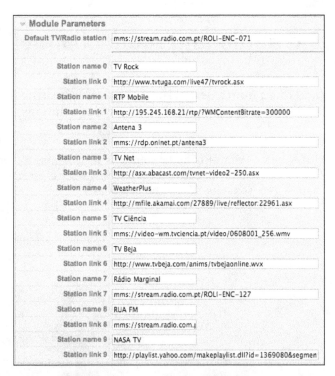

To download this extension, visit `http://extensions.joomla.org/` and search for "LCPlayer".

Joomla! and photo integration

Joomla! works well with images and the opportunities for displaying photos and galleries from external resources is vast. Here are some of the more popular extensions used for this purpose.

> A number of image extensions for Joomla! also offer the ability to display content from external resources.

UniversalPlayground - Flickr slideshow plug-in (P)

The UniversalPlayground - Flickr slideshow plug-in displays slideshows from your Flickr account with a simple lightbox effect:

This extension uses the phpFlickr library, Slimbox (a lightweight visual lightbox clone), and the TripTracker slideshow scripts.

A single photo, or complete gallery sets, can be displayed by entering a simple expression into your articles, for example: `[flickr photo=xxx]` (where *xxx* is replaced by the photo ID number).

The plugin contains numerous parameters for customization:

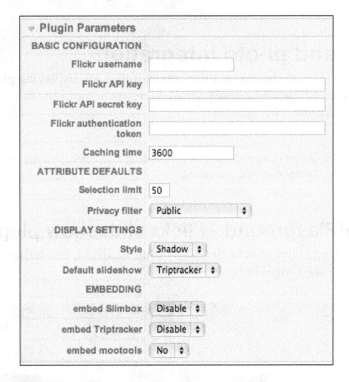

 A Flickr API key is required to enter into your plugin, and a link to this is available from the module and developer's website.

To download this extension, visit http://extensions.joomla.org/ and search for "UniversalPlayground - Flickr slideshow".

Flickr + Highslide (M)

The Flickr + Highslide module extension displays photos from Flickr within your Joomla! site using the Highslide JavaScript effect:

Highslide is an open source media and gallery viewer written in JavaScript. The module displays an elegant looking display of Flickr content and contains the following features:

- 13 unique ways of displaying your photos
- Eight different gallery styles
- Displays photos from a photoset
- Displays all photos of a user
- Displays photos in latest or random order
- Ability to change the size of images and thumbnails
- Ability to separate photos into pages
- Displays the titles of photos

The module will require your Flickr account ID. It also offers numerous styling parameters:

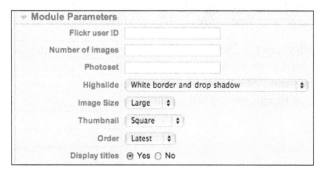

To download this extension, visit `http://extensions.joomla.org/` and search for "Flickr Highslide".

Joomla! and weather integration

For busy news and community portals, offering a weather forecast is a popular requirement. Google Weather is a popular resource for the source of weather information for these extensions, and this is due to the global solution it provides. There are numerous other weather extensions also; here are some popular ones.

Google Weather - Plugin (P, M)

The Google Weather - Plugin is a lightweight plugin that uses the Google Weather Forecast API to display the current weather in your Joomla! Articles:

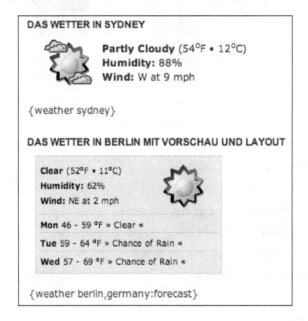

By using simple plugin tags to trigger the plugin, it is possible to include {WEATHER CITY, COUNTRY} into your content and the plugin will do the rest!

The plugin is installed via the Extension Manager and then configured using the Plugin Manager. Numerous styling options are available and the plugin can be configured using custom CSS. You can display the weather as often as you like using the plugin tags throughout your articles.

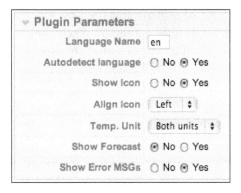

A Google Weather plugin is also now available, to easily display weather in a module position.

To download this extension, visit `http://extensions.joomla.org/` and search for "Google Weather".

Z Weather (C,M,P)

Z Weather is a component, module, and plugin that displays weather for U.S. cities using data provided by the National Weather Service. Forecasts, current conditions, and weather alerts are supported. Weather for either a single city or multiple cities can be displayed:

Numerous display options are available, including single-day and multiple-day forecasts, 3-hour (new!), 12-hour, or 24-hour forecast display, pop up weather window (overlib), and vertical and horizontal layout options.

The component, module, and plugin are installed via the Extension Manager and then configured using the applicable managers. Each element provides its own set of parameters and configuration options in order to display the weather as you would like:

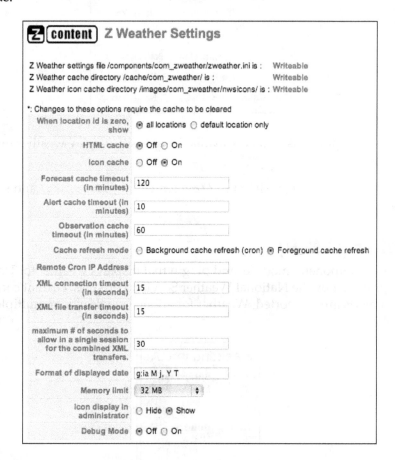

To download this extension, visit http://extensions.joomla.org/ and search for "Z Weather".

eWeather (C,M)

eWeather is a component (with an additional module) which will show a visually appealing display of current conditions and weather forecast in your Joomla! pages. The weather data is supplied by The Weather Channel via an XML feed:

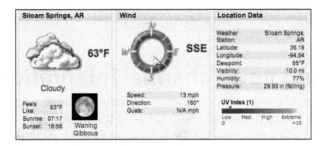

One nice feature of the component is to allow your site visitors to select their own city and the ability to see a five-day forecast. There is, however, some "Weather Channel" advertising throughout the display of information.

eWeather is a powerful component allowing configurations within the component configuration settings. These include:

- New overview and management of installed regions/countries
- Default configuration of a city
- Weather forecast for up to five days
- Date/time format freely definable
- Proxy definable

New icon styling packs are now available to customize the look of your site. An accompanying module is also available to display the weather in any module position:

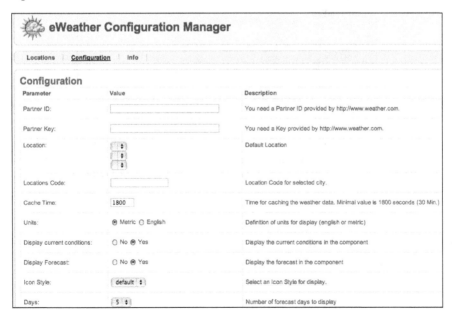

To download this extension, visit `http://extensions.joomla.org/` and search for "eWeather".

Joomla! and news channel integration

There are a number of good news channel extensions available to pull external news in and display this on your site pages. Using RSS techniques, it is possible to manually perform this process, but the following extensions make things nice and easy.

Google News (M)

The Google News Module embeds Google News stories into any module position on your site. It allows your site visitors to see the headlines and previews of **Google News**, which you have selected to show:

This module contains numerous parameters, including the ability to filter topics, adjust the size, country, and language that gets displayed. It is a simple module, but perfect for those wanting to easily display Google News in their Joomla! website.

The Google News Module is installed via the Extension Manager with configurations being set in the module.

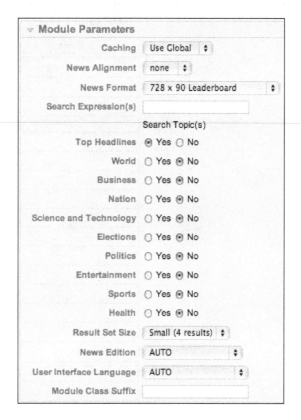

To download this extension, visit `http://extensions.joomla.org/` and search for "Google News".

Other resources and how to integrate them with Joomla!

There are hundreds of extensions that allow Joomla! to interact with external resources, here are examples of some of these.

Plugin GoogleMaps (P)

This extension is a plugin for displaying one or more Google Maps within articles, modules, or components for Joomla!.

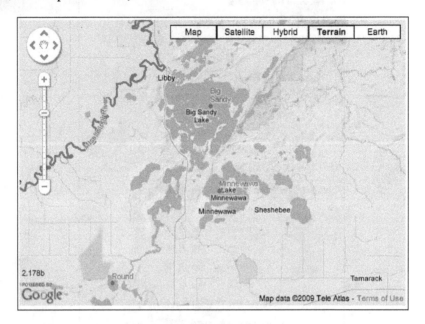

As with a lot of plugins, the map is displayed by using a special tag containing numerous parameters. These offer the ability to really customize your map contents and the following is a small selection of this plugin's features:

- Adjustable width and height
- Adjustable latitude and longitude
- Zoom controls
- Map markers
- Add selections and tooltips to your map

The GoogleMaps Plugin is installed via the Extension Manager with default configurations set in the plugin, with the ability to override with each instance of using the plugin trigger tag.

A GoogleMaps reference key is required to use most Google Map services and is a requirement for this plugin to work.

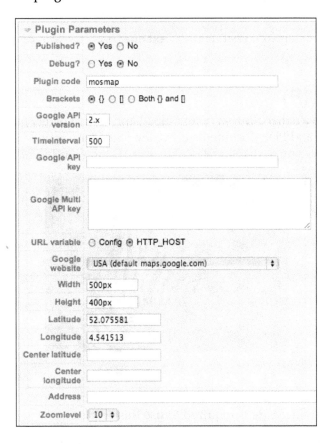

To download this extension, visit http://extensions.joomla.org/ and search for "Daylife News".

Ajax Whois (C,M)

The Ajax Whois extension is an international domain search and "whois" extension for Joomla! that utilizes the power of Ajax technology in order to allow your Joomla! website visitors to check for availability of domain name(s). The results of these searches are displayed instantly on the site:

The Ajax Whois component and module are installed via the Extension Manager with default configurations being set in the component. There are numerous display options available.

To download this extension, visit `http://extensions.joomla.org/` and search for "Ajax Whois".

SlideShare (P)

SlideShare is a service that allows you to upload and share PowerPoint presentations, Word documents, and PDF documents using the SlideShare service. This simple module then allows you to display SlideShare content in your Joomla! website:

A user account at SlideShare is required to use this service.

The SlideShare Plugin is installed via the Extension Manager with default configurations being set using the Plugin Manager:

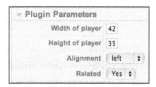

To download this extension, visit `http://extensions.joomla.org/` and search for "SlideShare Plugin".

Slick RSS (M)

Slick RSS allows you to parse and display external RSS feeds on your Joomla! website with a nice tooltip teaser feature:

Some features include:

- Configure number of items
- Display title and description
- Enable/disable images
- Limit word counts for title and descriptions

The Slick RSS module is installed via the Extension Manager with configurations being set in the Module Manager:

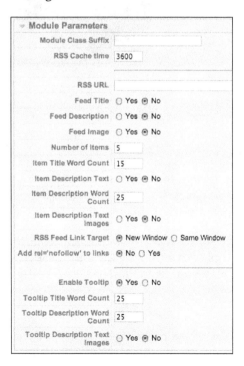

To download this extension, visit `http://extensions.joomla.org/` and search for "Slick RSS".

RokBox Plugin (P)

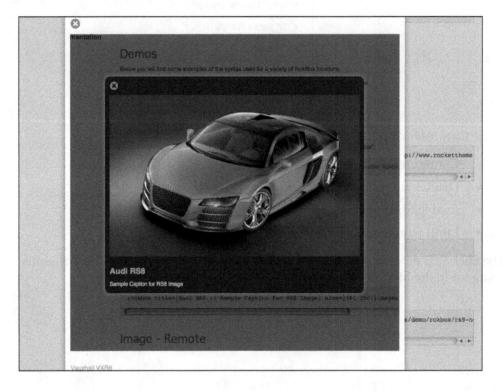

RokBox is a MooTools powered JavaScript slideshow that allows you to quickly and easily display multiple media formats including images, videos (video sharing services also), and music.

RokBox provides a theme system that allows you to create your own custom ones to fit your websites design. It includes two predefined themes, a light theme and a dark theme that will fit seamlessly into your site design.

RokBox is a nice all-in-one solution to present multimedia content off with professional effects. It can play external media sources such as YouTube videos as easily as it can play your own files.

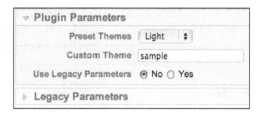

To download this extension, visit http://extensions.joomla.org/ and search for "RokBox".

Simple RSS Feed Reader (M)

Adding RSS syndicated content inside your Joomla! website is now super-easy and simple with the "Simple RSS Feed Reader" module:

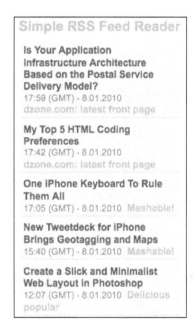

To use, insert the feed (RSS) URLs of the websites you want to syndicate in the module's settings, edit your module options, and then publish the module in your desired position. The module will display the latest feed contents in your module.

Simple RSS Feed Reader is based on the very popular SimplePie PHP class, which makes it easy to integrate syndicated content into your Joomla! website. The module supports everything from RSS 0.91 and RSS 1.0 formats, to the ever-popular RSS 2.0 format. It also supports the emerging Atom format, in both 0.3 and 1.0 flavors.

The module has a very fast, very efficient caching system. By caching the processed data rather than just the raw XML, the module is able to create a feed parser that's quick and should not cause excessive overhead on page loading.

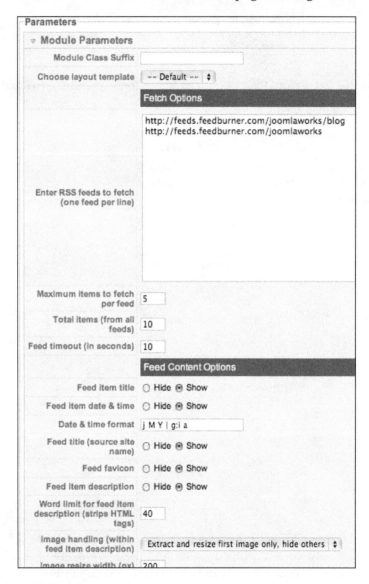

To download this extension, visit `http://extensions.joomla.org/` and search for "Simple RSS Feed Reader".

Summary

For regular users of the Web, there are a few key tools and social networking sites that may contain your profile and data. Every month there are improved integrations between these sites and other online resources, including Joomla!. All this helps to minimize account logins and the repetition of data in different places.

Web 2.0 is all about integrating yourself into the Web experience and sharing your information; being a part of the Web instead of just searching for material. Content from external resources can easily be embedded into Joomla! via the use of HTML code or custom extensions designed to collaborate with popular resources.

Joomla! lends itself well to displaying external data into its framework, as it does to broadcast some of its own content to other sources. New extensions are being developed at an astounding rate that provide solutions for collaborating with popular external web resources. This will only increase with time, as the Joomla! developer community helps to define integrations for the "next big thing" on the Web... whatever it may be.

8
Joomla! Templates and Multimedia

Joomla! Templates are the distinguishing factor between one Joomla! website looking just like the next. They contain the structural elements to display your Joomla! content, and deliver style and scripting information to the user's web browser.

As Joomla! Templates provide style information for your website, they naturally have an impact on the multimedia elements within your Joomla! site. Besides your site design and module formatting (often using images), templates may contain advanced JavaScript features that can enhance your site's multimedia capabilities.

This chapter is an overview of Joomla! Templates, how they work and how they can affect the display of multimedia content in your Joomla! site. Learn how templates can enhance multimedia capabilities as well as how they affect the way in which your Joomla! site is displayed on mobile web devices. It contains:

- What is a Joomla! Template?
- Template components
- Scripting and multimedia
- The mobile web
- Making your site mobile friendly
- Accessibility

What is a Joomla! Template?

Joomla! uses a template system to control the look, feel, and layout of your web content.

Joomla! has been designed so that the key processes for delivering your website have been separated out within its design, making Joomla! as efficient as possible and easily maintained as a piece of software:

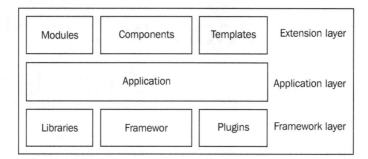

One of these elements is the Joomla! Template, which controls the overall layout, and distinguishes one Joomla! install from the next. Templates provide the structure to place various content elements (including components, plugins, and modules) on any given page in almost any part of the web page you choose. One of the most important factors for the success of your Joomla! website will be the information that you want to deliver to your audience, and how the template has been designed to achieve this. This is where a template design can make or break your Joomla! website:

When producing a website, the location of a number of elements will often remain constant. For example, menus, search boxes, banners, copyright, sidebars all typically stay in fixed positions on the page. Important styling information will be contained within your stylesheets (which control the fonts, colors, and placement of information) and this needs to be included, so it is also presented on every page.

This is why templates have been developed, and Joomla! is a perfect example of how they can be utilized effectively. You can either re-create all of the mentioned features on every web page you build for your site, or use a template structure to contain and deliver this information to every page. We as administrators simply "fill in the blanks" with our site content.

Template components

Joomla! utilizes templates for both the frontend views, and administration sections of the site.

The administration has one template (named **Khepri**) that comes installed as default and creates the style for your administration:

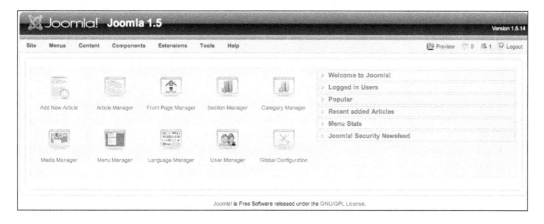

Joomla! Administration Templates are located within the `/administrator/ templates` directory. If you are looking to adjust your site administration template, take a copy of the default Khepri template and re-name the template folder with your new name. Make sure you re-name the XML references and then you can begin to customize your administration theme. There are third-party administrator templates also available, which can provide a completely new look for your Joomla! administration.

Templates for the frontend are contained within the /templates directory of Joomla!:

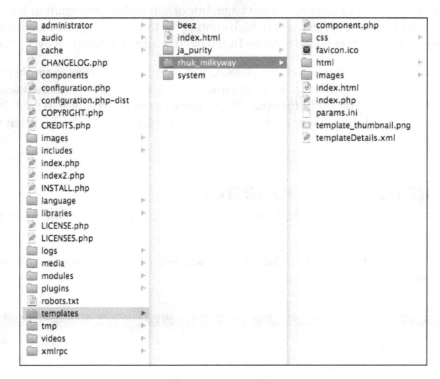

Your Joomla! Template contains a set of files and directories to sub categorize the contents. A typical Joomla! 1.5 Template structure will usually contain the following:

- index.php: This is a key file usually containing HTML and PHP logic for the display and positioning of modules and components.

- component.php: Provides the logic for the display of additional pages such as "E-mail this link to a friend", and the Printer Friendly page.

- css/template.css: The template CSS file is usually located within a CSS folder and handles the presentational aspects of the template, including specifications for fonts, headings, margins, image borders, list formatting, among others.

- templateDetails.xml: The templateDetails.xml is another key file which holds meta-information related to the template, and is used by the Joomla! Installer and the Template Manager. This file also contains a reference of module positions that the template utilizes.

- `template_thumbnail.png`: This image file could be a JPG, GIF, or PNG file. Generally, it's a 200 x 150 pixel image that is shown when the cursor is hovered over the template name in the Template Manager. This gives the administrator a snapshot view of the template before applying it to the site.

A typical Joomla! 1.5 Template will also contain the following directories:

- `css`: The `css` folder contains all the CSS files for the template.
- `html`: This folder usually contains the template override files for core output.
- `images`: The `images` folder contains all images that are used by the template. In popular commercial templates, it is not uncommon to have multiple subdirectories within the `images` folder, each containing their own color variations of the images.

Template folders for Joomla! usually contain all relevant files which relate directly to the template in use on the website. Therefore, images and other multimedia content that you use within your Joomla! Articles should reside within their own folders, and not be placed within the template folder.

Scripting and multimedia

When the majority of users hear the term "Multimedia", it may conjure initial thoughts of "Images" and "Video" content. The term is used to describe these prominent media elements; however, in this quickly evolving world of the Web, new features and interactive elements are presenting themselves regularly.

A number of commercial template providers are now creating feature packed template systems for Joomla! that not only contain the basic template elements, but also include numerous scripts, making the package more feature packed and versatile for users.

These features include sophisticated JavaScript drop-down menu systems, user-defined module ordering, mobile web themes, extensive typography options, and many more. While some of these features may not be considered as traditional forms of "Multimedia", they usually contain text, images, fonts, colors, and provide an interactive experience to the site user.

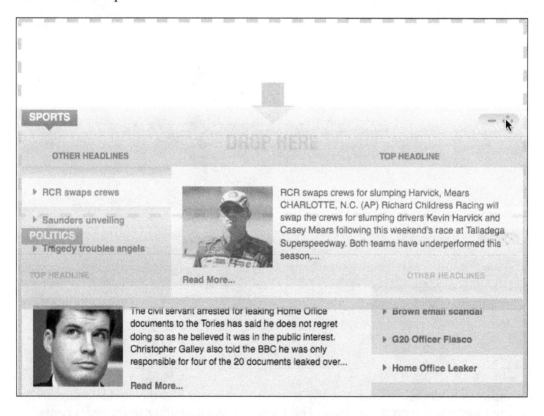

The previous screenshot shows the Solar Sentinel template from RocketTheme at `http://www.rockettheme.com`.

Mellow template—Yootheme

Mellow is a feature packed but simple and well organized template from YooTheme:

www.yootheme.com contains an abundance of scripting features, including the following:

- A powerful, flexible menu system: This includes numerous submenu options with icons, among others:

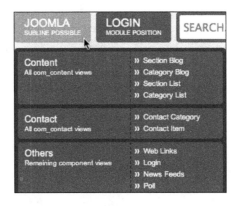

- Auto day/date adjustment: It uses a PHP script to adjust the day accordingly:

- Ten color options: Something for everyone in this line up:

- MooTools cooler fade-on menu item: Main menu and side menu items not only have a rollover, but a subtle fade in and out using JavaScript action to perform this.

- Detailed typography: Mellow contains an abundance of text formatting and headings style information, allowing your site text to easily contain numerous style elements:

- Back to top: Includes an icon at the bottom of the page, with JavaScript smooth scrolling back to the top feature:

Infuse—RocketTheme

Infuse by RocketTheme is a colorful and professional template which may suit a variety of purposes:

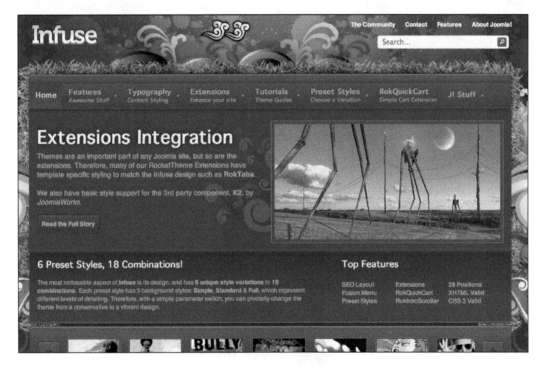

The Infuse template is an infusion of artistic flair and functionality. The theme boasts six individual and unique style variations:

1. Fusion: A powerful JavaScript-based drop-down menu system (including menu icons, submenu support):

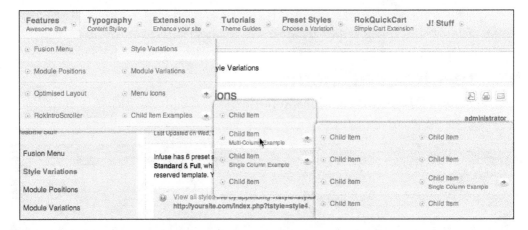

2. Style variations: With 18 options to choose from, the same template can take on a whole new look and feel with various theme options:

3. Optimized layout: Your centralized content will load into the page first, ahead of your side columns, making this an added enhancement for search engine optimization:

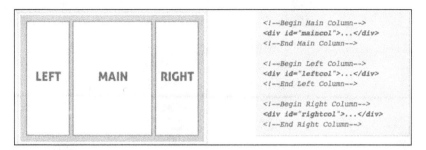

4. Typography options: Characterize your content and bring it to life with a range of fancy styling options:

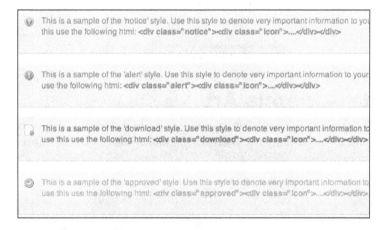

5. Back to top: Rather than your users having to scroll to the top of the page again, they can utilize the easy **Back to Top** hyperlink, which uses JavaScript to smoothly scroll to the top of the page:

6. Multi-module positions and variations: With 28 module positions and a range of styling options for each one, there is always a place to put something:

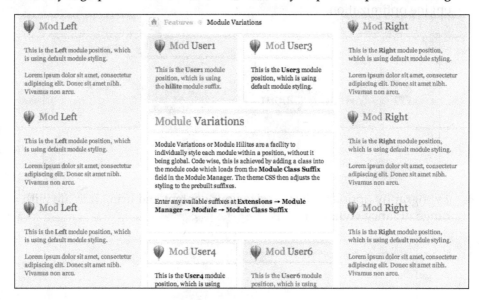

JA Halite—Joomla Art

JA Halite is a simple but striking template by Joomla Art, www.joomlaart.com. This template is packed full of features, including mobile support, color and style options, and menu options:

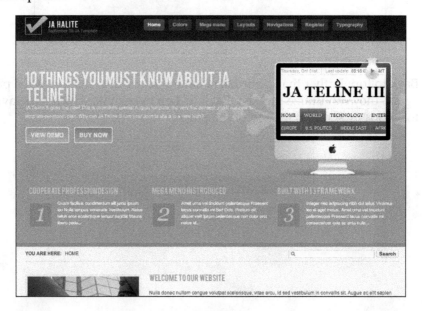

The features are:

- Handheld and iPhone support: This template will automatically simplify site content and styling when a mobile device is recognized:

- Multi-theme: Ten theme options with module variations within each theme:

- Numerous menu options: Four different menu options, including split menu, CSS menu, MooTools menu, and mega menu.

- Typography: This template contains some sophisticated pre-designed styling and formatting, making it easy for you to style your web text with numerous colors, styles, and icons:

Motion—Yootheme

Whether it is your cup of tea or not, the Motion theme from Yootheme is a feature-rich Joomla! Template, including a wide screen layout with powerful scripting to create numerous animations effects:

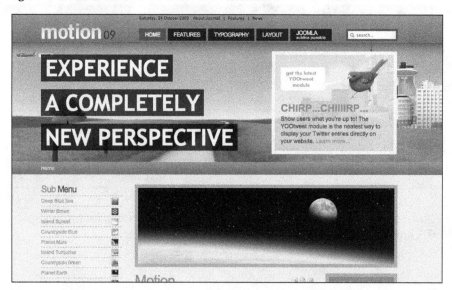

Each theme within this template carries its own animation which is achieved through a combination of graphics, CSS, and JavaScript. In the theme shown in the next screenshot, two boats scroll across the screen, as well as the background clouds subtly drift across the page:

The Motion template is really ten templates within one, due to its versatility of themes:

- Ten built-in themes: Including an abundance of graphics and animations within each theme:

- Auto day/date function: The date changes as the server day changes.

- MooTools menu: Menus with fancy effects such as sliding boxes and fading colors. Menu items can have explanatory subtitles and other powerful menu effects.

- PNG fix for IE: As only IE7 onwards supports transparent PNG image files, the Yootheme PNG fix enables PNG alpha transparency for inline and background images in the entire template.

- Tableless template overrides: Not only is the template's design tableless, but this template will make the whole content area tableless, which Joomla! usually renders as tables:

The list of templates could go on and on. As you can see, a template can completely change the look, feel, and complexity of your Joomla! web pages. Even the same template can be configured in a completely different manner than someone else may choose to. Picking the right template for your project can dramatically cut down on project time and expense, as well as offer you these additional multimedia features out-of-the-box.

The majority of new professional Joomla! Templates contain menu options, colored themes, and complex CSS. This means that the majority of well-built extensions that you add to your site will integrate into your template easily, and pick up appropriate template styling.

The mobile web

The term "mobile web" refers to web browser based services that are viewed using a mobile device such as a mobile phone, PDA, iPhone, and so on.

The number of mobile web users is increasing each year, and an entry on the popular Wikipedia page `http://en.wikipedia.org/wiki/Mobile_Web`, mentions: "In 2008, the total number of mobile web users grew past the total number of PC-based Internet users for the first time". This may come as a shock to some who have not utilized the mobile web service before, and to us as developers / administrators, it is important to note.

In the early days of mobile web devices, the only way to surf the mobile web was to browse using WAP sites. **Wireless Application Protocol (WAP)** is a secure specification that allows users to access information instantly via handheld wireless devices. WAP uses **Wireless Markup Language (WML)** as its primary markup language.

As the mobile web has evolved, WML has been superseded by a number of other technologies. The new technology standard is now **Extensible Hypertext Markup Language (XHTML)**.

XHTML is an extensible markup language that was designed as a subset of XML. This was to promote greater interoperability and the possibility of using standard XML tools to parse XHTML. Most mobile devices now recognize two flavors of XHTML:

- XHTML: The same markup language as is used by desktop web browsers
- XHTML – MP: The MP stands for mobile phone

One of the medium's greatest restrictions is that the mobile web still suffers from accessibility and usability issues. For example, mobile devices tend to have small screens making it hard to fit content into. Some devices try to mimic web browsers but still have the need to zoom in and out of web pages. Others face restrictions to run certain software, such as the Adobe Flash Player. And then there is the abundance of formats and connection issues.

Web developers are only now starting to consider taking the time to look into this subject and what can be done to make their websites usable to mobile web viewers. As Joomla! users, we have a number of testing procedures and options available.

 When developing for PC-based World Wide Web viewing, as developers, we need to take into consideration different web browsers and screen resolutions. When developing for the mobile web, there are even more considerations to take into account. This is mainly due to the large number of operating systems and screen sizes available on mobile devices.

Making your site mobile friendly

The main purpose of your website is to deliver your content to your audience as easily as possible, while allowing them to (hopefully) enjoy the experience. With most Joomla! Templates having been designed for desktop viewing, little consideration is often paid to the growing audience of mobile web users.

A number of methods can be implemented to adjust your site, making it more suitable for the mobile web medium:

Mobile users tend to be online to get information quickly and it is important to make this process as easy as possible for them. While your Joomla! Template might contain hundreds of graphics when viewed in a desktop-browser, and look very smart and stylish, mobile web users may be "out and about" and may simply want links to take them to the information they require. This generally means that a simplification of the content is required and often preferred for mobile web users.

Consider these adjustments

One of your best opportunities to developing a mobile-friendly Joomla! website is to begin with a well-formatted HTML valid codebase for your template, built with logical semantic markup. A well-structured code document will display cleanly, load in elements in an organized order, and should be usable on many devices due to the valid and well-organized code.

Areas of importance

One of the most important visual hotspots in your Joomla! Template will be the top-left zone. This is quite often where logos reside. Take note that you want mobile web users to be able to navigate easily and not zoom in and out or scroll all over your site page just to find a menu link. So if you are creating a custom mobile version of your website content, look for that top-left area to place a main navigation or a search function:

The previous image displays a web template for a PC based web browser, and a separate site template available for handheld devices.

Disabling images, CSS, and JavaScript

For older mobile devices, one of the best development methods available is to disable image CSS and JavaScript on your site pages, and see how it looks. Your site will take on a completely different look and feel with the main styling of the template removed, and you will see the natural layout of elements as they load on your page.

Take an on-demand approach with your multimedia

If you utilize multimedia in your website, think about offering these to the user when they request it, rather than bombarding the user with this information as they land on your website page.

Videos, images, audio, or other multimedia in your website can be presented to the user via hyperlinks to the intended content. This approach offers choice, and means that the user can choose to visit that content if they wish to, and not have it force-fed to them. If you are displaying the episodes of a podcast using Flash players, consider using a player that loads the media when someone chooses to play. This approach usually leads to well-structured sites that are quick to load and have a healthy "large content" feel to them.

Load in custom stylesheets or templates for mobile devices

With a combination of PHP, HTML, and CSS, it is possible for your Joomla! site to recognize particular mobile web devices and deliver specific stylesheets for these. By using this method, you can provide a simplified layout for your content, which makes page loading faster and easier for users to navigate your site pages.

There are a number of websites and tools that can help generate PHP code for recognizing particular devices viewing your website. Some PHP and CSS skills are required in order to achieve these results, but with efforts in this area, you can specifically target the mobile market with your Joomla! content. One such useful tool can be found at `http://detectmobilebrowsers.mobi/`.

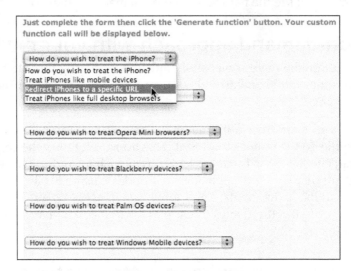

The site generator will allow you to tailor the code for your environment, and then download the applicable code for you to use. It is free for non-profit websites and donations are accepted for commercial use. For those with limited PHP knowledge, but like to get your hands mucky with some code play, this tool will be helpful.

For those with limited development skills, a number of Joomla! Extensions are also available.

Available extensions

There are a number of mobile web extensions now available for Joomla! that can help to make your site accessible for mobile devices, and decrease the technical knowledge required to make this happen.

PDA-plugin for Joomla! 1.5 (P,T)

The essence of the PDA-plugin for Joomla! 1.5 is that it activates a PDA template, or a mobile web-friendly template, for your Joomla! site instead of using the default site template:

▽ Plugin Parameters		
	Postprocessing (not recommended)	
PDA for PDA-user-agents	○ No ⊙ Yes	
PDA for subdomain	○ No ⊙ Yes	
Subdomain name	pda	
PDA template	pda	
Gzip compress	⊙ No ○ Yes	
PDA Homepage		
	Postprocessing (not recommended)	
Remove IMG	⊙ No ○ Yes	
Remove IFRAME	⊙ No ○ Yes	
Remove OBJECT	⊙ No ○ Yes	
Remove APPLET	⊙ No ○ Yes	
Remove EMBED	⊙ No ○ Yes	
Remove SCRIPT	⊙ No ○ Yes	

This plugin will determine if it is appropriate to activate itself, based on it recognizing the user agent of a mobile device. There are two ways to use this plugin:

1. Display the mobile version of a site for the mobile browser that is on the same link, http://yoursite.com/. It is possible to see both the full and mobile versions of a site depending on the device used for viewing. This is referred to as the multi-client approach.

2. Display the mobile version of a site for a subdomain. For example, for http://pda.yoursite.com/. This is referred to as the multi-site approach.

With this plugin, it is possible to use either of these approaches, or both.

Installation

There are two elements for the PDA-plugin for Joomla! 1.5. Firstly, you install the template, and secondly the plugin using the Joomla! Extension Manager.

The plugin will require publishing and contains a number of configuration options. The way the PDA-plugin works is to activate the PDA Template (or another template if set in the Plugin Parameters) so that your site will be simplified to work on mobile web devices.

This plugin takes the hard work out of placing code in to recognize different devices visiting your website, but you may still need to get your hands dirty by adjusting the included PDA Template to your liking.

To download this extension, visit `http://extensions.joomla.org/` and search for "PDA-plugin".

WAFL: Mobile Content Adaption (P,C,T,M)

Website Adaption and Formatting Layer (WAFL) was built to achieve device-specific content adaptation for your Joomla! website. It is still in alpha mode so has not reached the maturity of other Joomla! Extensions yet.

This plugin supports three modes of operation. The selected mode will be activated when the plugin detects that a request is coming from a mobile device:

1. Template switching: You will be able to select a template that will be used for mobile requests. The plugin contains a mobile template, which can be used.

2. Mobile redirect: The visitor will be redirected to a URL that you can specify.

3. Siruna: It is a fully managed solution for creating mobile web applications. When this mode is activated, the plugin will redirect any mobile requests to an instance of the Siruna platform. It will also deliver a mobile template (enriched with information for Siruna) to requests coming from the Siruna platform.

Installation

There is one extension to install that contains four different files:

1. **Plugin**: It intercepts Joomla! events so that mobile users get delivered mobile-enhanced content.

2. **Administrator component**: In the WAFL administration-side section, the web administrator will be able to change preferences to suit their site.

3. **WAFL template**: It delivers our basic version of a mobile template without taking screen widths and heights into account.

4. **WAFL module**: It is in fact a component wrapper to enable module ordering in the WAFL template.

The extension is installed via the Extension Manager.

The administration side of our extension can be found by clicking on **WAFL** in the **Components** menu. Here, you can change the look-and-feel of the mobile website version, or how you would like to have your mobile site configured and displayed.

You will need to check your mobile settings by surfing your website using a mobile device, or even better to look at a number of devices (just as you would when testing with Safari, IE6, IE7, and so on) to make sure all is as you require.

To download this extension, visit http://extensions.joomla.org/ and search for "WAFL Mobile Content".

Mobilebot for Joomla 1.5 (P)

Mobilebot 1.0 for Joomla! 1.5.x can detect visitors using mobile devices and change the Joomla! Template automatically.

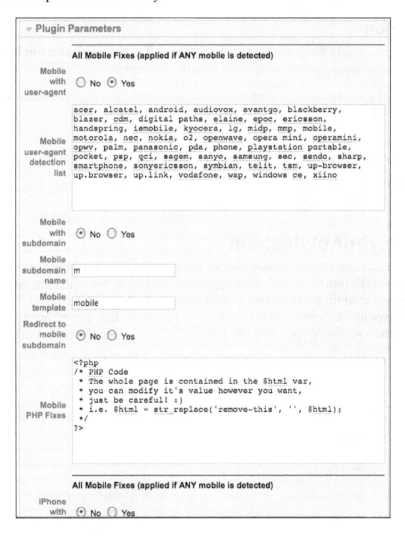

Mobilebot 1.0 for Joomla! 1.5.x has the following features:

1. It can detect iPhone, Blackberry, Android, and Opera Mini browsers separately and load a particular template for each of them.

2. It has two extra spaces so you can add your own custom mobile devices.

3. You can adjust your final HTML code with simple/regular expression PHP replacements. This can be done independently for each particular device.

4. If none of the specific devices are detected (or you just have one template for all mobiles), the plugin can also perform a general mobile detection and load a "generic" mobile template if configured accordingly.

Installation

Mobilebot is a simple plugin extension that is installed via the Extension Manager, and configurations are made within the Plugin Parameters.

To download this extension, visit `http://extensions.joomla.org/` and search for "Mobilebot".

Testing for the mobile web

The following is a list of measures that you can take to improve your Joomla! site's "mobile friendly" presence.

Disable your stylesheet

As has been mentioned previously, one of the easiest ways to test compatibility of your website is to remove the Cascading Style Sheet from the equation. As your stylesheet will contain an abundance of styling elements, it is important from an accessibility point of view for you to see "if that menu still appears" or "do I still have a search feature showing" on your site when you have removed the styling:

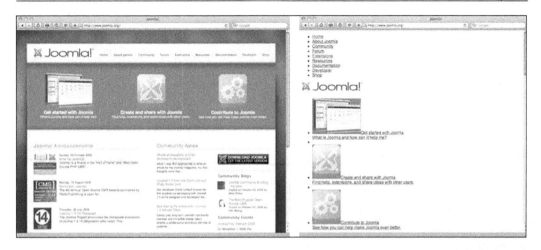

The previous image displays the joomla.org website with the Cascading Style Sheets on, and then turned off in the users' web browser.

Many older mobile devices still render unstyled raw HTML output. Hence, after turning off your stylesheet, you will get an idea of the semantic layout of your content and how this displays on your web browser. If your template and HTML content has been built according to web standards, then menu links and other main navigation features should continue to work.

If you use Mozilla Firefox, you can easily turn off the loading of stylesheets by going to **Menu | Develop | Disable Styles** on the Firefox browser.

Resize your browser

Resizing your browser window will give you a good idea about how your website will look when viewed on a mobile device that supports stylesheets. It is a simple but effective way to view your site on smaller screens:

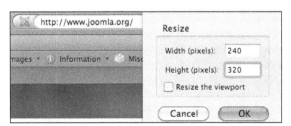

If you use Mozilla Firefox, http://www.firefox.com, and the "Developer Toolbar" plugin for it, https://addons.mozilla.org/firefox/60/, then resizing your browser is a piece of cake. Simply go to the **Resize | Resize Window** menu option, which will allow you to enter custom values for resizing your browser window.

Here are common screen resolutions for mobile devices:

- 128 x 160
- 176 x 220
- 240 x 160
- 320 x 240
- 480 x 320

Being aware of these screen resolutions and testing on them will help you optimize your web content accordingly. As you can see there are a number of different resolutions, and these are just the popular ones, so designing a site that works on the mobile web takes important consideration.

Borrow a phone to test with

This isn't hard to do, but it's a simple method that is often overlooked:

Talk with friends and colleagues and ask them to take a look at your site on their mobile device, and let you know what it's like. There are some great emulators available but there is nothing like viewing it with a physical device, possibly running various software versions.

Target your visitors, and what you want them to see

The goal for any website (not just mobile web) should be to deliver the most appropriate content to users. The goal might be to sell something, deliver important information, or simply offer learning material, but using good navigation and leading the user to this information quickly is the trick!

This goal is even more important when viewing content on the mobile web. This means that you may need to simplify a version of your website content in order to suit a mobile device. Using Joomla! Mobile Web Extensions or manually loading in a different template and CSS may also help with the process of simplifying the layout and display of your pages. At the end of the day, make sure what you are trying to deliver is concise information and users can get to their location easily.

Consider using a tool such as Google Analytics for monitoring your website statistics. The Google Analytics tool is free to use and can set goals, follow user paths, and closely monitor who is visiting what pages, and with what devices. Further information about Google Analytics can be found at www.google.com/analytics/.

Use an emulator

Desktop and web browser emulators are an easy and great way to view what your site will look like on different devices. As with most emulators, they don't always replicate the "real thing" and so are not as good as having a handset in your hand to test on. This being said, they are the next best thing (if they do work) and so here is a list of a few popular web emulators to test mobile web content on:

Emulator	Description	URL
Microsoft Pocket PC emulators	Documentation, sample code, header and library files, emulator images, and tools for building Windows Mobile 6 applications.	http://msdn.microsoft. com/en-gb/windowsmobile/ bb264327.aspx
dotMobi web emulator	An online emulator with Nokia N70 and Sony Ericsson K750 skins.	http://emulator.mtld. mobi/emulator.php
iPhone Simulator	A web-browser-based simulator for quickly testing your iPhone web applications.	http://www.testiphone. com/
Opera Mini Simulator	A live demo of Opera Mini 5 beta that functions as it would when installed on a handset.	http://www.opera.com/ mini/demo/

Emulator	Description	URL
TagTag emulator	Emulator to view mobile web pages on your computer. Enter the page address at the bottom of TagTag emulator and click on go. Browse the page like you would on your mobile phone.	`http://tagtag.com/site/info/emulator`
OPENWAVE	OPENWAVE® phone simulator is a free software development kit that makes creating innovative mobile applications even easier.	`http://developer.openwave.com/dvl/tools_and_sdk/phone_simulator/`

Accessibility

Accessibility for your Joomla! Template is an important topic to mention, as your template is the key container that delivers your Joomla! contents, hence it affects the output of every page on your website.

Accessible content

In order to make your site as accessible as possible, you may need to consider some of the accessibility topics mentioned in previous chapters. Always try to use valid HTML code to embed or display your content. If you are updating your Joomla! website regularly, then consider learning some basic HTML code. Turning off your WYSIWYG editor, in order to format your content manually will usually allow you to have cleaner HTML and it may be the start of a new career with the Web!

Secondly, it is important to offer alternative information to cater for users with disabilities. For example, if you link to a document full of text, consider making an audio version of this available for users who may be visually impaired. This "alternative option" approach can be applied to almost all major content additions to your website, whether it is text, audio, or video.

Accessible template code

With regards to the template itself, your `index.php` file contains all of the HTML markup and is at the core of every page that Joomla! delivers. It is a page, just like any HTML page, but has the extension `.php`, and contains PHP code to deliver the contents of your site. It is very important that this document contains valid HTML code, as validation errors will affect every page of your Joomla! website. To check for validation of your site, you can utilize online validation tools such as `http://validator.w3.org/`:

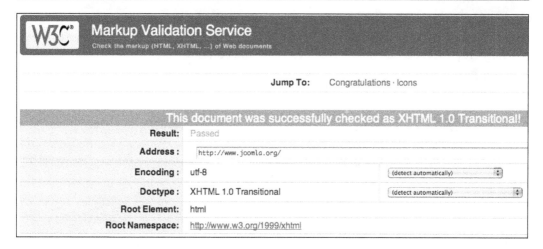

Here are a few key points to adhere to when building or adjusting your
Joomla! Template:

- Use valid HTML code.
- Do not build the HTML using `table` tags, `<table>`. Use the modern method
  of `div` tags, `<div>`, instead.
- Choose contrasting colors that can be easily viewed.
- Optimize graphics for the template.
- Use valid CSS code.
- Offer text-resize options (most major browsers now offer this feature, so
  make sure you use `em` values for font control in your CSS file).
- Test your template and site by using online validation tools.
- Test your website in all popular web browsers.

Fonts, colors, and contrasts

We all tend to choose font typefaces and color schemes that we think look great, but
as proven on the catwalk, one person's idea of style is not necessarily another's! You
may have utilized a default template, or used a pre-designed, third-party template
for Joomla! and settled for the pre-configured options. Although glossy images with
rounded corners and shadows / highlights look great in a perfect environment, there
will be users visiting your sites using mobile devices, many different web browsers,
and possibly with disabilities, which are important to consider.

Choosing the right color scheme is a rather simple but effective way of making your template more accessible. Try to use sufficient color contrast so users who are visually impaired do not have issues viewing the content:

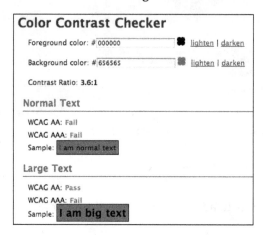

There are a number of tools available on the Web to test for color contrast, such as WebAIM, `http://www.webaim.org/resources/contrastchecker/`.

If your favorite colors are light green text on dark green backgrounds and you just have to use them, consider offering your site users the option to adjust the site contrast by loading in different stylesheets at their request. It is possible to achieve this using CSS and it uses a similar approach as if you are offering the user font size controls for text resizing. Most modern web browsers offer the ability to adjust font sizes. Try to use em values in your site CSS so that users can define their own font sizes in the browser if they so require.

Summary

Due to the nature of the Joomla! Template controlling layout and style properties of our website, it plays an important part in the accessibility of the site.

Templates can enhance multimedia capabilities by delivering JavaScript scripts that can provide additional multimedia features to the site. Templates usually contain a number of images within their presentation and styling, which have an effect upon the extensions we publish in our Joomla! site.

The mobile web is a rapidly growing environment and there are a number of things to check and test in order to make sure that your site can be viewed effectively on a mobile web device. Taking this further, it is possible to utilize some Joomla! Extensions that help create your own mobile web versions of your Joomla! site, making them available to a wider audience.

9
Joomla! Multimedia Project

In the previous chapters, we have covered a multitude of media types
(and respective elements) that are considered as different forms of media.
Put any number of these together and you have created multimedia!

In this last chapter, we follow a cookbook-style approach as we build a multimedia
packed Joomla! website from start to finish. We throw in some of the previously
mentioned techniques, as well as some new tips and tricks for good measure!

This chapter contains:

- An overview
- The site structure
- Multimedia features
- Accessibility and validation

Overview

This chapter is our playground! It is designed with a cookbook-style approach that
will enable you to include various media elements into a default Joomla! installation.

The whole idea is to play and throw things at our Joomla! installation, and learn
during the process. I am a firm believer that is not until we physically do something
(rather than just read about it), and create or break something (and hopefully fix it
again) that we learn how it really works!

If you have read this book and do not utilize the media features mentioned in it, then at least you are now aware of the multimedia capabilities of Joomla!, which is important when planning future projects. If you do utilize some of these features within your website, then you will end up with a feature-rich website containing many cutting-edge web features:

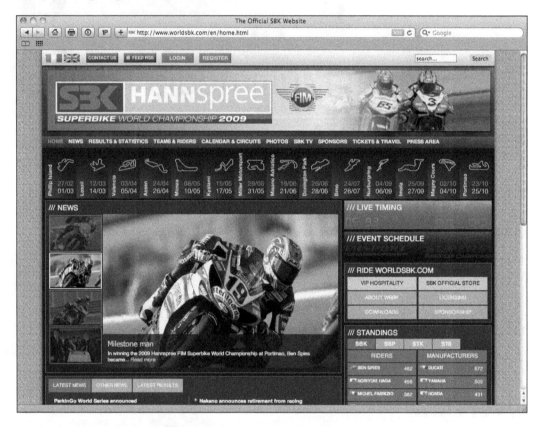

Preliminary advice

Before going further, it is important to point out the following information:

- **Please do not try the following on a live site**: It is best to always use a test website that contains a copy of the files and extensions, and a separate database.

- **Treat the following as a demonstration project and don't build for a live project**: It is very easy to copy over features to a new site, or replicate them once you know how. You will probably learn more by taking a laid-back approach to building a demo site, rather than being "up against the clock", trying to resolve an issue on a real project.

- **Take the time to read about the extensions that you use, and their supporting documentation**: Extensions have been written by numerous developers with varied experience, and agendas. Try to know what you are including within your website if possible.

- **If you install an extension and do not use it, then remove it**: Besides keeping your Joomla! site organized and uncluttered, it is best to remove code/files/folders from your server that are not being used. Leaving older code lying around can create security vulnerabilities.

- **Build the site for your users, not against them**: Once you have completed areas of development on your website, ask friends and family for their opinion about it. It is sometimes far too easy to become pre-occupied with "how something looks" and forget how users are going to navigate to it or use it effectively. A fresh viewpoint can only enhance the project.

- **Use the Joomla! Forums**: Joomla! was made for the community, and it's the community that makes Joomla! what it is. The forums are full of valuable information, and sometimes answers to issues that you have might only be a quick search away. If you don't find what you are looking for, post it on the forums and help build the knowledge base.

- **Keep Joomla! up-to-date**: Joomla! releases are made available for a reason and it is important to stay up-to-date with the software. With a well-structured design to the framework, there are now very few reasons to go near the core codework. Upgrading is usually an easy process, compared to some other web platforms. Remember to take a backup of your site files before performing any upgrade work, and to take regular backups whenever you can. There are some excellent Joomla! backup extensions which can be found at `http://extensions.joomla.org/extensions/access-a-security/backup`.

Getting started

Joomla! can be what you want it to be. It is built with flexibility in mind, and I have personally used it from one-page websites through to UK government projects that receive four million hits-per-month. The Joomla.org site alone receives near five million hits-per-month, and is a great example of how diverse the platform can be.

Joomla! is easy; with knowledge it can be installed within ten minutes and you have a dynamic database driven website out-of-the-box. At this point, the difference between "just another Joomla! install" and "your custom website" (that just happens to be built on the Joomla! Framework) is about knowledge, experience, content, and elbow grease!

And that's what we are about to do; create an environment where it is easy and safe to play in, go get our hands dirty and come out the other end with a working Joomla! website that is packed with multimedia features. You can then re-create these features easily on your live website, if required, as you would have the working knowledge to do so.

Local development

Local development takes place on your computer rather than on an external remote web server. Before you disregard this section, local development is your friend. Lets see how easy it is to get up and running with a local development environment.

With a range of tools available, it is now very easy to set up a local development environment which can mimic your live website. Local development is often seen as something that only spotty-faced coders who hang out in closets should be doing, but in fact it is the safest way to work on your website without affecting a live site environment.

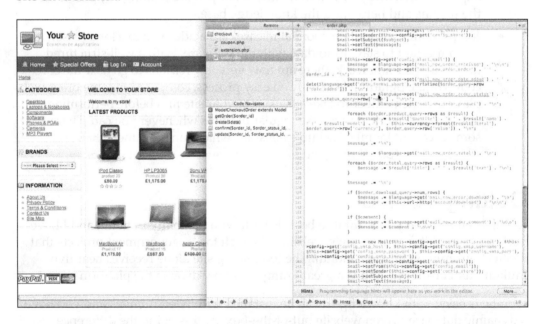

The reasons to run a local development server are as follows:

- Develop locally on your computer without being online.

- Make mistakes and put work on your site without it being searched and indexed by Google. We don't want to be halfway through something and have Google come along and make it available to the world.

- Test out your work before introducing the same features into the live environment.

- Developing with a localhost package such as MAMP, WAMP helps you understand the server and database relationship, which makes you more knowledgeable about how your Joomla! website works.

- Local server development is quicker. There is no need to FTP to your web server, and wait for pages to reload through slow internet connections.

- Local development server environments are free to set up and use.

There are numerous ways to set up a local development environment. The main requirements to run a Joomla! website on a server as follows:

- **Apache server**

  Apache makes the most popular web server software in the world. A web server is a program that serves the documents, images, and all other stuff you have on your website to the outside world.

- **PHP**

  PHP is a popular server-side HTML-embedded scripting language. PHP can collect form data, generate dynamic page content, and process cookies. It supports a wide range of databases including mSQL, MySQL, MS-SQL, ODBC, Oracle, and PostgreSQL. PHP also supports a wide range of protocols including IMAP, SNMP, NNTP, and POP3. PHP borrows from the best of the Perl and C worlds, and has hundreds of built-in functions to simplify most of the common tasks.

- **MySQL**

  MySQL is a very fast, multi-threaded, multi-user SQL database server. It can utilize multiple CPUs, supports many column types, and very large databases. Its speed, flexibility, and price (free) make it an attractive database option.

If you know what you are doing, then it is possible to install each of these on their own and configure your own local development environment, but for those of us who just want to get on with it, there are a number of excellent packages available which install these elements and create an easy-to-use local web server.

Some of the more popular packages available are:

Package	URL
WAMP — Windows	`http://www.wampserver.com/en/`
MAMP — Apple Mac OS X	`http://www.mamp.info/en/mamp.html`
LAMP — Linux (and other Unix)	Distribution dependent
XAMPP — Multi-platform — Windows, Linux, Solaris, Mac	`http://apachefriends.org`

The previous links will help provide advice for installation of these packages within your environment. For the purpose of this tutorial, I will show how easy it is to install the MAMP platform for Mac OS X.

Installing the MAMP package

MAMP stands for **Macintosh**, **Apache**, **MySQL, and PHP**. MAMP comes free of charge and can be installed in typical Mac fashion with just a few clicks.

MAMP will not compromise any existing Apache installation already running with your OS X, and you can install Apache, PHP, and MySQL without starting a script or having to change any configuration files.

1. Simply download the MAMP `.dmg` file from the MAMP website, `http://mamp.info/en/downloads/index.html`.

The previous image shows the MAMP website and the MAMP DMG file download option.

2. Click to run this file as you would install any other Mac OS X application.

3. Drag the application into your `Applications` folder and job done! You now have the MAMP server installed locally.

4. Once installed, click on the MAMP icon in the `Applications` directory to open the MAMP start control panel:

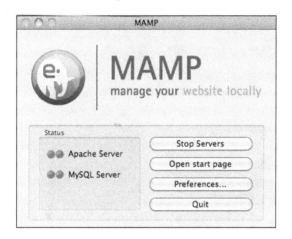

The MAMP control panel offers the following options:

- **Start/Stop Servers**: Allows you to easily start and stop your localhost Apache Server with a simple click.

- **Open start page**: Opens the default MAMP start page, where you have links to phpInfo, phpMyAdmin, SQLiteManager.

- **Preferences...**: Allows some configurable options for Apache port numbers, PHP versions, and other settings.

- **Quit**: Stops all services and shuts down the MAMP application.

By clicking on the **Open start page** option in the MAMP control panel, the following start page appears in your web browser:

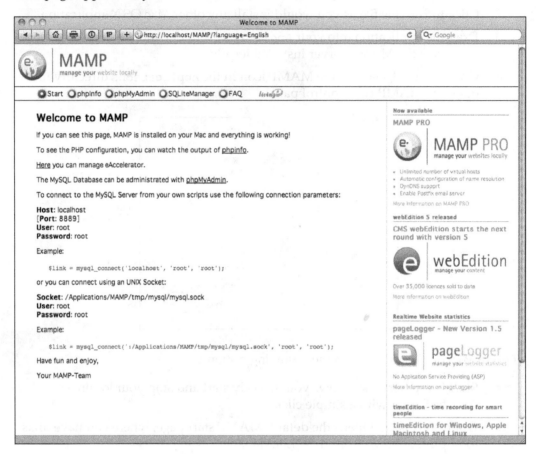

Links to the following tools can be found on this page:

- **phpMyAdmin**: Is a database management tool that is used to easily set up and manage MySQL databases.
- **phpInfo**: Provides a listing of PHP and server configuration information.

How to use MAMP

In your Mac's **Applications** folder, you will now find a directory installed for the MAMP application.

Inside the MAMP directory, you will see a number of folders and files. We need to look for a folder called `htdocs`. It is within this folder that you will place your new directories that contain your website files:

It makes things easier by creating a shortcut to your `htdocs` folder on your desktop (or in this case, the MAC Finder window) to enable easy access to our web repositories.

Here is an example of how you would configure a Joomla! website using MAMP:

1. Download Joomla! to your Mac from the Joomla.org website.

2. Unzip this download, and rename the folder to the project name of your choice. In this tutorial, we will call the unzipped folder **JMultimedia**.

3. Drag the new **JMultimedia** folder into your MAMP `htdocs` directory:

4. Make sure MAMP servers are turned on (using the MAMP control panel).

5. Open up a web browser and type in `http://www.localhost:8888`. MAMP defaults to using port 8888 on a Mac, so it is important to include this in your URL. It is possible to adjust the MAMP preferences to not use this by going to the **Preferences** area from the MAMP control panel:

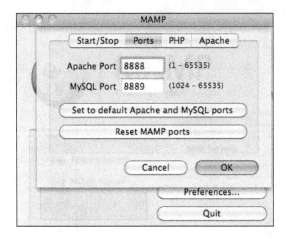

If we leave the settings as default, in order to reach our new Joomla! installation, the address that we need to type as our URL will be: `http://localhost:8888/JMultimedia` (assuming you called your project JMultimedia also).

With any luck, a Joomla! installation page will now show.

Before we begin the Joomla! installation, we first need to go and create a database, which thankfully is easy to do by using the phpMyAdmin tool that comes with MAMP.

Creating a local database

Open the MAMP control panel, and click on the **Open start page** option, or enter `http://localhost/MAMP/` into your URL bar. From here, we can use phpMyAdmin to create a new database and then run the Joomla! installer.

On the MAMP start page, a link to the **phpMyAdmin** tool can be found:

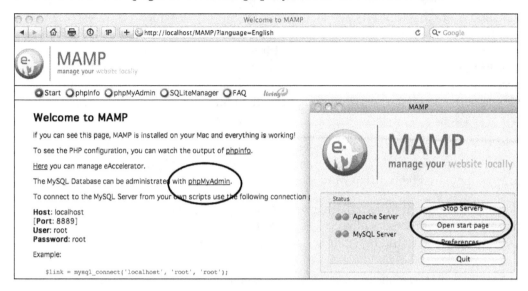

Clicking on this will take your browser to the phpMyAdmin tool home page.

To create a new MySQL database for your Joomla! installation, simply enter a new database name into the **Create new database** field and click on the **Create** button:

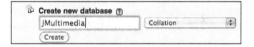

You can leave all other settings as default. Once the database has been created, you should now see this listed on the left-hand column showing the database listings.

It is now possible to proceed with the Joomla! installation via the Web Browser Installer, entering the details of your database during the installation process. Your database server will be `localhost` and the default username and password will be `root`:

Running more than one website locally

Creating more than one website locally is easy. Simply download or re-extract another copy of Joomla! from your download and then give the extracted directory a different project name, for example, JMultimedia2. Move this folder into the `htdocs` area of your local web server (in our case MAMP), and your project will then be accessible under the new URL `http://localhost:8888/JMultimedia2`, and they should show in a list when you navigate to the main localhost directory, for example, `http://localhost:8888`.

Create a new database for your new project, just as you did before, and then you are ready to install Joomla!. You can create as may local sites as you have space for, as long as they are given different names.

For those who want to install other server packages, such as WAMP for Windows or XAMPP, the process will be very similar to that of MAMP. Further installation assistance can be found by visiting the supporting documentation for each product.

Most of the free web server environments have been configured to run easily and openly on a local computer, providing ease of development. They have not been configured to be used as live web hosting servers, and because of open configurations, they should not be used to host a live website.

Remote server development

A remote host is one that you access via the Internet. It may be your own server or rented via a web hosting company. There are many different types of web hosting servers, including dedicated, virtual, and shared hosting, and many forms of operating systems running these servers. Whichever option you choose, it is important to check whether Joomla! is able to run in that environment and a checklist of requirements can be found at `Joomla.org` under the **Documentation** area.

Working on your site on a remote web server is a surprisingly common approach that is used by many people, including those new to Joomla! and the web development industry. Remote web development usually requires FTP access or some sort of web hosting control panel File Manager tool. It can be dangerous to work on the final site, because of the simple fact that once a file has been overwritten, there is no way of retrieving it easily without a backup copy. Internet connections can make the process very slow and sometimes FTP connections can corrupt files.

With that said, working on a remote server may offer the ability to closely match a development environment to the live environment and can also offer the ability to easily show clients the progress of a project. If you do not want to work locally for development, I suggest setting up a remote hosting space to mimic your live environment, and password protect this via `htaccess`. Server-side programs such as cPanel and Plesk all offer the ability to easily password-protect directories or domains, which will keep it private to you and stop search engines from referencing your development work.

If you are using either a remote hosting environment or localhost environment to perform the following additions to your site, please get into the habit of taking a backup of your database and files before proceeding with any of the following.

The site structure

The following assumes you have a working installation of Joomla! on your web server. If you have any issues during an installation, please search the Joomla. org website, `http://help.joomla.org`, and the forums to search for answers and assistance. Often, it may be a hosting environment issue rather than any Joomla! issue during the installation.

For the purpose of this tutorial we will be building on a new installation of Joomla!, without the default content installed. When working on a Joomla! website, I find it best to keep two tabs open in my browser window: One for the frontend of the Joomla! website, and one for the administration. For this tutorial, I will be working with Joomla! 1.5, the MAMP web server for local development, and the Firefox web browser:

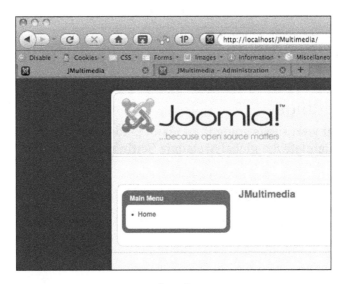

Things to consider when configuring from the start

During the Joomla! installation process you get the opportunity to enter in some basic site information, such as a website name, e-mail address, and site login username and password, but there are usually a number of other things that are worth configuring when first logging into your new Joomla! installation.

Global Configuration settings

The Global Configuration area of your Joomla! site contains some powerful site-wide settings. It is worth looking at these at the start of a project to see if these require adjustments.

Site Settings

There is one change we need to make within the **Site Settings** box, and it is a major one:

Change the **Default WYSIWYG Editor** to **Editor - No Editor**. This will give us more control and limit issues around entering custom code into your site.

Metadata Settings

If you know what your site is going to be about (and hopefully you do), then it is possible to pre-populate the global **Metadata Settings** at this stage:

Metadata Settings

Global Site Meta Description	The JMultimedia site is a feature packed an project about Joomla! Multimedia.
Global Site Meta Keywords	joomla multimedia,Joomla,joomla images,joom audio,joomla multimedia book, allan walker
Show Title Meta Tag	○ No ● Yes
Show Author Meta Tag	○ No ● Yes

Global metadata is presented on pages that do not contain their own metadata information and is valuable information for search engine optimization.

Populate the **Description** and **Keywords** boxes with content that directly relates to your web project.

SEO Settings

The **Search Engine Optimization (SEO)** area of the Global Configuration is probably one of those areas that most administrators will look into. Here we can enable search-engine-friendly URLs for our Joomla! website, which can really help with a more user friendly and search-engine-friendly website:

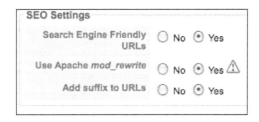

Because our Joomla! web content is created dynamically by the database, there are no physical files created for each article. This means that we need to utilize the SEO URL feature to change our URLs from long complicated strings that are not easily recognizable into more recognizable URLs that relate to the content displayed:

- SEF URLs turned off:

  http://localhost/JMultimedia/index.php?option=com_content&view=
  article&id=1&Itemid=2

- SEF URLs turned on:

  http://localhost/JMultimedia/seo-friendly.html

You will need to select **Yes** for all three fields, as shown in the previous screenshot and then click on **Apply** at the top-right of the Global Configuration page. We need to make one more adjustment to a file within Joomla! for the SEO feature to become active.

In order for SEO to work correctly, it needs to use a feature called `mod_rewrite`, which is installed on a web server. Most apache servers should have this feature installed, but if yours is not, then you will need to active it, or ask your web server support people to look at this. You can easily check if `mod_rewrite` is active or not by going to the **Help | System Info** menu link within your Joomla! administration menu. On this page, there will be a link labeled "PHP Information" and on this page use the browser window search bar to search for `mod_rewrite`. It should show in an area labeled "Loaded Modules".

If `mod_rewrite` is active, then we are clear to proceed, and need to rename a file named `htaccess.txt` (which is included at the root of your Joomla! install) to `.htaccess`. That is all that is required for search-engine-friendly URLs to work for Joomla!.

 Depending on your computer platform, there may be restrictions in renaming files beginning with a dot symbol. You may need to use an FTP program, such as the free and powerful FileZilla client, `http://filezilla-project.org/`, to rename your `htaccess.txt` file.

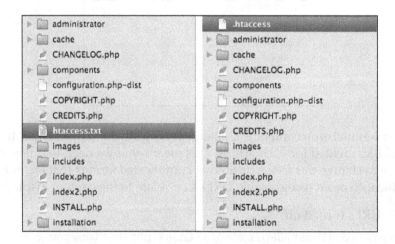

Right, back to the Global Configuration screen. There are three menu links at the top of the Global Configuration page. Click on the second one called "System". On the System page, there are a range of options relating to the hosting server, and how Joomla! interacts with this.

User Settings

This box contains **User Registration** settings. For the purpose of this project, I am going to turn off User Registration, as we have no requirement for users on the site at this stage. User Registration can be activated for the site at any stage:

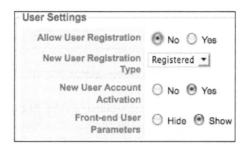

Media Settings

We looked at these in earlier chapters and they are important in allowing the Media Manager to work effectively. At this stage, we can leave these as default, but we may need to re-visit them, depending on what media formats we end up using on the site.

Debug Settings

Debug is used by developers to view additional information about the page that has loaded. It can help show diagnostic information and SQL errors. You can turn this feature on and off as you wish. If you know how to decipher the information, it is very useful for troubleshooting the build of a website.

Cache Settings

The website cache helps to optimize and improve performance of your site by creating a temporary copy of pages and delivering that information to the user, rather than going back to the database to retrieve it each time:

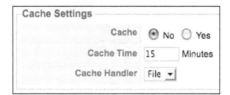

Caching can really come in handy on large production websites, but for development it can sometimes cause headaches with you making changes and not being able to view them. Let's turn caching off for now.

Session Settings

The Session Settings control how long a user can be logged in and inactive on the site before being logged out automatically. The default is **15** minutes and you can adjust it:

Be cautious of setting this too high, but let's change it to **30** minutes, else you will probably find yourself getting logged out of the administration area if you go off to get a cuppa.

Click on the third menu link called **Server** at the top of the Global Configuration page:

Mail Settings

The Mail Settings area of the Global Configuration may require your attention, depending if you require specific site **Mail Settings**:

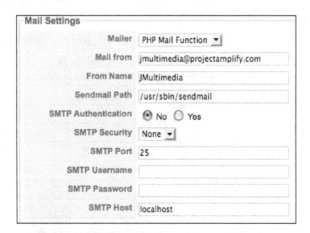

Generally these settings can be left at default, but if your site is not sending e-mails for some reason, this is the first place to look and check your e-mail configurations.

Once you are happy with your Global Configuration settings, make sure you click on the **Save** button at the top-right of the Global Configuration screen to save your changes.

Content parameters

The Article Manager in Joomla! contains a "Global Parameter" setting that sets the default options for your Joomla! Articles. You can override these within each article, but it is good practice to set these globally first, so you don't have to go back and adjust them later on.

The global parameter for articles is found at the top-right of the page when viewing the **Article Manager** screen:

When you click on the **Parameters** button, a new screen with a lightbox pop-up effect will display the available parameters. For this tutorial, let's adjust the following to "Hide":

- Author Name
- Created Date and Time
- Modified Date and Time

You can also adjust any other article parameters that you feel suitable for your project.

Front page

When you install Joomla!, the Main Menu item that links to your front page (or default menu item) will have the title set for this menu link to be the same as your site name.

Sometimes you may want your front page item to say something different, such as "Welcome to our site". You can adjust this front page title by visiting the default menu item to that page, in this case our **Home** menu link.

To adjust your title, go to **Menu** | **Main Menu** and click on the **Home** menu link.

On the right-hand side, under **Parameters (System)**, you will see the option to rename the menu link **Page Title**. Let's rename this simply to **Welcome** for now so you can see how this affects the Joomla! front page:

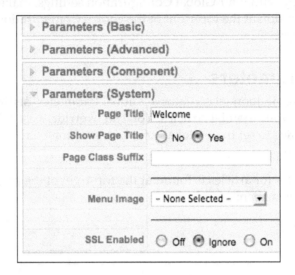

When we view the frontend of our website now, and click on the **Home** menu link, the page title will change from **JMultimedia** to **Welcome**.

Sections and categories

One more thing to do now, let's head over to take a look at our sections and categories.

Sections and categories are the foundations of our Content Management System administration. They are an option in 1.5 (meaning you don't have to utilize them). However, they do allow you to do two things if you choose to use them:

1. If you have a number of articles in your Joomla! website, then using sections and categories allows you to organize the content and display it accordingly. You can use filters when viewing the Article Manager page that can help you find articles easy. For sites that add new content regularly, this can really help to keep your site organized.

2. There are built-in features in Joomla! which can take advantage of this article organization. Menu item types (also called layouts) can link to sections or categories and automatically display the contents within these depending on the parameters you have set on that menu link. An example of this is the menu link to Section Blog, Section List, Category Blog, and Category List.

Many other Joomla! and third-party modules utilize sections and categories in order to display news items for that particular topic. By grouping all of your articles on a particular topic into one category, for example, Latest News, any new items you add to this category can be automatically displayed on your site pages via a module. We will look into this shortly.

Sections and Categories can be easily added from the **Content | Section Manager**, and **Content | Category Manager** menu links. You can also get to these areas from the icons located on the administration Control Panel:

If you keep an organized site, you will probably constantly visit these areas in order to add new sections and categories. For a start, I am going to put the following in place. To create a new section or category, simply click on the "New" icon at the top-right of the respective manager screens, and give the section or category a title, then click on **Save**.

Sections

Sections are as follows:

- Site
- Images
- Audio
- Video
- General
- News

Categories

Categories need to be located within sections, so create the following categories with the respective sections you just created:

- Site: Create a category called **General**
- Site: Create a category called **Legal**
- Images: Create a category called **General Image**
- Audio: Create a category called **Podcast**
- Audio: Create a category called **General Audio**
- Video: Create a category called **General Video**
- General: Create a category called **Content**
- News: Create a category called **Latest**

That should provide us with a basic organization structure that we can define further as required.

Choosing a template / theme for your site

A Joomla! Template is used to manipulate the way that content is delivered to the browsing device. Templates are extremely powerful elements to a Joomla! site and one of the defining factors between one site looking just like the next.

Fonts, colors, backgrounds, links, and the way our extensions end up displaying within the page are controlled or influenced by the Joomla! Template. It is for this reason that we need to choose a template that suits the purpose of the site. By this, I do not just mean the color scheme, but more so the layout and flexibility of displaying the type of content required easily to our users.

Templates can be added to a Joomla! install at any stage, and once added, they can be adjusted with a combination of HTML, CSS and PHP, image and JavaScript skills.

For the purpose of this project, I am going to utilize one of the built-in templates that comes shipped with Joomla! 1.5. In order to change to this template, we need to go to the **Extensions | Template Manager** menu link:

The **Template Manager** screen allows you to do two things, firstly you can set your site's Default Template from the area, and you can also go into each template to adjust any available Template Parameters.

Firstly let's select the radio button on the left, next to the template named **JA_Purity** and click on the "Default" icon on the top-right of the page. This will make the **JA_Purity** template the default for the site, and will now show on your page.

Secondly, let's click on the **Title** of **JA_Purity** to go and edit some of its parameters. Once you are on the Template Edit screen, you should see a list of parameters on the right-hand side. Adjust the following:

- **Template Width**: Auto (Fluid)
- **Horizontal Navigation Type**: Suckerfish Menu

You can adjust any other options as you wish and click on **Save** on that screen.

One more thing before we get down to business: A quick logo change for this template.

The JA_Purity template can easily be modified and is a great base for creating your own site's theme. Further customization tutorials for this template can be found by visiting `http://docs.joomla.org/Tutorial:Customising_the_JA_Purity_template`, or taking a look at the "*Joomla! 1.5 Template Design*", *Tessa Blakeley Silver*, *Packt Publishing* book at `http://www.packtpub.com/joomla-1-5-template-design-2nd-edition/book`.

To change the JA_Purity logo to a custom logo for your website, you will need to navigate to the JA_Purity template folder, which is located within your Joomla! fileset. If you are working locally, this is simply a case of visiting the following directories and locating the file `logo.png`: **htdocs | JMultimedia | Templates | ja_purity | images | logo.png**.

You will need to edit this in an image-editing program on your computer.

Once the file has been adjusted, save the new logo (with the same `.png` file extension) in the same directory as the original. The original file will be overwritten and your new logo will be displayed in its place. The default logo is 207 px wide by 80 px high. If you need to adjust the logo dimensions to suit your new logo, then we also need to make a change to the CSS file that is referencing the logo graphic.

There are two ways to edit the CSS for your template:

1. **External editing**

    Use an external editor on your computer by navigating to the following file and opening it with an applicable editing program: **htdocs | JMultimedia | Templates | ja_purity | css | template.css**.

    Within the `template.css` file, search for the `h1.logo a` style. It should be located around line 956 within the file:

    ```
    h1.logo a
    {
        width: 208px;
        display: block;
        background: url(../images/logo.png) no-repeat;
        height: 80px;
        position: relative;
        z-index: 100;
    }
    ```

    Adjust the applicable height and width values for your new logo dimensions and click on **Save** on this file.

2. **Internal editing**

    You can also edit the `template.css` file using the built-in Joomla! CSS Editor in the Joomla! Administration. Here are the steps:

    ◦ Navigate to **Extensions | Template Manager**.

    ◦ Click on the **JA_Purity** template to view the Template Edit mode.

    ◦ Click on the **Edit CSS** icon at the top-right of the screen.

    ◦ Select the `template.css` radio button, and press the "Edit" icon at the top-right of the screen.

    ◦ Use your browser search feature to search for `h1.logo a`. Edit the following values:

    ```
    h1.logo a
    {
        width: 208px;
        display: block;
        background: url(../images/logo.png) no-repeat;
        height: 80px;
        position: relative;
        z-index: 100;
    }
    ```

If you have made logo adjustments to your site, the new logo should now appear when you view the frontend of your website:

Before we proceed, refresh this page a few times in your web browser. You will notice that the JA_Purity template contains a nice feature, which is randomly changing the top-right header background image. So without actually adding any multimedia features to our website yet, we already have the following media elements in place:

- Multiple images (including gradient and other template-styling images, in fact, an impressive 19 images are now loading into my web page)
- Text (including font adjustment controls)
- Styled text using fonts from our CSS
- Template image

Multimedia features

Now this is where the fun begins. The following section separates out the media features, and categorizes them into headings such as "Adding Video Features", "Adding an Image Gallery", and so on. We will use both built-in Joomla! features and a range of third-party extensions in order to achieve a media-rich working website.

Text content

Due to the fact that there is no applicable content to drop into this web project, I will include some Fake Latin textural paragraphs to help establish some throughout the project. Fake Latin text is very useful for simulating how a site page can look with textual content. It is also an option when the client may not have delivered the content "copy" to you. A Fake Latin text generator can be located at the following website: `http://www.4guysfromrolla.com/demos/latin.asp`.

Module positions

Module positions play a role of allowing you to display processed code within different areas of your template. There is a neat trick you can add to your browser URL in order to see where module positions are located within a Joomla! Template. Simply enter in the following at the end of your main URL: `/index.php?tp=1`. So the full URL should look like: `http://localhost/JMultimedia/index.php?tp=1`:

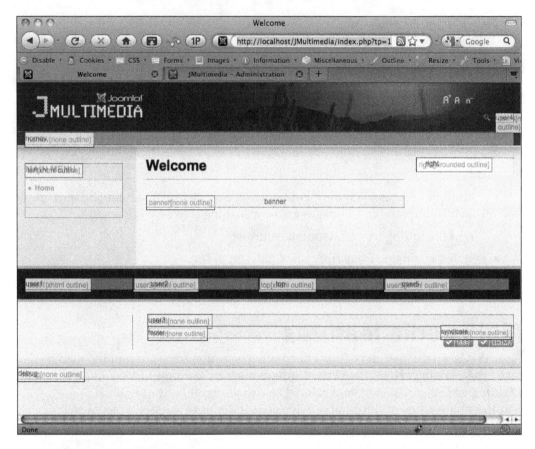

In most Joomla! Templates, this will display the available positions on the page and give you a helpful reminder of their names and locations within the template.

You can achieve the same effect by visiting the **Extensions | Template Manager** screen and clicking on the template name you wish to preview. On the Template Edit screen, a preview button is located at the top-right of the page.

Adjusting the menu

By default, our Joomla! Installation has the Main Menu module published in the left-hand column. The JA_Purity template has a built-in module positioning and styling for your Main Menu to be displayed in a horizontal position underneath the logo area. To make your Main Menu show in this position, perform the following:

1. In your Joomla! administration, navigate to the **Extensions | Module Manager** screen.

2. Locate the **Main Menu** module and click on its title in order to edit it.

3. In the **Details** area of the page, adjust the following parameters: **Show Title = No, Position = hornav**:

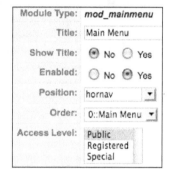

4. Click on **Save** on this page and view the frontend of the website. Your side menu that was located in the left column will now show up in the menu bar under the site logo:

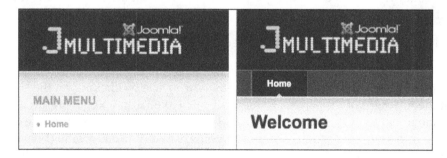

Using this horizontal navigation area will help maximize the display space.

Front page features

There are a number of ways to display content on a Joomla! website's "Home Page".

The front page component

The Joomla! front page is a default view of the com_content component. This component allows you to control how your home page is displayed. The com_content component has the ability to display multiple articles on the front page, helping to create a magazine-type display of your articles. The front page layout is configured by the parameters associated with the **Home** link in the Main Menu.

To customize the look and feel of this, within the administration, navigate to **Menus** | **Main Menu** and click on the **Home** link to edit it.

On the right-hand side, under **Menu Parameters**, you can adjust the number of articles to be displayed and the number of columns to be shown in your front page. Let's set the numbers as per the following image:

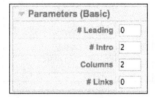

Once you have changed the values, click on **Save** on that screen to save your changes, and that is all we need to do now in this area. If you refresh the frontend of your website, you will see no changes yet, but we have set the display now for when we add some content.

Let's add a few articles into our website, so we can start to build our front page features.

Navigate to the Article Manager and create a new article by clicking on the "New" icon at the top-right of the screen. Remember our Fake Latin text generator; it will now come in handy! Go grab some fake text (or use real text if you prefer) and paste this into your new article. Make sure you give your article a Title (I have used "Article 1") and place this into the Section called "General" and Category called "Content". Make sure the article is "Published" and also "Published on the front page", then click on **Save** at the top-right of the screen.

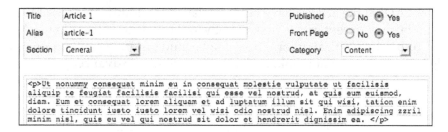

When you have clicked on **Save**, you will be taken back to the Article Manager screen. We want to repeat this process, so we have at least three to four articles displayed. Hence, use the "Copy" feature on the Article Manager screen in order to clone the article:

1. In the Article Manager, click on the left-hand side radio button next to the article you wish to copy.

2. Click on the "Copy" article icon at the top-right of the screen.

3. Choose the section and category you wish to copy the article into (in our case, "General – Content"), and then click on **Save**.

4. Click on the title of the new article to edit it. Once in the Edit Article screen, adjust the Title and Alias of the article (Article 2, 3, 4, and so on) and make sure they are set to a published state and viewable on the front page).

If all of your copied articles have been published, when you look at the frontend of your site, you should now see two of them shown on the Joomla! front page. This is because we told our "Home" menu link to display two articles only, and to show two columns:

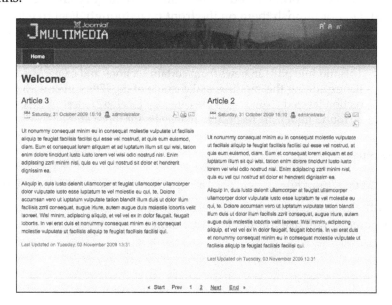

You will notice that the articles have been displayed randomly. It is possible to show them by most recent article first, the physical ordering of them in the Article Manager, or by alphabetical order. These display and ordering configurations are all made in the "Home" menu link, under the **Parameters (Advanced)** section:

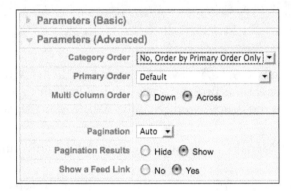

Adding a module to display our latest news

There are a number of other features available for the front page; let's add a module extension that nicely displays articles that are located within a certain category. The module we will use for this is called "ThumbsUp" and is available from the Joomla! Extensions page.

Before we can use this module, we need some content to be displayed within it. Repeat the process you used to create and copy articles, but this time make sure they reside within the section labeled "News" and the category labeled "Latest" and are published. Do not publish them on the front page though. Feel free to add any images into your content items in order to add some color and interest to the pages.

This module pulls in news from certain sections and categories. Before editing this module, make a note of the ID number with the section labeled "News" and the category labeled "Latest". These can be found under the respective managers for those areas.

Follow these steps:

1. Visit http://extensions.joomla.org and search for "ThumbsUp".

2. Visit the extension developer's website and download the extension to your computer. (I will use the stable 1.3 version.)

3. Upload this extension in the Joomla! administration, using the **Extension | Install / Uninstall** feature.

4. In the administration, navigate to **Extensions | Module Manager**, and click on the title of the "Latest Articles with Thumbnails" module to edit it.

5. Adjust the parameters of the following:

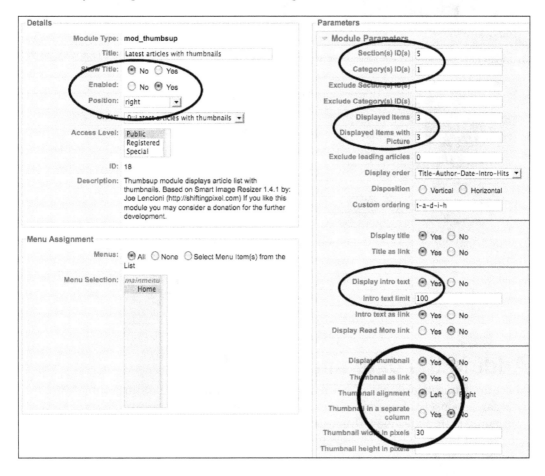

Feel free to adjust any other parameters that you require. If you look at the front page of your website now, it is starting to get some depth to it quickly:

Adding the date and time

There are a number of ways to add a time and date function to your Joomla! site. This can be a useful feature to users in news, magazine, or busy web portals. Some commercial templates may already contain this feature, and simply require it to be activated. Others, like the JA_Purity template, do not have this option, so we will proceed to include it.

1. Method 1

    Insert the correct PHP, JavaScript, and / or HTML code into your template manually. There are a number of pre-built scripts available on the Web that display the time and date on your site pages.

2. Method 2

Use an available Joomla! Extension such as the Date and Time module. Here are the steps:

   ° Search the Joomla! Extensions area for "Time" at
     http://extensions.joomla.org.

   ° On the results page, click on the category labelled **Date & Time**, and this module will be displayed.

   ° Visit the extension developer's website and download the extension to your computer.

   ° Upload this extension in the Joomla! administration, using the **Extension | Install / Uninstall** feature.

   ° In the administration, navigate to **Extensions | Module Manager**, and click on the Title of the "Date2" module to edit it.

Adjust the Module Parameters as you wish. I am going to use the "JavaScript" feature to check the time (so seconds show in real time), and I will publish the module to the "Left", which will show in a left column in our template. I am also going to turn off the module Title:

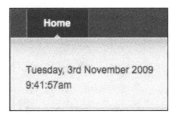

It is worth noting that these time and date features will work off the server time. Hence, if working locally, you will see your local computer time.

Adding a search feature

All sites that have any form of content need a search feature to allow users to find this easily. The JA_Purity template has built-in styling for a search box already included within the template's CSS, so adding a new search feature to our site will be very easy.

1. In the administration, navigate to the **Extensions | Module Manager** screen.

2. Click on the **New** icon at the top-right of the screen to create a new module.

3. From the available list of options, select the **Search** link and click on the text in order to load a new search module:

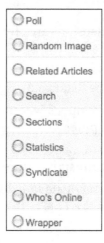

4. Make sure the title is not displayed, but the module is enabled. It will need to be published in **user4** position, which will display it at the top-right of our web page:

5. Click on **Save** on that module, and if you look at the frontend of the site, you will see your new search box displayed below the font size controls:

Personally, I feel the default black background is a bit dark to see, so a quick change to the template CSS file can adjust that. I will set the search background to white, and the search text to black:

```
#ja-search .inputbox
{
    width: 120px;
    border: 1px solid #333333;
    padding: 3px 5px;
    color: #000000;
    background: #FFFFFF;
    font-size: 92%;
}
```

Remember to save your changes and you should see these reflected in your site.

Adding images

As you have seen throughout the course of this book, images can be easily added to Joomla! Articles and Modules and formatted as you require. There are, however, some powerful image extensions for Joomla! that we will now utilize within our site.

Adding an image gallery

Image galleries are one of the most popular extensions at Joomla.org, hence there are a number of excellent options available.

Hopefully, you have had a good read of Chapter 4, *Adding and Managing Image Content*, and have found image solutions you require for your projects. For this tutorial, I am going to utilize a few extensions to display images throughout the site.

Image gallery using Phoca Gallery

Phoca Gallery is a heavyweight contender for displaying beautiful photo galleries in Joomla!. It is a feature-packed solution, so much so that you could probably write a book on it in itself!

That said, we are quickly going to add this to our site in order to create a feature rich photo gallery using this component, module, plugin. I will cover the basic steps, however for detailed support the developer's website and Joomla! Forums will be able to provide a wealth of knowledge:

1. Search the Joomla! Extensions area for "Phoca Gallery" at http://extensions.joomla.org.

2. Visit the extension developer's website and download the following extensions to your computer:

- **Phoca Gallery Component**: Powers the main Phoca Gallery features.

- **Phoca Gallery Search Plugin**: Allows your Joomla! search feature to also search Phoca Gallery images.

- **Phoca Gallery Slideshow Plugin**: Displays a slideshow of images from a selected Phoca Gallery category {pgslideshow id=...|width=...|height=...|delay=...|image=...}. For an image, O: original, L: large, M: medium, S: small. Example: {pgslideshow id=1|width=100|height=100|delay=3000|image=M}.

- **Phoca Gallery Image Module**: Displays random images from the Phoca Gallery Component.

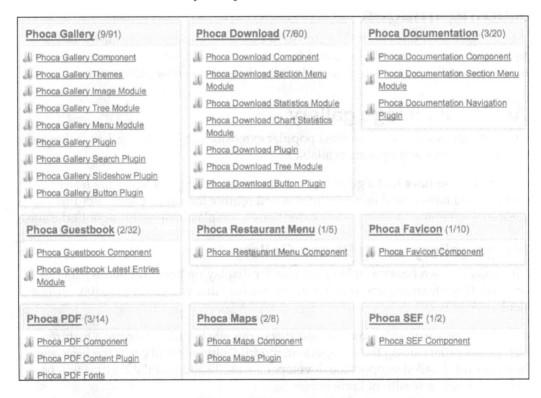

Phoca Gallery (9/91)
- Phoca Gallery Component
- Phoca Gallery Themes
- Phoca Gallery Image Module
- Phoca Gallery Tree Module
- Phoca Gallery Menu Module
- Phoca Gallery Plugin
- Phoca Gallery Search Plugin
- Phoca Gallery Slideshow Plugin
- Phoca Gallery Button Plugin

Phoca Download (7/60)
- Phoca Download Component
- Phoca Download Section Menu Module
- Phoca Download Statistics Module
- Phoca Download Chart Statistics Module
- Phoca Download Plugin
- Phoca Download Tree Module
- Phoca Download Button Plugin

Phoca Documentation (3/20)
- Phoca Documentation Component
- Phoca Documentation Section Menu Module
- Phoca Documentation Navigation Plugin

Phoca Guestbook (2/32)
- Phoca Guestbook Component
- Phoca Guestbook Latest Entries Module

Phoca Restaurant Menu (1/5)
- Phoca Restaurant Menu Component

Phoca Favicon (1/10)
- Phoca Favicon Component

Phoca PDF (3/14)
- Phoca PDF Component
- Phoca PDF Content Plugin
- Phoca PDF Fonts

Phoca Maps (2/8)
- Phoca Maps Component
- Phoca Maps Plugin

Phoca SEF (1/2)
- Phoca SEF Component

3. Upload these extensions to the Joomla! administration using the **Extension|Install / Uninstall** feature. (Tackle the component last as you will need to run an installer for the component once it has been uploaded).

4. In the administration, navigate to **Extensions | Plugin Manager**, and enable the search and slideshow plugins.

5. In the administration, navigate to **Components | Phoca Gallery**, and on the main Control Panel page, click on the icon "Categories". Set up a new category by clicking on the "New" icon at the top-right of the page. Let's give this a title of **Images** and click on **Save** on that page (note that you can revisit all of these options to define them as you require).

6. Adding images can be done using various methods, with Phoca allowing you to use a Flash-based and Java-based upload feature to upload multiple images quickly.

I will use the multiple image feature to add a number of images into my new "Images" Category. The first step is to upload the images, and then once they are uploaded, you associate them with a category. This provides a mail image resource for future reference.

Once your images have been uploaded, choose the "Images" Category (that we will put them into) and click on the **Save** button at the top of the screen. Depending on the number of images you upload, you will probably see a processing screen appear for a period. The page should refresh after processing and you will see your new images loaded into the **Image** area:

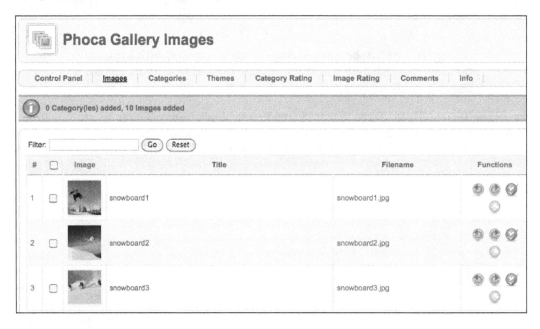

To display these in your website, we need to create a new menu link to this gallery.

Navigate to **Menu | Main Menu**, and create a new menu item to **Phoca Gallery | Phoca Gallery Category Layout**. The new menu item edit page will show and we need to give our menu link a title called "Image Gallery".

On the right-hand side of this screen are the available parameters for the new Phoca Gallery menu link. Firstly, we need to choose the category to link to—**Images**. The following parameters contain a vast array of options, and can allow you to manipulate your gallery colors, layout, features, and so on. You can set these at a global level in Phoca Gallery, but having overrides at the menu item level means that each gallery (or link to a gallery) that you create can contain the various options you require. For now, let's click on **Save** on this menu item and see the results.

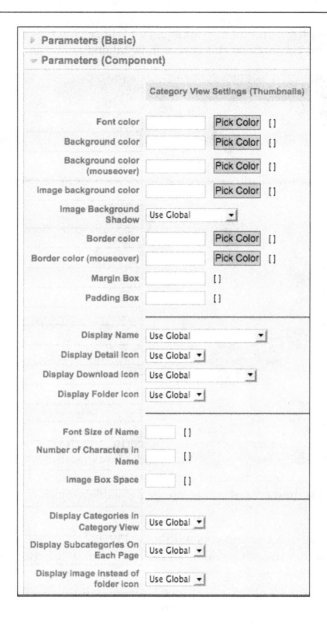

If you now look at the frontend of your site, you will see the new menu link in the Main Menu. When you click on this, you will be taken to your new image gallery:

As mentioned, Phoca Gallery is extremely powerful and flexible. Almost anything can be achieved with time and effort. We could allow download links on our images, special effects on each transition and further image information. We can even allow image ratings and comments, if we install the available plugins from the Phoca Gallery site.

Phoca also contains main parameters within the Phoca control panel, as well as options and overrides in each menu link that you create to the component. Have a good play about and you can get some great results using Phoca Gallery. It is a very suitable solution for larger image galleries that require the structure of gallery categories and other image features. We will leave this component for now and move on with a few other image features.

Image Gallery in articles, using BK-Thumb

BK-Thumb is a multi-purpose image plugin for Joomla! that can automatically create thumbnails and pop ups of the original images, as well as resize the full-size images or add a watermark to them. It can do some pretty powerful stuff for a plugin, so we will take a quick look at it for our site. To install BK Thumb, follow these steps:

1. Search the Joomla! Extensions area for "bk thumb" at
   `http://extensions.joomla.org`.

2. Visit the extension developer's website and download the extension to
   your computer.

3. Upload this extension to the Joomla! Administration, using the
   Extension | Install / Uninstall feature.

4. In the administration, navigate to **Extensions | Plugin Manager**, and click on
   the title of the BK-Thumb plugin to edit it.

BK-Thumb contains a number of parameters, all creating quite a different look and
feel to the presentation of your images. I suggest you adjust these as you feel the
need to, but for now let's make sure the plugin is enabled and click on **Save** at the
top-right of the screen.

In order for BK-Thumb to do its work, we need a new content article called
"BK-Thumb" and to make this reside within the section labeled "Images" and the
Category labeled "General Image". Within your content item, insert some text and
upload a good-size image by using the "Image Upload" button at the bottom of the
content article. For a suitable size, aim for a pixel size between 600px and 700px width
or height, depending on the image layout.

In order to display our new image feature, we need to link to this article from the
Main Menu. To do this, simply create a new link on the Main Menu and link to
Articles | Article Layout:

Give your menu link a title (BK-Thumb), and on the right-hand side, select the "BK-Thumb" article you created. One more thing to do here, that is under the parent item on the left column; choose your existing "Image Gallery" menu link. This will start building a submenu under the "Image Gallery" menu. Remember to save your new menu item by clicking on **Save** at the top-right of the screen.

When you view the frontend of your website (refresh the page), you should now see the submenu item "BK-Thumb" shown under the "Image Gallery" menu Link. This will take you to the page that displays a nice, new automatic thumbnail of your larger image in the content article

 If you can't see the submenu item in the **Administration | Extensions | Module Manager | Main Menu** module, make sure the parameter "Always show sub items" is set to "Yes".

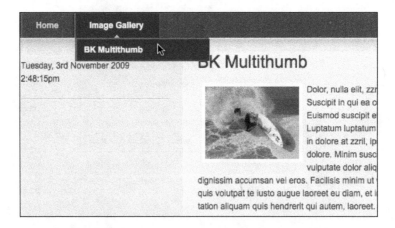

BK-Thumb can automatically pick up multiple images, add captions, titles, and so on. It contains some great features for a plugin. I suggest playing around with it to see if it suits your projects. You may notice that BK-Thumb also affects some other images on your website, so this solution will be suitable for some people and not others.

Multimedia display using RokBox

I mentioned previously that one of my favourite extensions is RokBox by Rocket Theme; this is due to its diversity to display multiple types of content. RokBox is a MooTools-powered JavaScript slideshow that allows you to quickly and easily display multiple media formats, including images, videos (video sharing services also), and music. Here's how to use it easily in your site:

1. Search the Joomla! Extensions area for "RokBox" at `http://extensions.joomla.org`.

2. Visit the extension developer's website and download the extension to your computer. (You can install the Content Button as well, but we definitely require the main `rokbox-system.zip` file).

3. Upload this extension in the Joomla! administration, using the **Extension | Install / Uninstall** feature.

4. In the administration, navigate to **Extensions | Plugin Manager**, and enable the "RokBox" plugin:

The RokBox plugin is triggered by using a special tag, or link code, in content items and modules. The developer's website contains a helpful documentation page and forums. You can find the main RokBox page at `http://www.rockettheme.com/extensions-joomla/rokbox`.

The way RokBox works is really simple. All potential RokBox links need is an extra element within them to work with any hyperlinks: `<a>`. This element is used to put the following code into your link: `<a rel="rokbox" href="/...">example</a>`. When RokBox finds a hyperlink that contains this information, RokBox will take it into consideration. Using this method means you can use RokBox in modules and not just articles. If you do want to use RokBox within a Joomla! Article, then you can use another method (the following tags) which RokBox is built to recognize:

```
{rokbox...}link to the file{/rokbox}
```

There are many other parameters we can add to this basic tag, to start displaying the title and other information for your media:

```
{rokbox size=|100 50| text=|my rokbox| thumb=|images/thumb.jpg|
title=|Head :: Text| album=|photos| module=|login|}images/image.jpg{/
rokbox}
```

The choice of which way you reference your media is up to you. More information can be found within the RokBox documentation.

For now, let's create a new custom HTML module by navigating to the **Extensions |
Module Manager** screen, and clicking on the "New" icon, and then on "Custom HTML" to create a new custom module.

Give the module a title called "RokBox" and make sure the position is set to "Left".
Then we need to enter the following into the "Custom Output" area of that screen:

```
<a href="images/stories/image1.jpg" title="Image 1 :: Image
Description" rel="rokbox[600 400]">Link to RokBox Image 1</a>
```

The previous code adds a hyperlink to the text called Link to RokBox Image 1 , gives
it a title of Image 1 and a description of Image Description, and opens the image
using RokBox in a window size of 600 by 400 pixels. Make sure you have an image
uploaded in your /images/stories folder with the correct name, then click on the
Apply button at the top-right of the screen to apply your changes.

When you view the frontend of your website you should now have a text link to the
RokBox feature:

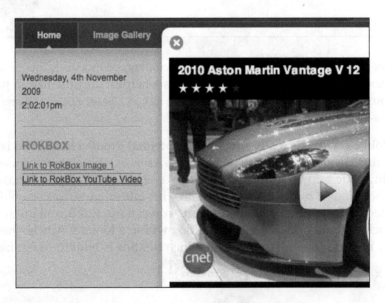

RokBox can be used as we have here, or you could insert an image with the RokBox link around it, effectively creating a thumbnail link to the RokBox content. Many options are possible, including using RokBox to create image galleries with thumbnails.

Adding video features

Video is the media element of the moment! As highlighted earlier in this book, there are some great video features now available for Joomla!, so let's crack on with these and integrate some into our project.

RokBox, here we go again!

As the RokBox plugin can also play video, let's add to our RokBox side module to display a YouTube video below our recently created RokBox image link. Here are the steps:

1. Open up the RokBox module in **Extensions | Module Manager**.

2. Add the following code to the custom output box:

```
<p>
<a href="http://www.youtube.com/watch?v=6RWQz0Q7_zY"
title="Cars :: 2010 Aston Martin Vantage V 12"
rel="rokbox[425 373](demo)">Link to RokBox YouTube Video</a>
</p>
```

The code is broken down as follows:

- The link is to a YouTube hosted video.
- The title is Cars.
- The description is 2010 Aston Martin Vantage V 12.
- It will open in a RokBok window sized 425 px by 373 px.
- The text is Link to RokBox YouTube Video. I have placed paragraph tags around this in order to create spacing with the image link that we created earlier.

Click on **Apply** at the top-right of the page to save the changes.

In the frontend of your website, you will now see a new text link, which opens a YouTube video using the RokBox plugin:

Let's make an adjustment to our code, so we can display a thumbnail image for the link. The code now will look like this:

```
<p><a href="http://www.youtube.com/watch?v=6RWQz0Q7_zY" title="Cars
:: 2010 Aston Martin Vantage V 12" rel="rokbox[425 373](demo)">
<img src="images/stories/astonmartin_thumb.jpg" title="Aston Martin"
alt="Aston Martin" height="159" width="180" /></a></p>
```

I have made a thumbnail graphic for the video and placed this within the /images/ stories directory. You can see that I have put paragraph tags around the code to provide some clearance between our first text links. If you click on **Apply** on the module now, you will see your new graphics displayed instead of a text link:

It is possible to use RokBox to display galleries of videos and display these throughout modules and in articles. I think you will agree that it's a great multimedia extension!

Video using hwdVideoShare

If you are after a hefty YouTube type video approach, the hwdVideoShare video sharing gallery is an open source (GNU GPL) video sharing Joomla! Extension that functions like websites such as YouTube. It features multiple uploading tools for large media uploads. The component supports numerous video formats.

Let's take a look at setting this up for our project:

1. Search the Joomla! Extensions area for "hwdVideoShare" at `http://extensions.joomla.org`.

2. Visit the extension developer's website and download the extension to your computer.

3. Unzip the downloaded file first before uploading it to Joomla!. The package contains numerous extensions within the ZIP file.

4. Upload the `com_hwdVideoShare.gzip` file to the Joomla! administration, using the **Extension | Install / Uninstall** feature. In the administration, navigate to **Components Menu | hwdVideoShare**. On this page, you get an option to install sample video data. Agree to the non-commercial license and click on the "Finish Setup" icon on that page:

After the setup has completed, you will see a page with options to clean things up and run maintenance on the video component. Leave all settings as they are and click on the "Run Tools" icon at the top-right of the screen. The maintenance should run and refresh the screen.

Now let's see what we have so far after installing the main component with some default data. In the administration, navigate to the **Menus | Main Menu** and click on **New** at the top-right of the screen to create a new menu item. From the available list, select **hwdVideoShare** and then from the sublist select **Video Homepage**:

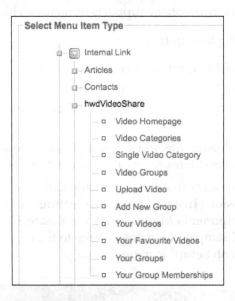

Give the menu link a title called "Video Gallery" and click on **Save** at the top-right of the screen. If you now view the frontend of the site, you will see a new menu item linking to the hwdVideoShare component:

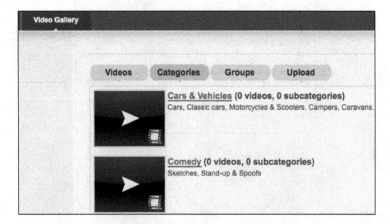

The hwdVideoShare component is a big one, and full of video features as are displayed on the author's demonstration site. It is possible to create a full-blown video hosting service such as YouTube (within your Joomla! site), or you can simply offer videos nicely categorized and lock down frontend uploading features. I would love to spend more time populating this component and adding video features, but I feel that the supporting documentation explains all the features of this extension. For now, we need to carry on and add some more multimedia features to our project.

Videos within articles using FlowPlayer

For the majority of you, being able to place videos within your articles is probably a technique that you will require often. The FlowPlayer uses a Flash-based video player that plays a video file easily in your articles by using the plugin tag:

```
{flowplayer}URL_Video{/flowplayer}
```

The FlowPlayer is available as a Joomla! Plugin so you can add to your articles, or also as a module to place in any module position you require. To add the FlowPlayer into Joomla!:

1. Search the Joomla! Extensions area for "FlowPlayer" at `http://extensions.joomla.org`.

2. Visit the extension developer's website and download the extensions to your computer.

3. Upload both the video and plugin extensions to Joomla! using the **Extension | Install / Uninstall** feature.

4. Navigate to the **Extensions | Plugin Manager** and publish the **Content – FlowPlayer** plugin:

 There is another plugin called Flow Player that was installed for use with the hwdVideoShare component. Make sure you enable the **Content – FlowPlayer** plugin which is the one we just installed.

The plugin also contains additional parameters, so you might want to take a look at these while enabling the plugin:

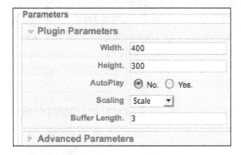

Once the plugin has been enabled, navigate to **Content | Article Manager** and create a new Joomla! Article named "Videos". Select the Section labeled **Video** and Category labeled **General Video**; this simply helps with the organization of our content and media. We need to enter in some text for the article, and then enter the following code to activate FlowPlayer and link to your video file:

```
{flowplayer}URL to Video{/flowplayer}
```

This file can reside within your website file system:

```
{flowplayer}images/video/dog.mov{/flowplayer}
```

Make sure you save your article, and head over to create a new menu link to display this article. I am going to make this a submenu link of the **Video Gallery** link, similar to what we did for the audio link, and call it "Video Page".

Want to do something similar but link to a YouTube video instead? Unfortunately due to a licensing issue, the FlowPlayer cannot play YouTube content, but we have other options.

Using the QTube extension to display YouTube videos

As you are now aware, there are a number of multimedia extensions that provide the flexibility of displaying multiple media types. These are very useful because you only require one plugin or extension to cater for numerous situations.

A simple but specialist plugin worth mentioning though is the QTube plugin. If you think that all of your video content is going to come from YouTube hosted videos, then take advantage of the small footprint that this plugin creates. It does what it says on the tin, and that is playing YouTube videos within your Joomla! Articles.

Like the FlowPlayer, QTube offers a module and a plugin, so you can play videos from YouTube either in module positions or within articles. To install these extensions, follow these steps:

1. Search the Joomla! Extensions area for "QTube" at
   `http://extensions.joomla.org`.

2. Visit the extension developer's website and download the extension to your computer.

3. Upload both the extensions to Joomla! using the
   Extension | Install / Uninstall feature.

4. Navigate to the **Extensions | Plugin Manager** area and click on the **QTube** plugin title to edit. Here you can configure the plugin parameters you require, and make sure the plugin is enabled. Click on **Save** and we are ready to roll!

Here is the plugin syntax required in its simplest form:

```
{qtube vid:=xxx}
```

In place of xxx, you must put the unique identifier assigned to the video from YouTube.com. To obtain it, simply visit the YouTube site and look at your browser's address bar while you are watching the video you want to include. You will see a URL like this:

http://www.youtube.com/watch?v=CQzUsTFqtW0

The CQzUsTFqtW0 part is the unique movie identifier, so our QTube code will become:

```
{qtube vid:= CQzUsTFqtW0}
```

All we need to do now is to insert this into our article, so let's head back to our Video Page with the FlowPlayer video in it and insert our QTube code in also.

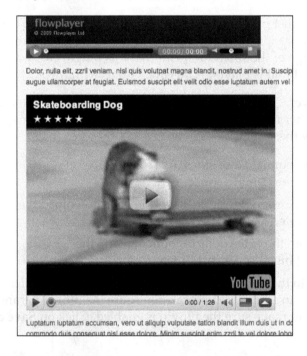

Checkout the documentation for the QTube player; you can adjust player size, add border and color, among other features.

Let's quickly publish a video using the QTube module. Navigate to the **Extensions | Module Manager** screen and click on the **QTube** module. You can configure this as you wish. I have placed it to the left, under my RokBox module, and have configured a width and height so that my video fits into the left column. I have chosen to show it on all pages and have saved the module.

When we now view the frontend of the site, you can see the new QTube module playing a video in the left-hand side column:

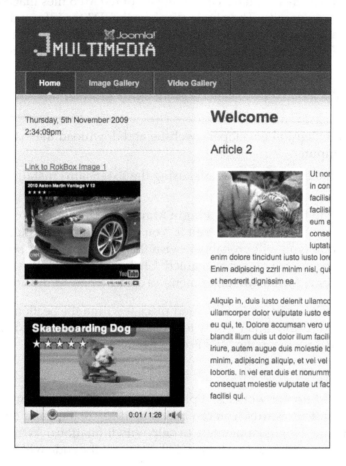

There are numerous other parameters and features for styling and playing videos using the QTube plugin and module. It really is a simple, but very easy, way to embed YouTube videos into our Joomla! site.

Adding audio features

Audio tools for Joomla! are a fantastic way of not only offering music and interviews to your site visitors, but it can be utilized to help offer content to users with disabilities. There are some great audio extensions available and we will add a few to our project now.

MP3 Browser

The MP3 plugin will create a table containing all of the MP3 files that are present in any directory you specify. The plugin displays the ID3 tag information for title, album name, track length, and size. It produces a link to download the MP3 files and an embedded MP3 player to play each MP3 file. It really is a neat bit of kit! To install this feature:

1. Search the Joomla! Extensions area for "MP3 Browser" at
    `http://extensions.joomla.org`.

2. Visit the extension developer's website and download the extension to your computer.

3. Upload the extension to Joomla! using the **Extension | Install / Uninstall** feature.

4. Navigate to the **Extensions | Plugin Manager** area and click on the **MP3 Browser** plugin title to edit it. You can configure the Plugin Parameters you require (you will probably re-visit them once you have seen it in action), and make sure the plugin is enabled. Click on **Save** and then navigate to the **Content | Article Manager** menu to create a new audio article.

Create a new article, calling it "Audio" and place it within the Section **Audio** and Category **General Audio**. Enter in any text you wish, and then the following plugin tag syntax to activate the MP3 Browser plugin:

```
{music}directory path to the music folder{/music}
```

The way the MP3 Browser works is, it picks up any MP3 files residing within a directory you point it towards. You can play one file or 20 files, and options are available within the Plugin Parameters to help with limitations. Assuming you had some MP3 files within a directory called /audio/, the code will look like this:

```
{music}/audio/{/music}
```

You will need to click on **Save** on your article and create a new top-level menu link to it, and you should now see something similar to the following:

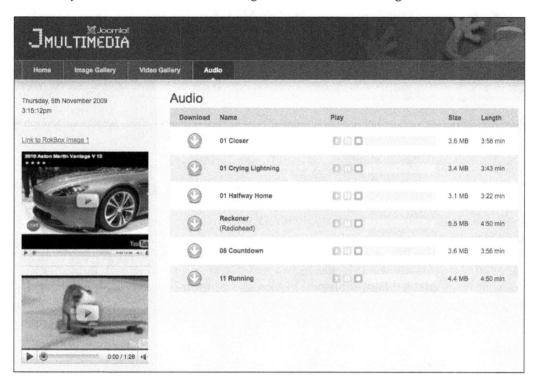

Simple MP3 Player

Simple MP3 Player is an easy to configure MP3 player module that uses a Flash-based audio player. It has various styling options and can be used as a multiplayer with playlists as well as a single player with only control buttons. The module comes with language support, with English and German language files included.

Simple MP3 Player is a versatile player that we can put into any module position, so let's add it:

1. Search the Joomla! Extensions area for "Simple MP3 Player" at http://extensions.joomla.org.

2. Visit the extension developer's website and use the download link on the right-hand side of the page.

3. Upload the extension to Joomla! using the **Extension | Install / Uninstall** feature.

4. Navigate to the **Extensions | Module Manager** area and click on the **Simple MP3 Player** module title to edit it.

The module has not only been well designed, but the author has considered putting documentation into the module, so you have an easy reference guide to all of the Module Parameters. The main fields to populate are the following:

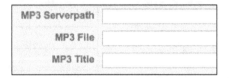

You can enter details to your audio directory into the server path, enter the MP3 filenames into the MP3 file (separating them with a pipe, |, symbol), and then enter in some MP3 titles for the tracks (separated with a pipe symbol). There are plenty of other adjustments this module allows, such as player color and layout, but for now make sure it's enabled and published in the right column. Then click on **Apply** and you will see the results shown on your site:

You may want to revisit the module to customize it, and the supporting documentation will make this job easy.

RokBox for audio

You can use RokBox to play audio files also with the nice JavaScript pop-up box that the viewer's audio player will play within.

To use it, head back to your RokBox module in the administration and enter the following syntax:

```
<a href="PathToAudio" title="Audio Title :: Audio Description"
rel="rokbox[200 100](audio)">Link to RokBox Audio File</a>
```

We have done exactly the same as our image and video files, except adjust the values for the audio file. I am going to save this module and view my updated side module:

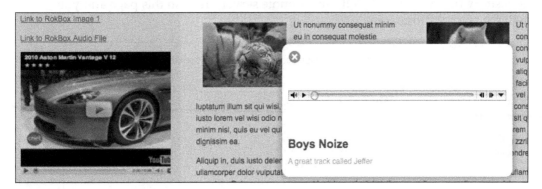

Adding podcasts

There are numerous ways to add podcasting capabilities to your Joomla! project, and more details on this can be found in Chapter 5, *Using Audio in Your Joomla! Website*. For now, there is one very important and wonderful extension we will add to our project. The Joomla! Podcast Suite by Joseph LeBlanc contains a component, module, and plugin and is a great bit of kit to offer easy podcasting capabilities. Here is how to install and use it:

1. Search the Joomla! Extensions area for "Podcast Suite" at http://extensions.joomla.org.

2. Visit the extension developer's website and download the component, module, and plugin to your computer. (Download links are clearly listed on the developer's site.)

3. Upload the extensions to Joomla! using the **Extension | Install / Uninstall** feature.

4. Navigate to the **Extensions | Plugin Manager** area and enable the **Content – Podcast** plugin (there are no Plugin Parameters to set).

5. Navigate to the **Components Menu | Podcast Suite | Manage Clips**.

You will see that a notice informs you that you will need to upload some audio MP3 content into the following directory: /components/com_podcast/media/.

It is possible to change this to any path you wish through the **Parameters** button on the **Manage Clips** screen. Once you have uploaded a file (or several) into your repository (usually via FTP if it's to a remote server), refresh this page and you will see your audio content:

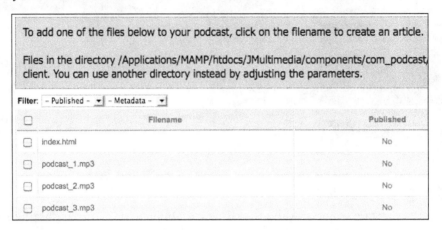

The Podcast Suite is unique in that the component generates a new Joomla! Article and places a tag to the audio file within this. Then it uses RSS capabilities in order to produce the podcast feed.

To create the first podcast, click on the title of one of your audio tracks. You will see the following screen:

You will need to populate the fields with applicable information, and then click on the "Save and Publish Article" icon at the top-right of the screen. This will actually create a new article and pre-populate it with some of the previously entered information. This is now simply a Joomla! Article, so you can revisit it at any stage if you wish to enter in further information. Make sure that you select the section "Audio" and the Category "Podcast" to help with article organization, and that the article is also published. Then click on **Save** at the top of the page.

Now our first podcast has been configured, we can do two things:

- Create a Menu link to this from a Menu.
- Publish the Podcast Module to display our new feed.

Now we're going to go publish our Podcast Module. Navigate to **Extensions | Module Manager** and click on the **Podcast** module to edit it. There are a number of parameters you can set, but for now let's enable the module, publish it on the right-hand side column, and adjust the module ordering so it shows at the top of the right-hand side column. Click on **Apply** to save your changes and take a look at the frontend of the site. There you will see the new Podcast module, and if you click on the icon, you will be taken to an RSS page. (The address is similar to the following address: `http://localhost/JMultimedia/index.php?option=com_podcast&view=feed&format=raw`.)

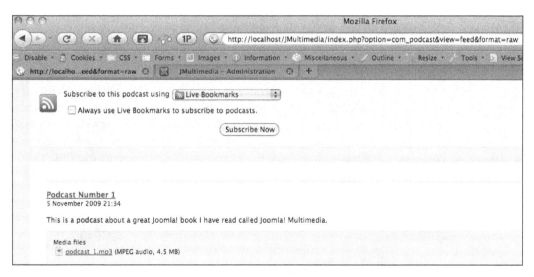

Here you will be able to view your podcasts. You may want to go back into your module and adjust some of its parameters to define the look you require. Here is my new module after a few adjustments:

When new podcasts are added to the Podcast Suite, they will be shown automatically, and any users subscribed to these feeds will be notified of the new podcasts that are available.

I have rushed through this pretty quickly in order to show you the basic process, but there are other features available in the Joomla! Podcast Suite. In the administration, click on **Menu** | **Main Menu**. Create a new menu link to **Articles** | **Article Layout**, and select the Joomla! Audio Article that was just created for your first podcast. Create a link called **Podcast Number 1**, and make it a submenu of the main audio link. Once you have saved this new menu item, visit the frontend of your site to view the results:

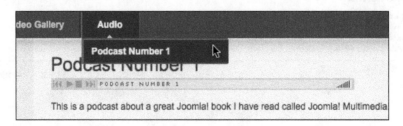

You will now see that the Joomla! Article contains a nice Flash MP3 player where our podcast tag resides. So not only does the Podcast Suite allow you to publish podcast feeds, but you can play the audio and display it within your site articles.

 If you would like to create a link to all of your podcasts, simply create a menu link to a Category Blog Layout. Each time you add a new podcast article to your site, and locate it within the correct section and category, it will automatically be available to your site visitors.

Adding social profiling features

Social networking is the big thing. It's all about networking and groups, the integration of information from different sources, and opportunity for cross-publicizing it.

This section will help you add a few of the most popular social networking features into Joomla!.

Easy Twitter Status

Easy Twitter Status is one of the easiest (and non-commercial) twitter message extensions available. It contains the following features:

- Twitter username
- Tweet display limit
- Which timeline to show
- Show avatar
- Avatar size
- Enable default style or use your own customized style
- Show follow link

 In order to use this extension, you will require a Twitter account at `http://www.twitter.com`.

The rest is easy, let's add it now:

1. Search the Joomla! Extensions area for "Easy Twitter Status" at `http://extensions.joomla.org`.

2. Visit the extension developer's website and download the extension to your computer.

3. Upload the extensions to Joomla! using the **Extension | Install / Uninstall** feature.

4. Navigate to the **Extensions | Module Manager** area and click on the **Twitter** module to edit it.

You will see the module preferences available. As with all modules, you can hover over the parameter title to obtain a tooltip description that will help explain the fields.

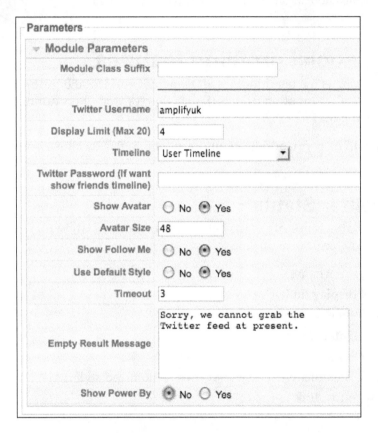

In my demonstration, I have also made a change to the module title, published it on the left column, and under the Menu Assignment area we want to make this module available on just the **Home** menu link:

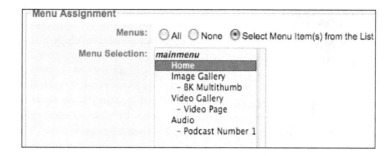

Now that we have published the module on the left-hand side, it could make our left column quite long as compared to the other content published on the front page. Let's go into our "RokBox" and "QTube" modules and only make them assigned to the menu links related to our video examples:

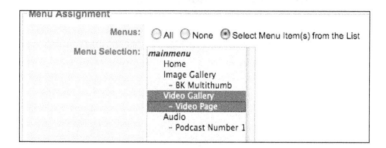

The Easy Twitter module should now only show on our Home Page menu item and pull in our latest Twitter messages. Styling for this can be adjusted with CSS, and may also be affected by the current styling within your `template.css` file:

Twitter Follow Me

The Twitter Follow Me module displays a choice of simple eye-catching graphics displayed within your Joomla! page and links to your Twitter account. Users who wish to follow your Twitters can easily reach them by clicking on the provided link.

Follow these steps to install this module:

1. Search the Joomla! Extensions area for "Follow Me" at `http://extensions.joomla.org`.

2. Visit the extension developer's website and download the extension to your computer.

3. Upload the extensions to Joomla! using the **Extension|Install / Uninstall** feature.

4. Navigate to the **Extensions|Module Manager** area and click on the **Follow Me** module to edit it.

The module contains a number of self explanatory parameters. I have selected the following:

For this module to sit well within our current template, I have selected to display it in the bottom-left of the site page, and have adjusted the module's title so it is not displayed. This Twitter Follow Me module can actually be placed within any available module position as it utilizes another display method compared to usual modules. Here is a screenshot of how it looks in my project:

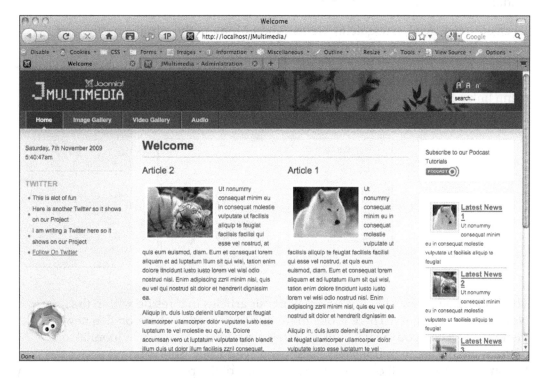

For those who want to provide an easy link to their Twitter accounts, this is a five minute eye-catching solution.

There are many other extensions that enable you to communicate with external social networking resources such as Facebook, MySpace, Flickr, and so forth. I suggest playing with a few to see if they provide the functionality you require for your projects.

Adding RSS features

With RSS being the perfect medium to display and provide site information, it is important to offer some RSS feeds from our site project.

There are a number of RSS extensions available to display Joomla! RSS feeds.

The creation of RSS feeds for Joomla! has been covered in Chapters 5 and 6, so here is a summary to create one using the built-in Joomla! RSS creation feature.

Joomla! has the ability to generate its own RSS feeds. These are created automatically when we create a new menu item to either the front page feature, or a menu link to a section or category.

To create a new feed, navigate to **Menu | Main Menu** in the administration and create a new menu item. Under the "Select Menu Item Type" screen, select "Articles" and then select "Category Blog Layout". The Category Blog Layout option will create a new menu link to articles that reside within our selected category. Give the new menu link a title of something like "Latest News", and on the right-hand side of the page, select the section and category **News / Latest**.

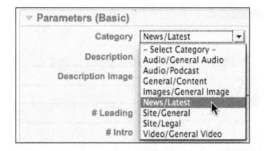

This will create a new blog layout for all of our articles that reside within the **News / Latest** category. There is one more thing we need to check on this new menu item. When you create a link to either a section or category in Joomla!, one of the available menu options will be **Show a Feed Link**. This is found under the **Parameters (Advanced)** options on the right side of the page:

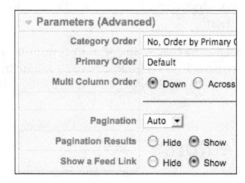

Click on **Apply** to save your new menu item and view the frontend of the site. A new Main Menu option should now be available and when clicked upon, it should take you to a blog layout of your articles:

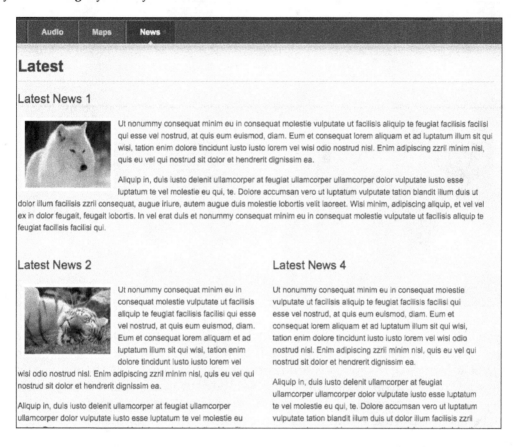

If you look in your browser URL address bar, you should now see that an RSS feed has been recognized on this page and an icon displaying it is shown:

When clicked on, this will offer the user the ability to subscribe to two feed types. The respective RSS feeds will show, allowing the user to subscribe to them:

If you like you can take this feed URL, and create either text hyperlinks around your site to promote it, make a nice icon to publish on your site pages, or use an extension module to recognize feeds created from your site and automatically show a nice feed icon when it finds them. Either way, when we add new articles into this section and category, our new content will be displayed on our RSS feed and anyone subscribed will be able to easily view your new website content.

RSS feeds can only be generated on the front page layout, to a section, or to a category. They can include video, audio, images, and other multimedia content and provide this directly to your subscribers, rather than them having to come to your site to obtain it.

Adding map features

There are a number of great mapping features for Joomla!, most of them utilizing the Google Maps application which has become one of the most powerful mapping tools available on the Web.

Googlemaps Plugin

Googlemaps Plugin for Joomla! displays one or more Google Maps within your articles. It is a perfect method for dropping mapping features easily into your site.

Although, perhaps not considered as traditional multimedia, maps contain a range of text, images, and scripting features, as well as provide an enhanced interactive feature to your site visitors. Let's drop one into our project:

1. Search the Joomla! Extensions area for "Googlemap" at
   `http://extensions.joomla.org`.

2. Visit the extension developer's website and download the extension to your computer. (For Joomla! 1.5 make sure you take a version with that listed in the filename.)

3. Upload the extensions to Joomla! using the **Extension | Install / Uninstall** feature.

4. Navigate to the **Extensions | Plugin Manager** area and click on the **Google Maps** plugin to edit it.

There are lots of **Plugin Parameters** to configure, and you will probably re-visit these to tweak them as you need to:

For now, enable the plugin and click on **Save**. Navigate to **Content | Article Manager** and create a new article.

Name your article "Google Map", and select the Section "Site" and Category "General". Within your article, we need to place the plugin code. The code works as follows: Usage: {mosmap parameter='value'|parameter='value'|...}. For example:

```
{mosmap width='500'|height='400'|lat='-36.843288'|lon='174.770508'}
```

There are many available parameters that you can add to this code, and the Googlemaps Plugin really is powerful. To use them, make sure you put a pipe symbol (|) in between the parameters and make sure there are no breaks within your plugin code. Here are some of the available parameters:

Parameters	Description
width	Adjust to whatever you want, although if it's too small, you won't see very much.
height	You must put the units behind the number such as 100% or 400px.
lon, lat	For the coordinates or address to search for the coordinates (use the standard of your country).
zoom	Can be anything, as specified in the Google Maps API.
zoomType	Can be small or large. This controls the type of zoom function displayed. It can also be none, so there is no zoom control.
zoomNew	Can be 1 for continues zoom, and double-click and zoom, or 0 for click to center (default 0).
zoomWheel	Can be 1 for mouse wheel zoom and 0 for no mouse wheel zoom (default 0).
mapType	Can be Normal (default), Satellite, or Hybrid.
showMaptype	0 for no Maptype controls and 1 shows Maptype controls (default 1).
Overview	0 for no overview window in bottom-right corner, 1 shows the overview, and 2 for overview enabled but closed initially (default 0).
text	Is for the marker that will show on the map in a balloon/information window. If you don't want to see the text, just set text=" ", and it will not display. The text is the data displayed above the location pin. Usually it would be used to display an address or hyperlink. A hyperlink uses the format: < a href=linkAddress target=linkTarget title=linkTitle>linkName< /a>. Don't use (double) quotes.
marker	Is for opening the information window (1 default) or closing the information window (0) initially.
dir	For adding get directions form for a route at maps.google.com to the coordinates.

Parameters	Description
tooltip	Is for the marker to have a tooltip when the mouse is on the marker (don't use HTML).
address	Is for an address to search for the coordinates.
gotoaddr	For a search field and button so the user can search an address on the map (default 0).
kml	For a URL to a kml file to load as an overlay on the map for multiple markers or a route.
align	Is for placement of the map in the content (left, right, center, or none).

Drop some code into your article and save it. Then create a new menu item to the map's article. I have simply called mine "Maps" and made it a top-level menu item. Your Google Map should now show within your Joomla! Article.

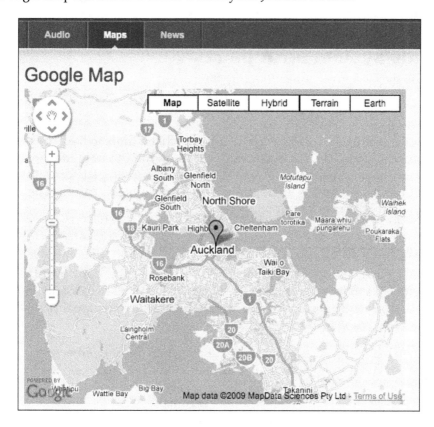

There are a number of Google Map modules also available, that offer the ability to easily place Google Maps within module positions. These are located at http://extensions.joomla.org.

Creating a custom error page

A nice personal feature for any web project is to create your own custom error pages. Joomla! uses the `/templates/system/error.php` file to handle several HTTP status errors, including "403 Forbidden", "404 Not Found", and "500 Internal Server" errors. These different status codes are information delivered by the server to the client, for different reasons.

Personalizing your error pages can help the user with further information, and really show that you have taken the time to consider them, when things on the site may not function correctly. Your custom error pages may contain multimedia items, as they are simply HTML web pages.

There are a number of ways to create a custom error page for Joomla!. The one I am going to use requires you to get your hands dirty with some code, but it is quite easy to perform.

Override system error page

To override the system error results, copy the `/templates/system/error.php` file into your own `/templates/<active template>` directory. In our case, this will be: `/templates/ja_purity/error.php`.

If it finds one, Joomla! will use the `error.php` file that it finds in the active template, in place of the system file. This is a nice approach, as you can upgrade Joomla! but your custom `error.php` file will always stay within your template directory, which should not be affected during an upgrade. This `error.php` file can then be formatted as desired, usually to match your template.

Override system error page styling

If you want to change the styling of this page, we also need to copy over the following file: `/templates/system/css/error.css` and place this copy into your `/templates/<active template>/css/error.css` file. In our case this will be: `/templates/ja_purity/css/error.css`

Next, update the `/templates/ja_purity/error.php` file to reference the new location of our stylesheet by changing this line: `<link rel="stylesheet" href="<?php echo $this->baseurl; ?>/templates/system/css/error.css" type="text/css" />`, which will now become: `<link rel="stylesheet" href="<?php echo $this->baseurl; ?>/templates/ja_purity/css/error.css" type="text/css" />` so that it points to our copied CSS file. You can now make adjustments to your CSS file as desired to style your error page results.

We have now taken duplicates of the two files concerned. Joomla! will look for these files in our template, before using the default ones in the system template. By adjusting our `error.php` page and `error.css` file, we can completely customize the way in which our error page is displayed. Unfortunately, it is not possible to go into the details of creating a new page, but by viewing both of the default files, you should be able to make the changes you require, even if it is a logo change or background color change on the page.

A few things that good **404 Page not found** error pages should contain are:

- A link to the website site map.
- A link to the website home page.
- Relevant links to popular pages.
- A search feature. (Google offers a facility through its WebMaster Toolkit to drop in some easy search code.)

Use images, text, and styling, as well as some of the mentioned features, but keep it as usable and simple as possible. 404 pages tell the user that the page they were looking for cannot be found. By offering the previous information, you can help your site visitors get to somewhere else easily. The last thing you want is a full page of site navigation, images, and other content to distract the user from getting to the information they required.

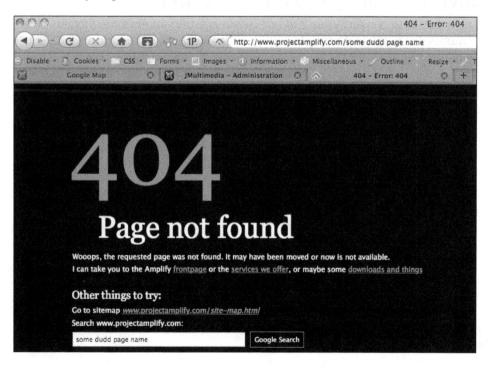

Changing the site favicon

The word "favicon" is short for "Favorites Icon". It is a 16 x 16 pixel icon that is associated with your website, and appears on the web browser's address bar and bookmark's favorites menu. In Firefox and Internet Explorer 7 / 8, it also appears on the browser tab.

Joomla! comes shipped with its own site favicon file. Unless you know how to change it, most people just leave that as default. The favicon, however, is actually quite easy to adjust and is a small feature that can help personalize your project and give it a professional touch.

Create the image

In most situations, you will probably want to use your organization logo, or some part of this to be displayed as the favicon. You will need access to a graphic editor in order to create this image so that it fits within a 16 x 16 pixel square. It is best to save this as either a PNG or GIF file format.

Convert the image to an ICO format

The next step is to convert your PNG or GIF image into another file format. There are a number of ways to do this, but the easiest tool that I have found is an .ico file generator located at `http://tools.dynamicdrive.com/favicon/`.

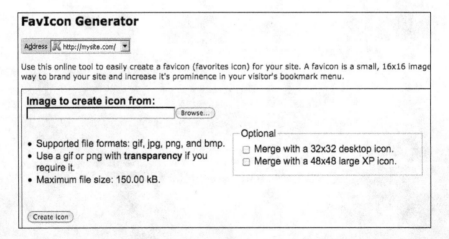

Simply upload your graphic and click on **Create Icon**. Then save the new file on your computer.

Replace the existing favicon

The favicon is located within your active Joomla! Template directory. This is actually applicable for both the frontend and administration displays, hence you can create a different favicon for each if you wanted to. As we have assigned the JA_Purity template to our project, we need to look within our Joomla! file structure and replace the favicon.ico file, within the **ja_purity** template, with our new favicon file. Make sure your new file is named favicon.ico else it won't be recognized — /templates/ja_purity/favicon.ico.

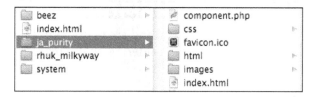

Viewing the new favicon

If you have followed the previous procedure, created the graphic and the favicon.ico file, placed the file into your active template directory, then all should be good to go. If you cannot view your new favicon, then chances are the web browser has cached the original favicon file.

For most browsers, it will be best to navigate away from the Joomla! page (say open google.com or another web page), clean out your browser cache, restart your web browser, and re-open your Joomla! project. This method should ensure your browser loads in the new favicon.ico file.

And the rest...

As you have seen throughout the course of this book, and on the ever growing Joomla.org website, there is a wealth of extension features that can be used to enhance the Joomla! Content Management System. These provide a diverse range of added functionality with most being easy to install and user friendly. They offer "out-of-the-box" features for little-to-no expense, compared to a developer's time to create these for your project.

We could keep going with this site and throw a multitude of extensions at it, building a feature packed multimedia site. One important point to mention is that every extension available for Joomla! has been written by a different developer, with varied skill levels and purposes for making it available. It is good practice to remove any extensions that you are not using on a live site, and to assess the code of extensions when possible, rather than just adding them into a live project and assuming all is hunky dory.

Accessibility and validation

If you have developed your project locally, and are ready to put this on a live server, then there are a number of steps worth considering before making it live.

Accessibility

We have covered this topic a number of times throughout the chapters of this book. It is a very important subject and one that often gets overlooked.

There are numerous levels of accessibility and the subject can be taken to extremes, where sometimes a website is so dull and unusable because people have tried to make it as accessible as possible. The opposite can also be said, but this usually requires a lot of time and consideration to make the site glossy and rich, while considering many user abilities. The most important consideration is that if we are offering valuable information to our visitors, we make alternative content available in some way.

An example of this in our project could be the Google Maps page. For a number of reasons, some users may not be able to view that great looking Google Map. So, let's make the contact details listed under the map, or a text description of why the map is on the page.

Always try to get a range of users to view your site and provide their feedback. With the nature of the fast paced Web now, it is easier for your site visitors to close your web page if they have an issue with it, rather than take the time to write a notification to tell you about it. Quite often, there can be fairly major issues relating to a site that the developer may not be aware of until someone finally tips them off.

Testing in a range of web browsers is a very important step, and relying on honest feedback from friends, family, and colleagues can be helpful when developing a project. I have seen beautiful sites in Firefox, only to find out they don't work, or look poor in Internet Explorer, and it is better for you to find this out from your own quality control processes, rather than your client (or site visitors) pointing it out.

Here are some general considerations to take into account when checking through your final web project:

- Does the site have valid HTML?
- Does the site have valid CSS?
- Does the site have clear navigational mechanisms?
- Does it provide clear alternatives to auditory and visual content?
- Does it perform in terms of page-load speeds?
- Does the site have broken links?
- Do aspects of the layout break if the font size is increased in the user's browser?
- Are there sufficient color contrasts?
- Are all hyperlinks descriptive?
- Does the site work in IE 6-8, Mozilla Firefox, Safari, Opera, Chrome?
- Is the site accessible with CSS switched off?
- Does the site work in hand-held browsers?
- Does the site include detailed metadata?
- Does the site work well in a range of browser sizes?
- Does the site have a useful 404 error page?
- Do your URLs work without the WWW?
- Does the site have a favicon?

Online validators

One way to help make your site more accessible is to make sure it validates to at least a baseline of requirements. There are a number of web-browser based, and online, validation tools available to help with the validation process.

If I run a local validation on the JMultimedia project home page, I receive 50 errors and 33 warnings on that page. Now that leaves some work to do if I am trying to get this site to validate before it goes live. These errors can all add to making the site unusable under various circumstances, so it is important that I try to reduce the main errors.

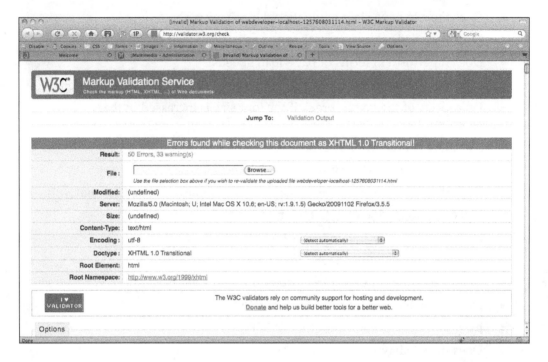

Having taken a quick assessment of these validation errors, it seems that there are one or two extensions that have been used which are causing a majority of these errors. Our options now are to:

- Try to fix what is causing the errors.
- Uninstall the extension and look for another solution.
- Disregard these and go make a cup of tea (I do not recommend this one, although there is nothing wrong with a cuppa).

A great way to start with solving validation errors is to make sure your template validates. You can check this by creating a new Joomla! Article with a simple `<p></p>` tag within it, save it, and create a menu link to it. Visit that page in the frontend. Next, make sure no modules are loaded onto that page and then try to validate it using a browser validation tool, such as the "Web Developer Toolbar" for Mozilla Firefox, or an online validation site, such as `http://validator.w3.org`.

The results will highlight the basics of the template structure and whether there are any issues with the way it has been structured. From here, you can start to introduce page elements and find the culprits easily, or check the validation tool results to find out exactly where the issues are.

Wrapping up

If you have developed your project locally, then the next steps will be to move it to a remote web server. This is usually performed via FTP or shell commands. There are some good articles on the Joomla! help site regarding this procedure.

In true Joomla! fashion, there are even a number of extensions to help with this process, one worth mentioning is JoomlaPack. JoomlaPack is a site backup utility enabling you to take a copy of your website and database, and reinstall this on any capable Joomla! server.

JoomlaPack not only allows you to move your site from a local development environment to a remote server, but it also provides you with an easy site backup feature to use whenever required. You can find JoomlaPack by searching for JoomlaPack at `http://extensions.joomla.org`.

I wish you good luck with your web projects.

Summary

This chapter used a cookbook-style approach to take a working copy of Joomla! and enhance the framework so it includes a range of multimedia features.

We highlighted setting up a local development environment to create a safe and easily-usable development area, where we can assess extensions, and develop our project.

A range of extensions were installed and Joomla! features configured within our working copy, highlighting how easily Joomla! can be extended to a media-rich working website.

Finally, we wrapped up with some accessibility testing and highlighted the moving of our site to its final residence.

Extension Types and How to Install Them

In order to take advantage of the full range of features that Joomla! can offer, you will at some stage need to install extensions to your Joomla! package. Installing extensions for Joomla! is an easy task, thanks to the design of extensions, and the **Extension Manager** tool that is included in Joomla!:

 Please make sure that you take a backup of your files and database before installing any third-party extensions into your Joomla! site.

Extension types

The term **Extension** is a generic term used to describe five main categories of "extendable elements" for your Joomla! site. These are:

Plugins

Plugins are powerful extensions that add additional functionality to your website. Plugins can work on different levels, for example, the content, the search, or system-wide levels:

An example of a plugin may be to add an easy tag into your Content Article which will embed a movie easily with no extensive HTML code, or to enhance the Joomla! search system to also search an included extension.

You can manage your plugins from the **Extension Manager | Plugin Manager** menu link.

Components

A **Component** can add completely new features to your Joomla! website and they can often be classed as mini-applications in themselves:

Components add great features such as "shopping carts" and "directory listings" to your site, and once installed they can be located under the **Components** menu. Components usually have various elements to them and contain additional sub-menu links to configuration and management screens.

Modules

Modules are extensions that help to deliver information on a page to the end user:

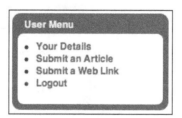

They can display information from simple HTML output to complex information delivered by the system, and they show this on your site pages. Modules are often associated with components as they provide information to the web page. An example of a module could be a simple weather report, a poll question, or a listing of events that is generated by an Events component.

Modules are managed in the **Extensions | Module Manager** area.

Templates

A Joomla! **Template** influences the entire design and structure of your web pages:

You can easily create a completely different style for your database-driven website by using a Joomla! Template. Templates contain module positions which help to organize and provide structure to your published modules.

Templates often contain numerous parameters for adjustments, and these are available as template options within the Template Manager in the Joomla! Administration.

Languages

Languages are a core feature of Joomla! and the packages of these translate the entire Joomla! interface including the frontend and administration of your Joomla! site:

Languages are managed in the **Extensions | Language Manager** area.

How to install

One of the easiest ways to install extensions is to download the extension and have a copy located on your computer. Besides retaining a copy of the original extension files, extensions have been written so they can be easily installed with the Extension Manager doing all of the work:

Log into your Joomla! Administration and navigate to the **Extension Manager** menu item.

In the **Upload Package File** section, click on the **Choose File** button to navigate your local computer in order to find the extension that you want to upload. Once selected, click on the **Upload File & Install** button:

You should receive an **Upload Success** message on the site. Your extension may require you to go and configure some parameters, or publish plugins and modules that were installed as part of the extension package.

How to uninstall

Extensions for Joomla! 1.5 can be uninstalled easily by clicking on the **Manage** menu item on the Extension Manager page.

Place a tick in the checkbox next to the extension you wish to uninstall, and click on the **Uninstall** icon located at the top-right of the page.

Your extension will be uninstalled with a message confirming this on the screen.

Index

Packt Open Source Project Royalties

When we sell a book written on an Open Source project, we pay a royalty directly to that project. Therefore by purchasing Joomla! 1.5 Multimedia, Packt will have given some of the money received to the Joomla! project.

In the long term, we see ourselves and you—customers and readers of our books—as part of the Open Source ecosystem, providing sustainable revenue for the projects we publish on. Our aim at Packt is to establish publishing royalties as an essential part of the service and support a business model that sustains Open Source.

If you're working with an Open Source project that you would like us to publish on, and subsequently pay royalties to, please get in touch with us.

Writing for Packt

We welcome all inquiries from people who are interested in authoring. Book proposals should be sent to authors@packtpub.com. If your book idea is still at an early stage and you would like to discuss it first before writing a formal book proposal, contact us; one of our commissioning editors will get in touch with you.

We're not just looking for published authors; if you have strong technical skills but no writing experience, our experienced editors can help you develop a writing career, or simply get some additional reward for your expertise.

About Packt Publishing

Packt, pronounced 'packed', published its first book "Mastering phpMyAdmin for Effective MySQL Management" in April 2004 and subsequently continued to specialize in publishing highly focused books on specific technologies and solutions.

Our books and publications share the experiences of your fellow IT professionals in adapting and customizing today's systems, applications, and frameworks. Our solution-based books give you the knowledge and power to customize the software and technologies you're using to get the job done. Packt books are more specific and less general than the IT books you have seen in the past. Our unique business model allows us to bring you more focused information, giving you more of what you need to know, and less of what you don't.

Packt is a modern, yet unique publishing company, which focuses on producing quality, cutting-edge books for communities of developers, administrators, and newbies alike. For more information, please visit our website: www.PacktPub.com.

Learning Joomla! 1.5 Extension Development

ISBN: 978-1-847191-30-4   Paperback: 200 pages

A practical tutorial for creating your first Joomla! 1.5 extensions with PHP

1. Program your own extensions to Joomla!

2. Create new, self-contained components with both back-end and front-end functionality

3. Create configurable site modules to show information on every page

4. Distribute your extensions to other Joomla! users

Joomla! 1.5 Content Administration

ISBN: 978-1-847198-04-4   Paperback: 212 pages

Keep your web site up-to-date and maintain content and users with ease

1. Add, edit, and manage content, from articles and text to images, audio, and video

2. Quickly master the administration area of your new web site and make yourself familiar with the navigation and how the content is organized

3. Get to grips with managing users, slaying spam, and other activities that will help you maintain a content-rich site

4. In-depth caoverage for content administrators and end users of a Joomla! site with plenty of practical, working examples and clear explanations

Please check **www.PacktPub.com** for information on our titles

Joomla! 1.5 Template Design

ISBN: 978-1-847197-16-0   Paperback: 284 pages

Create your own professional-quality templates with this fast, friendly guide

1. Create Joomla! 1.5 Templates for your sites

2. Debug, validate, and package your templates

3. Tips for tweaking existing templates with Flash, extensions and JavaScript libraries

Joomla! E-Commerce with VirtueMart

ISBN: 978-1-847196-74-3   Paperback: 476 pages

Build feature-rich online stores with Joomla! 1.0/1.5 and VirtueMart 1.1.x

1. Build your own e-commerce web site from scratch by adding features step-by-step to an example e-commerce web site

2. Configure the shop, build product catalogues, configure user registration settings for VirtueMart to take orders from around the world

3. Manage customers, orders, and a variety of currencies to provide the best customer service

4. Handle shipping in all situations and deal with sales tax rules

Please check **www.PacktPub.com** for information on our titles

Mastering Joomla! 1.5 Extension and Framework Development

ISBN: 978-1-847192-82-0   Paperback: 488 pages

The Professional Guide to Programming Joomla!

1.   In-depth guide to programming Joomla!

2.   Design and build secure and robust components, modules and plugins

3.   Includes a comprehensive reference to the major areas of the Joomla! framework

Joomla! with Flash

ISBN: 978-1-847198-24-2   Paperback: 260 pages

Build a stunning, content-rich, and interactive web site with Joomla! 1.5 and Flash CS4

1.   Build an attractive web site integrating Flash objects into Joomla!

2.   Create stunning photo galleries with Flash transition and animation effects

3.   Use interactive Flash-based maps, charts, animations, videos, MP3 players, logos, headers, and banners in Joomla!-based web sites

4.   Turn your Joomla! web site into a feature-rich multimedia enhanced site through this step-by-step easy-to-follow guide enriched with screenshots

Please check **www.PacktPub.com** for information on our titles

Joomla! 1.5 SEO

ISBN: 978-1-847198-16-7   Paperback: 300 pages

Improve the search engine friendliness of your web site

1. Improve the rankings of your Joomla! site in the search engine result pages such as Google, Yahoo, and Bing

2. Improve your web site SEO performance by gaining and producing incoming links to your web site

3. Market and measure the success of your blog by applying SEO

4. Integrate analytics and paid advertising into your Joomla! blog

Joomla! 1.5 Development Cookbook

ISBN: 978-1-847198-14-3   Paperback: 360 pages

Solve real world Joomla! 1.5 development problems with over 130 simple but incredibly useful recipes

1. Simple but incredibly useful solutions to real world Joomla! 1.5 development problems

2. Rapidly extend the Joomla! core functionality to create new and exciting extension

3. Hands-on solutions that takes a practical approach to recipes - providing code samples that can easily be extracted

Please check **www.PacktPub.com** for information on our titles